Theology Ablaze

Celebrating the 50th Anniversary Year
of Unitarian Universalism

Cheers + blessings /
Tom O-T
10/23/11

Theology Ablaze

Celebrating the 50th Anniversary Year of Unitarian Universalism

Tom Owen-Towle

Flaming Chalice PRESS

Flaming Chalice Press™
3303 Second Ave.
San Diego, CA 92103
Tel: (619) 933-1121
Website: www.tomo-t.com

10 9 8 7 6 5 4 3 2 1
First English Edition 2011
Printed in the United States on SFI certified sustainable paper

ISBN 10: 0-8352-5031-8
ISBN 13: 978-0-8352-5031-3
Library of Congress Control Number: 2010942220

Cover chalice image by Donna Hamilton
Cover and book design by CenterPointe Media
www.CenterPointeMedia.com

SUSTAINABLE FORESTRY INITIATIVE
Label applies to the text stock
Certified Fiber Sourcing
www.sfiprogram.org

TABLE OF CONTENTS

PREFACE

One of my most important and enjoyable stints of continental duty to our Unitarian Universalist Association has been service on the Commission on Appraisal from 2003 to 2009. Fortuitously, our weighty work of independent review for those six years was entirely devoted to furthering the theological literacy and resourcefulness of our religious movement. That mission was right down my alley, stretching my mind and feeding my soul from start to finish. You will note references to our commission's labor throughout *Theology Ablaze*.

I am indebted to my teammates on the Commission during those challenging yet productive years: Orlanda Brugnola, James Casebolt, Barbara Child, Megan Dowdell, Pete Fontneau, Joyce Gilbert, Mark Hamilton, Bev Harrison, Earl K. Holt III, Linda Weaver Horton, Janice Marie Johnson, Manish Mishra, Don Mohr, Arthur Morrison, Michael Ohlrogge, and Jacqui C. Williams. We often quibbled, but our passion for promoting an authentic and robust Unitarian Universalist theology was unquestioned.

Theology Ablaze is a summation volume of my reflections upon Unitarian Universalist theology, a process that began with *Living the Interdependent Web: An Adult Series on Unitarian Universalist Principles* (1987, published by the UU Denominational Grants Panel), continued with *Freethinking Mystics With Hands: Exploring the Heart of Unitarian Universalism* (Skinner House Books, 1998), then *Wrestling With God: A Unitarian Universalist Guide for Skeptics and Believers* (Barking Rocks Press, 2002), and most recently was articulated in *Growing a Beloved Community: Twelve Hallmarks of a Healthy Congregation* (Skinner House Books, 2004).

I would offer special thanks to Matthew and Joan Greenblatt of CenterPointe Media for designing and laying out a most beautiful book as well as to three Unitarian Universalists allies: John Davis, for his ongoing assistance; Virginia Dunn, for her superb editing;

and to Donna Hamilton, whose gorgeous chalice image—made from applique, fabric paint and ribbon—graces the cover. And, yes, immense kudos and love to our grandson, Owen Chapman, whose wisdom and watercolors are sprinkled throughout the pages of this book.

Foremost, I want to pay profound homage to my life-mate, Carolyn Sheets Owen-Towle, with whom I have shared both a professional ministry and theological banter for 40+ years. She and I remain lively partners in shaping the theological discourse of the Unitarian Universalist heritage we cradle in common.

Tom Owen-Towle
Fall 2010

FOREWORD

I have always had an ambivalent relationship with theology. I have felt sympathy for the observation (I think it was from Julian Huxley) that the difference between a philosopher and a theologian is that a philosopher is looking in a dark room for a black cat that isn't there and a theologian would *find* the cat. That is why in theological school I took as many philosophy courses and as few in theology as I could manage and still graduate.

And yet I call my feelings about theology "ambivalent," not irredeemably hostile. On the one hand, I think that most traditional theology is gobbledygook, nonsense—literally not grounded in sense, not true. I haven't read everything that the so-called "new atheists" like Sam Harris and Christopher Hitchens have written but of what I have read, I would guess that 80-90% is factually correct and logically irrefutable. "Can God create a stone heavier than God can lift?" I used to shout at those who dared dabble with divinity.

On the other hand, even back in theological school I recognized that the rational and linear was only one part of human experience and a relatively narrow part at that. The older I get, and the more deeply I become acquainted with human frailty and limitations (to say nothing of the evil and tragedy that stalk the world), the more obvious it is that the poet Wallace Stevens was right when he observed that "the truth depends upon a walk around a lake."

Scholars have long ago concluded that economics is hardly a science; that human beings often act contrary to their political and financial self-interests; that people make decisions (on everything from the brand of soap they purchase to whom they decide to marry) on grounds that could hardly be attributed to the faculties of the left-brain alone. And if that is the case with economics, politics, finances, and both trivial and momentous decisions, how much truer must it be of ultimate questions: concerns like "Why is there Something rather than Nothing?; "Why do bad things happen to good people?;

"Is there a meaning to life beyond the mundane and everyday elements of our existence?" These are theological questions and they begin as, Robert Frost said poems do, with a lump in the throat, not an algebraic logarithm.

When I thought a few years ago that I had prostate cancer, I learned everything I could about the science of the matter, but I also took myself regularly for long walks by the sea, because I knew that if I were to confront the challenge successfully, the state of my spirit would be as important as the extent of my knowledge. The things of the spirit go by many names—faith, God, oneness—but they are all grounded in something that we can call theology—not the "Queen of the Sciences," as it was called for many centuries, but the sweet, earnest, bumbling attempt by us human beings to take serious things like hope, death, iniquity, and transformation *seriously*.

Fortunately, we have in Tom Owen-Towle an extraordinarily able interpreter on that journey. In this lovely book, Tom does not talk theology as non-sense; rather he grounds his theological observations in *common*-sense, distilling the profound from the cauldrons of our lived experience.

And a good thing it is too for Unitarian Universalism—to learn that we need not trade in hooey in order to touch the holy. For far too long we have been suspicious of religious language and often with good reason, but it has been at the expense of our souls. By "souls" I mean those parts of us that yearn to live life deeply and seek out its most touching revelations.

Unitarian Universalism may not believe that we have souls in the traditional sense but who among us would be proud to be a person *without soul?* Yet that is what we would be, if we walled ourselves off from pleasure, mystery, pain, and possibility simply because we cannot always understand them.

Tom Owen-Towle helps us, then, to restore our souls just as he believes that the soul of Unitarian Universalism is redivivus or reborn. I hope he's right about that, because there is enough of the shallow and the petty at large in the world without a religion adding to it!

But whether he's ultimately correct about the trend-lines of our faith, he offers us here guidelines for our lives and that is a gift in and of itself and a reminder to me—and perhaps to you—that there is more to theology than meets the skeptic's eye.

REV. DR. WILLIAM F. SCHULZ
President and CEO, Unitarian Universalist Service Committee

CATCHING FIRE THEOLOGICALLY
(1961–2011)

*Theological reflection is a way to align what we believe with who we are.
Such reflection helps a congregation preach what it practices,
and practice what it preaches.*

*Theology is the best tool for congregations to speak the truth about the
relationship between the human and the divine.
We neglect the responsible use of theology at our own peril.*
—Anthony Robinson

The religious way is the deep way...the way that dips into the heart of
things...that sees what physical eyes alone fail to see,
the intangibles at the heart of every phenomenon.
—Sophia Fahs

One's 50th year is indeed an impressive milestone at
which one may well pause to take an accounting.
—Jane Addams (1860–1935)

On May 15, 1961, the Unitarian Universalist Association (UUA) officially became a corporate entity when consolidation of the American Unitarian Association (AUA) and the Universalist Church of America (UCA) was legally enacted. When Unitarian Universalists gather for General Assembly in June of 2011 in Charlotte, North Carolina, it will mark the 50th anniversary of the formation of the UUA. Clearly, this is a momentous passage worth celebrating.

During our Jubilee Year, it's imperative, as Addams urges, to "pause to take an accounting," to review the theological growth during our first half-century of existence as the Unitarian Universalist Association of free yet interdependent congregations. 2011 is a golden opportunity to re-articulate what resides at the core of our identity and mission as a progressive religion.

Our 50th anniversary is the watershed occasion to make our theological assumptions more explicit both for those who inhabit and for those who dwell beyond our ecclesiastical premises. Now is the time to demonstrate how our theology is ablaze with radiance and illumination.

There have been sizable social, demographic, and technological changes during the past fifty years, occurring both within and beyond our institutional walls. *THEOLOGY ABLAZE*, while not ignoring these cultural shifts, will focus its attention upon the spiritual evolution of our merged enterprise. This volume will appraise the depth and breadth of our theological development over these past five decades. As with the metaphor of the mythical African *sankofa* bird, we will review the past to more consciously blaze our path ahead.

Although psychologists and sociologists of variant stripes have acknowledged, over the centuries, our pervasive human drives for sexual connection, social power, and possessions, theology recognizes the fundamental yearning in our makeup for what William Sheldon has called "the craving for knowledge of the right direction—for orientation." Theology, at its most mature, does just that: it orients our scattered minds and slakes our thirsty souls.

Let's go back a bit further, some 75 years, to gauge the theological mood in both Unitarianism and Universalism.

The Universalists, at the Universalist General Convention in 1935, crafted their confession in clarion terms:

The BOND OF FELLOWSHIP in this Convention shall be a common purpose to do the will of God as Jesus revealed it and to cooperate in establishing the kingdom for which he lived and died.

To that end... WE AVOW OUR FAITH in God as Eternal and All-Conquering Love,
In the spiritual leadership of Jesus,
In the supreme worth of every human personality,
In the authority of truth known or to be known,
And in the power of men of good will and sacrificial spirit to overcome all evil and to progressively establish the kingdom of God.
Neither this nor any other statement shall be imposed as a creedal test.

This Universalist avowal of faith was fully intended to be a religious declaration, without lapsing into dogma.

The report of the Commission of Appraisal to the American Unitarian Association (1936) was entitled *Unitarians Face a New Age.* (Sound reminiscent of what our adherents must have contemplated in 1961, considered again in 1984, and are envisioning in 2011?)

Listen to the perceptive admonitions of the Unitarians seventy-five years ago:

> *What Channing, Emerson, Parker, Henry W. Bellows, and Thomas Starr King did for their generations must be done anew for ours, but their formulas will not serve to meet our need. The genius of the Unitarian movement has been its power to adapt the vocabulary and practices of a religion whose roots are sunk deep into the past to new knowledge, new conditions, and new situations.*

As the classic hymn by James Russell Lowell declares: "new occasions teach new duties. Time makes ancient good uncouth." Undoubtedly, our pre-eminent duty in 2011 is to clarify, promote, and embody the contemporary message of Unitarian Universalism in the larger world, to keep stoking our flame both within and beyond our household of faith. Our delicate mission is to stay ablaze without being consumed.

Other lessons saluted in *Unitarians Face a New Age* are acutely relevant upon our 50th anniversary:

- "Our institutional maturity is at stake"...our goal is "the transformation of the denomination as a whole into a positive and forward-moving faith."

- This report warned liberal religion of the "prevalence of indefiniteness...and the demand for greater definiteness.... avoiding with the utmost care any suggestions of an official creed."

Plainly, both traditions, Universalist and Unitarian, were committed to forging strong theological statements, while embracing latitude for freedom of belief.

We move ahead twenty-five years, to the time of consolidation: the birthing of the Unitarian Universalist Association.

The initial statement of the purposes and principles of the

Unitarian Universalist Association, adopted in 1960, was a basic and succinct confession. Most commentators would contend that our two religious heritages joined forces essentially for organizational reasons. At that juncture, there was neither sufficient will nor energy to engage in depth theology.

Yet they managed to produce Principles that weathered well for 25 years (1961–1984):

The Association, dedicated to the principles of a free faith, shall:

Support the free and disciplined search for truth as the foundation of religious fellowship;

Cherish and spread the universal truths taught by the great prophets and teachers of humanity in every age and tradition, immemorially summarized in the Judeo-Christian heritage as love to God and love to humankind;

Affirm, defend and promote the supreme worth and dignity of every human personality, and the use of the democratic method in human relationships;

Implement the vision of one world by striving for a world community founded on ideals of brotherhood, justice, and peace;

To serve the needs of member societies;

Organize new churches and fellowships and otherwise extend and strengthen liberal religion;

Encourage cooperation among people of good will in every land.

Additionally, it's revealing that one of the first documents produced, after the 1961 union, was overtly theological in nature, *The Free Church in a Changing World* (1963). The council, under the leadership of Dana Greeley, president of the newly minted UUA, coordinated the work of six study commissions comprised of religious professionals, academics, writers and artists, nonprofit administrators, and others.

In its formative section, *The Free Church in a Changing World* defines "theology as a critical and creative intellectual attempt to express, clarify, defend, reconstruct a religion"…adding that "religion is related to theology as practice is to theory…and we should never mistake theology for religion, or assume that the concept of theology can adequately substitute for the breadth and depth of religion."

We move ahead. In 1981, the UUA Board of Trustees appointed a committee specifically to consider a revision of the 1961 Article II (Principles and Purposes). The 1961 formulation, while serving adequately for the coming-of-age period of Unitarian Universalism, was found to be too patriarchal, hierarchical, and anthropocentric. It was time to address two major shifts in our evolving cultural consciousness: feminism and ecology.

There were other changes in language and sensibility which produced the existing Article II (Principles and Purposes). Not only was it adopted almost unanimously in 1984, but it also has lasted virtually unchanged for yet another 25 years (except for the "earth-centered traditions" amendment in 1995). Here stand our current Principles and Purposes:

We, the member congregations of the Unitarian Universalist Association, covenant to affirm and promote:

The inherent worth and dignity of every person

Justice, equity, and compassion in human relations

Acceptance of one another and encouragement to spiritual growth in our congregations

A free and responsible search for truth and meaning

The right of conscience and the use of the democratic process within our congregations and in society at large

The goal of world community with peace, liberty, and justice for all

Respect for the interdependent web of all existence of which we are a part.

The living tradition we share draws from many sources:

Direct experience of that transcending mystery and wonder, affirmed in all cultures, which moves us to a renewal of the spirit and an openness to the forces which create and uphold life

Words and deeds of prophetic women and men which challenge us to confront powers and structures of evil with justice, compassion, and the transforming power of love

Wisdom from the world's religions which inspires us in our ethical and spiritual life

Jewish and Christian teachings which call us to respond to God's love by loving our neighbors as ourselves

Humanist teachings which counsel us to heed the guidance of reason and the results of science, and warn us against idolatries of the mind and spirit

Spiritual teachings of Earth-centered traditions which celebrate the sacred circle of life and instruct us to live in harmony with the rhythms of nature.

Grateful for the religious pluralism which enriches and ennobles our faith, we are inspired to deepen our understanding and expand our vision. As free congregations we enter into this covenant, promising to one another our mutual trust and support.

The Unitarian Universalist Association shall devote its resources to and exercise its corporate powers for religious, educational, and humanitarian purposes. The primary purpose of the Association is to serve the needs of its member congregations, organize new congregations, extend and strengthen Unitarian Universalist institutions, and implement its principles.

As social analyst Warren Ross put it: "to a truly astonishing extent the Principles and Purposes have been woven into the fabric of our denominational life," even, as some would aver, bordering upon the edge of "creedalism."

Commitment to fanning our theological flame was evident throughout the ensuing UUA presidencies. O. Eugene Pickett, during his administration (1979–1985), admonished:

The old watchwords of liberalism—freedom, reason, and tolerance—wor-
thy though they may be, are simply not catching the imagination of the
contemporary world. They describe a process for approaching the religions
depths, but they testify to no intimate acquaintance with the depths them-
selves. If we are ever to speak to a new age, we must supplement our seek-
ing with some profound religious finds.

The Gospel of Luke in the Christian scriptures offers a compelling story about the depths, about the summons to delve toward a
profounder theology as a progressive faith. The biblical narrative
relates that after a frustrating night of fruitless labor, Peter and his
companions were cleaning their nets before going home. Unex-
pectedly, Jesus appeared on the bank, right off shore, teaching the
multitudes. As they pushed in on him, Jesus got into Peter's boat and
asked him to pull out from the shore. Then Jesus directed Peter to
"put out into deep water and spread out your nets for a catch."

Peter initially resisted Jesus' request: "Master, we've worked hard
all night long and caught nothing." Peter eventually relented: "…
but if you say so, I will spread out the nets." They then caught such
a vast number of fish that their nets began to tear. They called their
companions to come help with a second boat, and the final catch
filled both boats almost to the sinking point.

Jesus' invitation to drop our nets into the depths can be seen
as an overture to a bolder exploration of our individual souls and
communal bonds as Unitarian Universalists. In the past half-century
we have grown less frightened to leave the surfaces of existence
and have proven more willing to dive downward into an expanded
consciousness of theology. We are becoming freer and more focused
in climbing off our elevated perches, vacating the comfortable surrounds of the familiar and provable, and plumbing the depths of our
Unitarian Universalist treasure-trove of theology where authentic
suffering and joy, mystery and meaning await us.

I would reference a fragment of a Rainer Maria Rilke poem, as an anniversary acknowledgment of our maturing Unitarian Universalism:

> *You have not grown old, and it is not too late*
> *to dive into your increasing depths*
> *where life calmly gives out its own secret.*

In his first General Assembly address (1979), President Pickett also broached one of the hallmark features of his tenure—staunch commitment to theological pluralism:

> *Let us provide an atmosphere in which those among us of all theological persuasions—the Christians, the humanists, the existentialists—may fully explore and boldly express their worldviews without defensiveness, belligerence, or dogmatism. For too long, pluralism as a value has received our lip service. Now let pluralism become at last a real source of our vitality and strength. Ours will never be one world, but many. Let them be spoken with confidence and vigor. By rights, ours ought to be the richest theological milieu of any denomination in modern experience.*

This high-sounding viewpoint was validated in Pickett's own spiritual quest. Although he considered himself a religious humanist, Pickett was grounded in existentialism, respected the wisdom of the Jewish and Christian heritages, and remained open to the stirrings of transcendent revelation. Since President Pickett embodied a posture of pluralism, he could authentically entertain and promote the range of theologies circulating in our diverse association. Unitarian Universalism has only solidified its commitment to religious inclusion in the years since Pickett's regime. We unreservedly subscribe to Luke's admonition: "Wisdom has many children" (7:35).

President William F. Schulz kept our flaming chalice afire in his own fashion. In 1992, Schulz published *Finding Time and Other Delicacies*, a compilation of trenchant essays that explores the multiple topics of spirituality, liberalism, theology, Unitarian Universalism, church and ministry, the public world, and our global faith. The heart of Schulz' theology is captured in this personal and forthright declaration:

> *That the blessings of life are available to everyone, not just the Chosen or the Saved;*
>
> *That Creation itself is holy—the earth and all its creatures, the stars in all their glory;*
>
> *That the Sacred or Divine, the Precious and Profound, are made evident not in the miraculous or supernatural but in the simple and the everyday;*
>
> *That human beings, joined in collaboration with the gifts of Grace, are responsible for the planet and its future;*
>
> *That every one of us is held in Creation's hand—a part of the interdependent cosmic web—and hence strangers need not be enemies;*
>
> *That no one is saved until we All are saved where All means the whole of Creation;*
>
> *That the paradox of life is to love it all the more even though we ultimately lose it.*

The sixth President of the UUA, John Buehrens (1993–2001), contributed his fair share toward fanning our faith's flame, mainly through producing (with co-author, Forrest Church) one of the most popular volumes in our consolidated history, *Our Chosen Faith: An Introduction to Unitarian Universalism* (1989). Buehrens' entire presidency was an intentional effort to render our theology more definite, to keep our religion ablaze:

Many denominations are known according to their form of polity or or-

ganization, such as the Episcopalians or specific practices such as the Baptists...our communions, however, are named after doctrines. Unitarianism refers to a belief in the unity of God, and Universalism affirms salvation for all people. The two come together to form the most doctrinally free of all of denominations, which, ironically, has two doctrines in its name.

Theology is seemingly imbedded in the DNA of our consolidated liberal religion: Unitarian Universalism.

Nonetheless, there has been criticism of our current Principles and Purposes (1985) as being too pedantic as well as lacking in spiritual depth. Although well-liked, they sound procedural, even platitudinous. Article II spurs us neither to profound feeling nor to dance. Even Committee Chair Royal Jones "wondered aloud if many of us would, on our death bed, ask to have the Purposes and Principles read to us for solace and support."

However, I doubt whether conventional Christians would choose the Apostles' Creed to be read at the time of their earthly departure. My mother, who died at the age of nearly 96—an ardent Presbyterian for 55 years—wanted my brother and me to hold her hands and calm her brow, verbalizing, at most, a simple prayer bathed in hope and love, when her farewell drew nigh.

At time of death, solace is seldom found in doctrines for any religious devotee, be we liberal or conservative. Rather, comfort arrives via touch, tears, silence, and soothing sentiments.

I personally believe that we're all held in the grasp of a loving and Infinite Spirit—"rest assured," as our Universalist forebears put it. We harbor no need for confessions, scriptures, creeds, or recited portions of our Purposes and Principles to reassure us during our final exit. The clasp of both loved ones and the Eternal One will suffice.

A related criticism points to the lack of lyrical punch in our current Article II. Where's the spark? Undoubtedly, if we'd commissioned the finest poet laureate in our movement to do the job, the words might zing and sway more. However, our Purposes and Principles were a communal effort, striking evidence of the power and pertinence of "living the interdependent web" rather than opting for unbridled individualism. It's impossible for a group, let alone an entire faith, to craft inspirational poetry. That's why we've prompted the artists, bards, and musicians among us to produce noteworthy creative contributions, based on the content of Article II, over the past quarter-century.

This timely 1985 restatement of our Unitarian Universalist faith and mission was generated by neither a band of brilliant theologians nor savvy bureaucrats. Article II emerged as a document largely of, for, and by Unitarian Universalists. In a profound sense, our Purposes and Principles have furnished an impressive and unusual confession in the religious world, precisely because it was a covenantal one, from start to finish. Jones minced no words:

This is the result of three years' work…it is a piece with literally hundreds of authors and editors. Many of you spoke in powerful chorus. Some of you spoke alone, but in words which somehow carried a weight beyond your own. What results has sifted through the minds and hearts of the committee members. But at root it has been your document. Born of our historical statements, it has been hammered out on the anvil of our criticism and prayer. In this, it may be unlike any earlier religious affirmations in the traditions of humankind, including our own. For it contains, not merely what an intuitive few have perceived to be shared convictions but what has emerged from the widest actual participation of which we are capable at this time.

A watershed event, also signifying our theological renaissance, was the sermon by UUA president William Sinkford, entitled "The Language of Faith," preached at First Jefferson Unitarian Universalist Church in Forth Worth, Texas, on January 12, 2003. Sinkford put it passionately: "We need some language that would allow us to capture the possibility of reverence, to name the holy, to talk about human agency in theological terms."

I applaud Sinkford's bold and unerring call to initiate a movement-wide conversation about "expanding our vocabularies if we are to be able to develop our faith fully in our own lives, and if we are to be able to share it with others." Our former president's prodding has occasioned greater theological awareness and livelier dialogue in our Unitarian Universalist ranks. Sinkford kept kindling the fires of our faith.

However, I think our seventh president was too severe when he said:

> *I realize that we have in our Principles an affirmation of our faith which uses not one single piece of religious language. Not one…*

On the contrary, cognates of the words "inspired" and "spiritual" occur some six times in our Principles and Sources. One can scarcely miss the reverential power of phrases such as "encouragement to spiritual growth" and "direct experience of that transcending mystery and wonder…which moves us to a renewal of the spirit and an openness to the forces which create and uphold life."

This latter claim, in point of fact, presents a poetic reference to trans-human realities that undergird us: a presence named by some Unitarian Universalists as the Spirit of Life, by others as the Great Spirit, and still others as an Eternal Spirit…but a Spirit nonetheless, actually multiple in nature, as in "forces."

There exist other "reverence" allusions as well in this foundational document: the "transforming power of love"; the summons to "respond to God's love by loving our neighbors as ourselves"; and our most familiar theological touchstone, namely, "respect for the interdependent web of which we are a part." If these phrases from our sources don't evoke a "language of reverence," what do they suggest?

That your or my preferred view of the sacred would be explicitly quoted in our present-day principles and sources can scarcely be expected. After all, it was a document framed not by independent wills but by an interdependent web of folks.

Nevertheless, in this germinal sermon, Sinkford does confirm our theological maturation as a movement, echoing the signature argument of this book:

> *I believe that Unitarian Universalism is growing up. Growing out of a cranky and contentious adolescence into a more confident maturity. A maturity in which we can not only claim our Good News, the values we have found in this free faith, but also begin to offer that Good News to the world outside these beautiful sanctuary walls. There is a new willingness on our part to come in from the margins.*

Additional evidences of our theological evolution from 1961 to 2011 are reflected in a spate of books specifically on theology, composed from Unitarian Universalist perspectives and published by our own Skinner House Press: *Being Liberal in an Illiberal Age: Why I am a Unitarian Universalist* by Jack Mendelsohn; *Transforming Liberalism: The Theology of James Luther Adams* by George Kimmich Beach; *Faith Without Certainty: Liberal Theology in the 21st Century* by Paul Rasor; *Christian Voices in Unitarian Universalism,* essays edited by Kathleen Rolenz; *Soul Work: Anti-racist Theologies in Dialogue,* edited by Marjorie Bowens-Wheatley and Nancy Palmer Jones; and *Reason and Reverence: Religious Humanism for the 21st Century* by William Murry; to name but a sampling.

Just recently, "What Moves Us: Unitarian Universalist Theology," a new *Tapestry of Faith* adult program, by Thandeka, became available online. This curriculum offers a pathway for both developing a personal theology and learning about the theological strands of our Unitarian, Universalist, and Unitarian Universalist heritages.

Moreover, across the land copious poetry, prose, and songs have been penned about and from our distinctly Unitarian Universalist stories and sources. At fifty years of age, members of our movement are turning more and more for instruction and inspiration grounded in our own faith legacy.

We are reclaiming, as well as crafting anew, rituals, symbols, and tales drawn from our magnificent "living tradition." Without a doubt, we have been catching fire theologically!

Note that the proposed 2009 Article II revision (compiled by the Commission on Appraisal and approved unanimously by the UUA Board of Trustees) urged, for the first time since our consolidation in 1961, the inclusion of our own distinct heritages:

> *The Unitarian heritage has affirmed that we need not think alike to love alike and that God is one. The Universalist heritage has preached not hell but hope and courage, and the kindness and love of God.*

This yoked shift toward both historical appreciation and theological depth indicates a readiness in Unitarian Universalism to scrutinize who we are and where we've come from, to acknowledge our religious identities, and to resemble our roots.

Related has been the tendency to become low-key evangelists for our chosen faith. Unitarian Universalists seem willing to affirm and promote our theological virtues and values at home and work, in the public square and via the media. Countering the tendency to "hide our light under a bushel," this marketing resurgence has betrayed a sea change in our demeanor during the past five decades. We are deliberately fanning our flame.

Our current Principles and Purposes are overt about creating a unified, corporate witness toward affirming and promoting our theological virtues. The benedictory paragraph that follows the Sources furnishes clear-cut marching orders: "Grateful for the religious pluralism which enriches and ennobles our faith, we are inspired to deepen our understanding and expand our vision."

Furthermore, Unitarian Universalists are exhorted to "organize new congregations" and to "extend and strengthen Unitarian Universalist institutions and implement its principles." In short, as adherents who pledge to live evangelistically, we have been duly commissioned to light fires in cold rooms around the globe...to spread the "good news" contained in our progressive theology.

Evangelism signals Unitarian Universalism's unyielding promise, as a full-service religion, to stretch our interdependent web to encircle yet one more sister or brother. Evangelism ensures, in the words of William Sinkford, "that no one is left behind."

In the mature religious journey, reaching within and reaching beyond are coupled postures. Evangelism is the direct outcome of an embodied theology. According to the *Fulfilling the Promise* survey (1998), over 75% of Unitarian Universalists felt something substantial missing in our faith. It was identified as "spiritual discipline and depth."

Amidst the data collected by our Commission on Appraisal from 2006 to 2009, on the route toward a possible revision of the current Principles and Purposes, there existed considerable interest in adding the concept of "discipline," echoing what was affirmed in our 1961 statement: "the free and disciplined search for truth." The Latin root for discipline means to listen. A disciple is one who listens, pays heed, stays close, and dwells in shared tutelage.

Evidently, folks have felt that for Unitarian Universalism to become a more successful faith in our modern world, it sorely needed to become more disciplined and demanding. While concurring with that diagnosis, I acknowledge the reasoning of Royal Jones (chair of the Commission that produced our current Article II), who contended that the shift from free and *disciplined* to free and *responsible* meant that our religious search would not be a solitary endeavor but a communal enterprise. Nonetheless, it seems prudent to include all three terms in our evolving confession of faith: free, disciplined, and responsible.

Additionally, there's been a growing number of Unitarian Universalists in recent decades participating in personal and communal spiritual practices, including usage of disciplines grounded in our own 19th-century Transcendentalism—particularly journaling, conversation, sauntering, and prayer.

Small-group ministries and covenant groups have been catching fire in our congregations, eagerly probing theological themes such as forgiveness, love, grace, and hope. Consequently, it should come as no surprise that the bedrock advertising slogan of our contemporary Unitarian Universalist outreach has become: "nurture your spirit...help heal our world"...a forthright theological imperative. While Unitarian Universalists will continue to disagree fervently on theological particulars—that's the nature of our identity and quest—there exists mounting agreement that, upon turning fifty, ours is decidedly a theological enterprise.

In essence, turning fifty has planted our movement squarely on the path of "engaged spirituality," without signs of a slowdown. We're noticeably turning on and turning up the theological volume in our ranks. More frequently than ever, we're showing up at the community tables of interfaith dialogue, contributing our particular theological perspectives with burning zeal and passion.

There's more evidence of a fired-up theology in Unitarian Universalism. Our Commission on Appraisal, a body elected by the General Assembly delegate body, whose "mission is to provoke deep reflection, energizing and revitalizing Unitarian Universalism," chose to produce its most recent four-year report on *Engaging our Theological Diversity* (2005). This book explicitly recommended:

> that we mobilize an association-wide effort, building upon the findings of this report, to develop and articulate a deeper understanding of who Unitarian Universalists are as a religious people and what shared commitments the UU faith calls us to affirm as well as what challenges we face at this particular time.

Commissioners also developed their own working definition of theology, which supplemented the one stated earlier by the 1963 panel:

While the root words of the term theology refer to "reason or discourse about God," these questions assume a much broader understanding of its meaning. In modern usage, the definition of theology is understood to include the full range of religious and philosophical beliefs (not just theistic ones) and our human understanding of the meaning and purpose of life and of Ultimate Reality.

That definition is exemplified in THEOLOGY ABLAZE, where specific themes have been chosen to underscore "our human understanding of the meaning and purpose of life and of Ultimate Reality."

Engaging Our Theological Diversity was a shameless call for Unitarian Universalists to embrace greater theological literacy and to create safe and welcoming circles of genuine theological discourse in our congregations. This volume has been widely used in our congregational settings, selling out within the first year after its publication by Skinner House.

The Commission on Appraisal wasn't done with theology. We followed up the 2005 report, with a substantial revision of Article II (our current Principles and Purposes), laboring steadily on this project from 2006 to 2009.

The COA received, collated, and processed spoken and written input from hundreds of congregations, countless identity groups, and thousands of individual Unitarian Universalists. The proposal lost by thirteen votes, in a hotly contested discussion during the 2009 Salt Lake City GA plenary. Its defeat appeared primarily due to a failed process where folks, beholden to our current Constitution, were unable to proffer amendments. Without the ability to make substantive changes, delegates felt disempowered and were essentially resigned to stick with the current Article II.

The COA's proposed revision was laden with fresh and widely contributed theological concepts such as beauty, joy, divine and human love, right relationship, forgiveness, and reconciliation...none of which reached the floor for significant dialogue.

While changes to our present Article II must wait for future conversation and votes, the grass roots theological blaze in Unitarian Universalism continues unabated.

Another seismic shift in the landscape of Unitarian Universalism has been our burgeoning interest in systematic theologies, especially innovative and hybridized versions like process theology, which combines the rich resources of the arts, philosophy, and the sciences. The core law of the universe according to process thought is change itself. True power is always relational and flowing, as Unitarian Universalist Bernard Loomer noted. And "God, or Creative Interchange, is the integrating process at work in the universe," according to our premier process theologian, Henry Nelson Wieman. God is not a perfect or static presence but rather stands free to grow, evolve, and suffer just as we human beings do.

In our fifty years of existence as a consolidated religion, Unitarian Universalism has also incorporated the insights of feminist theologies of variant stripes that salute a plethora of motifs, such as images of the Goddess, inclusion, sacredness of the ordinary, a deep ecological consciousness, strategic risk-taking, relationality, and the passion for love, justice, and creativity in the world. Unitarian Universalist minister Shirley Ranck summarizes:

> *Thea-ology of the future must have a new root metaphor—a web of intricate interconnections.*

Liberation theology has been the most difficult perspective for "liberals" to address, largely because of our class and cultural privilege. Nonetheless, Sharon Welch, Fred Muir, Patricia Jimenez, and Paul Rasor, among others in our ranks, have explored the salient features of this theology, which challenges Unitarian Universalist beliefs and behaviors to diminish institutionalized poverty, oppression, and violence. Liberation theology focuses upon the pervasive concern of "those on the underside of history" to take control of their destinies, in order to live decent, free, just, and fulfilled lives. The Latin word *liber*, from which both liberal and liberation surface, was the name of an ancient deity of deliverance and growth.

Perhaps a place for Unitarian Universalists to start is with our sixth principle—espousing liberty and justice for all, where "all" necessarily embraces the poor and marginalized. Growing from a liberal (in thought) to a liberating (in deed) religion is never easy, but "easy" should never qualify as a descriptor for Unitarian Universalist theology.

It's no wonder that the proposed revision of Article II—a review that caught the religious imagination of thousands of Unitarian Universalists from across the land—should roundly recommend new theologies for inclusion: "mysticism, theism, skepticism, naturalism, and process thought, as well as feminist and liberation theologies."

Harvey Cox, prominent Protestant theologian, used to chide us for being "thick on ethics but thin on theology." That critique no longer holds traction, whether in our personal spiritual quests or in our congregational discourse. There's a conspicuous theological revival occurring within Unitarian Universalism. We're fanning the flames of our faith; we're catching fire theologically.

Across the span of the past half-century, we've experienced systematic thinkers in our Unitarian Universalist ranks beckoning us to claim, clarify, then embody the foundational themes of our theology. It's been tempting to forget that Earl Morse Wilbur, eminent Unitarian historian, in his 1952 foundational volume, *The History of Unitarianism in Transylvania, England, and America,* lifted up freedom, reason, and tolerance *not* as "the final goals to be aimed at in religion," but rather as "conditions under which the true ends may best be attained." Their role, according to Wilbur, was to assist us in discovering, then living, "the final goals" of our progressive faith.

Wilbur advances: "Only if the Unitarian movement…finds its fulfillment in helping us to live worthily as children of God and to make our institutions worthy of the Kingdom of Heaven, will its mission be accomplished." Obviously, Wilbur's governing mission for

Unitarianism was theological in spirit and substance.

In 1961 we were launched as a consolidated movement. In 1985, we were coming into our own as young adults. Now in 2011, during our mid-years, it's time to expand the horizons of our united histories and theologies. Ours is the generation to fulfill our promises as a beloved community with a civic circumference. It's the era of our existence to ensoul "the transforming power of love" through keeping our flame ablaze.

Our current President, Peter Morales, upon assuming leadership of our movement in 2009, openly urged fellow Unitarian Universalists to continue our theological growth. In his first letter to our *UU World* magazine, Morales writes:

> *We want our movement to change...the true challenges before us are spiritual.*

THEOLOGY ABLAZE heartily seconds Morales' motion for us to expand our religion, both numerically and spiritually, by intentionally cultivating, deepening, and embodying our theology.

EXPLORING OUR CORE
THEOLOGICAL THEMES

It is our watch now! Come great hearts, come dreamers and singers and poets, come builders, come healers, come activists, come those of the soil and those who command the might of machines.
Carry the Sacred Flame to make light the windows of the world. It is we who must be keepers of the flame. It is we who must carry the imperishable fire. It is our watch now! It is our watch now!
—Max Kapp

INTRODUCTION

After a brief historical analysis of the past 50 years, THEOLOGY ABLAZE will now explicate the salient traits of our theological renaissance during those decades. This second section furnishes a theological primer for usage both by individuals and congregations, as Unitarian Universalists continue the quest to nourish our spirits while serving the world. We will pay heed to the wisdom of our illustrious 20th-century theologian, James Luther Adams, that: "the principle things that concern me in theology are *intimacy* and *ultimacy*..."

THEOLOGY ABLAZE seeks to achieve that same rhythm of intimacy and ultimacy, as it balances personal and universal concerns crucial to our progressive religion during its golden epoch. Consequently, the themes explored are a mix of the prophetic and pastoral, as our theological reality gazes inward and outward, engaging both the passive (being vulnerable, broken, and in need of comfort and healing) and active (being creative, serving, and useful) sides of the robust, soulful life.

The specific theological topics that will be scrutinized are: gratitude, covenant, Sabbath, beauty, evil, God, faithfulness, interdependence, the sacred, peace and nonviolence, grace, embodiment, suffering, silence, love, prayer, justice, salvation, joy, mystery and wonder, self-care, forgiveness and reconciliation, hospitality, hope, death, and evolution.

Each of these theological themes will be developed in a separate essay that comprises an entire chapter within Section II. Some issues for personal reflection and discussion will follow each theme. It is the author's hope that individual readers and group participants will be motivated to convert their comments and claims into commitments, for Unitarian Universalism, at its truest, celebrates deeds, not merely study and talk.

The qualities are ordered primarily for balance and rhythm.

Naturally, overlaps and interconnections will exist among them. Furthermore, the list is hardly exhaustive, since each Unitarian Universalist would add or subtract if writing her/his own book on the core tenets of progressive theology.

The goal of *THEOLOGY ABLAZE* is to salute our governing virtues, recognizing that *virtue* in Latin connotes "power." If we honorably explicate, then embody, our major ideals, Unitarian Universalism will become an empowered and empowering presence in the 21st-century orb of religious conversation.

However, we must pursue these themes with suitable caution rather than excess, since as the late Unitarian Universalist minister, Forrest Church, reminds us in his book *The Seven Deadly Virtues* (1988): the theological virtues of any tradition can become deadly when malpracticed.

In truth, these chosen theological topics are familiar to all world religions. While we harbor our distinctive approach and angle, Unitarian Universalism certainly possesses no corner on any of them. Our aim is to view these classic traits through our own progressive lens. We engage them with the sole purpose of sustaining the Creation we earthlings hold in common. While occasionally reeling sideways or bouncing backwards along its religious journey, Unitarian Universalism, at its best, remains steadfast on course toward fanning our flame. That comprises our chief theological and organizational mission for the next half-century and beyond.

As a religious enterprise, we haven't completely realized these bedrock themes, nor will we ever, but we're set on the path. We've been bursting from spark to blaze. In 2011, we're consciously recognizing, then engaging, these theological topics as integral to our way of doing religion in the contemporary world. As Unitarian forebear Charles Dickens put it: "By the time we hit fifty, we have learned our hardest lessons. We have found that only a few things are really important." Contemporary Unitarian Universalism is grasping that one of our mandatory tasks is doing theology in a constructive, compassionate, and communal way. Blessedly, our flame is oft-burning with an intense light accompanied by beneficial heat.

THEOLOGY ABLAZE explicitly focusing upon our theological maturation as a movement from 1961 to 2011, is addressed to Unitarian Universalist adults, for both individual and congregational use. With good fortune, Unitarian Universalist adults will then be motivated to share their own theological fire with our children and youth.

I remember one woman in my congregation lamenting: "We adult Unitarian Universalists desperately want to pass on our theological convictions to others, especially our own offspring, yet we're rarely willing to start by dialoguing with each other." Such mentality must be outgrown as we pledge to ignite, then stoke, the flame of our chalice, from this day forward.

THEOLOGY ABLAZE can be flexibly employed at weekend retreats, for religious education training workshops or series, small group ministry, leadership development seminars, and Board goal-setting sessions. Portions of it can also be adapted for a newcomers' miniseries or a one-time Unitarian Universalist orientation.

I envision Social Action committees—perhaps strategic planning and evangelism task forces too—using this book as theological grounding for witness and action in the larger world.

There will be considerable appeal to outsiders as well, folks who are interested in a free and responsible religion that commits itself to open-minded theological banter.

I invite readers to utilize *THEOLOGY ABLAZE* in ways adaptable to your own congregation, cluster, district, or seminary.

Sound theology, like good music, needs not defense so much as rendition.

GRATITUDE

*I am grateful for what I am and have. Thanksgiving is perpetual. It is
surprising how contented one can be with nothing definite—
only a sense of existence.*
—Henry David Thoreau

*I thank You God for most this amazing day:
for the leaping greenly spirits of trees
and a blue true dream of sky;
and for everything which is natural
which is infinite which is yes*
—E. E. Cummings

In my 44 years as a parish minister in the Unitarian Universalist
fold, I've observed a resurgence of the virtue of gratitude. More
is being written about thankfulness, and more is being conveyed
in congregational life from a bearing of outright appreciation.
Unitarian Universalists seem to be an increasingly thankful lot: less
contentious, less self-sufficient, and less smug. We willingly summon
sources of strength beyond our creation. We resonate with the Buddhist attitude that to possess the life we wish, we must be fully present
to the life we have.

There are countless melodies and readings in our new hymnals
that focus exclusively upon gratitude. A couple examples. First,
"We Are Not Our Own" (#317 in *Singing the Living Tradition*), self-
explanatory in its declaration that we're connected to and shaped by
the earth itself:

*We are not our own. Earth forms us,
human leaves on nature's growing vine,
fruit of many generations,
seeds of life divine.*

Second, "O Brother Sun" (#1066 in *Singing the Journey*), a poem grounded in naturalistic theism and adapted from St. Francis of Assisi:

O Brother Sun, you bring us light, all shining 'round in fiery might.

O Sister Moon, you heal and bless, your beauty shines in tenderness.

O Brother Wind, you sweep the hills, your mighty breath both freshens and fills. O Sister Water, you cleanse and flow through rivers and streams in ice and snow.

O Brother Fire, you warm our night with all your dancing colored light.

O Sister Earth, you feed all things, all birds, all creatures, all scales and wings.

O Sister Death, you meet us here and take us to our God so near.

O God of Life, we give you praise for all your creatures, for all your ways.

Both hymns recognize that human existence is an exquisite gift of grace, a blessing beyond our control or conception.

O. Eugene Pickett's responsive reading "We Give Thanks This Day" (#512) has become one of our signature pieces since the initial printing (1993) of *Singing the Living Tradition*.

Max Kapp's poem entitled "Gratitude" (from *To Meet the Asking Years*, 1983) captures the essence of our thankful spirit:

Often I have felt that I must praise my world

For what my eyes have seen these many years,

And what my heart has loved.

And often I have tried to start my lines:

"Dear Earth," I say,

And then I pause

To look once more.

Soon I am bemused

And far away in wonder.

So I never get beyond "Dear Earth."

And here's a portion of another meditation manual piece by Unitarian Universalist minister Robert R. Walsh (1992):

Since we have not earned Bach—or crocuses or lovers—the best we can do is express our gratitude for the undeserved gifts, and do our share of the work of creation.

In addition, notice that following the principles and sources in our current Article II (adopted in 1985) there resides an unabashed ode to thanksgiving:

Grateful for the religious pluralism which enriches and ennobles our faith, we are inspired to deepen our understanding and expand our vision.

The sensibility of gratitude is bedrock to stoking the flame of our liberal religion.

It's said that gratitude isn't an emotion or virtue of youthfulness, a status that expects everything to come as a matter of course. As we grow older, feelings of thankfulness blossom. That surely seems to be the case for our maturing Unitarian Universalism in midlife, an era when we're declaring our gratitude, both individually and communally, for the unspeakable favor of existence itself.

In a Pogo episode, Churchy LaFemme sits wailing in the back of the rowboat after seeing a newspaper headline: "Sun Will Burn Out in Three Billion Years, Killing All Life!" Churchy cries, "Woe is me, I'm too young to die." Porky reprimands him, saying, "Shut up, you're lucky to be here in the first place!"

And so we are. Lucky to be here in the first place! The mathematical odds of our being born are incredible—something like one in 700 trillion. No two snowflakes are alike; no two humans are the same either. Even identical twins differ. It's truly a marvel that each of us, irrepeatables, walks the earth at this very moment in time.

In *Cat's Cradle*, a fanciful science-fiction novel, Kurt Vonnegut (whose family were founders of our Indianapolis Unitarian Church) suggests this same perspective through the Bokonist death ritual. The Bokonists, you see, serve God by lying down on the floor, raising their legs, and massaging each other's feet, sole to sole, while communing with God.

When one of the old Bokonists is about to die, she recites the prayer, "God made mud. I was some of the mud that got to suit up and look around. What memories for mud to have! I loved everything I saw! Lucky me, lucky mud!"

If we're bold enough to wear this attitude all the way until our death, then like the Bokonists, when the time comes to release our consciousness back to the greater planetary pool, we can shout: "How blessed I was to live—lucky me, lucky mud!"

None of us asks to be born. There's no special merit involved with our arrivals. We didn't earn the privilege of life. We were lucky. Whether we look at existence scientifically or religiously, it's a miracle, a wonder, a gift of grace. Every morning I get up, I try to take a deep breath and shout forth: "Wow, it's good to be alive. I'm downright lucky to be here. I'm taking nothing for granted. I'm going to live this blessed day...full-bore!"

To be honest, at my age I don't always spring out of bed upon waking. I sometimes crawl or stumble out, usually straightway to the bathroom—but, nonetheless thankful for the gift of yet another unearned 24 hours.

Let me relate the story of how gratitude and I joined forces. It was a clumsy start. My parents were worried about me as a toddler, because I didn't seem willing or able to muster detectable words until about five or so. Fortunately, I was suffering from no psycho-physical malaise of any consequence; I was just extraordinarily withdrawn. Perhaps, like the biblical Mary, I was pondering things in my heart. Who knows? Yet, once I started to talk, albeit late, I emerged in sentences, and look at me now—words are my trade.

Well, shortly after I first started to talk, I remember my Mom pulling me aside and saying, "Tommy, we're not quite sure how many words you're going to be able to muster in the days ahead. So, before you get going, I've a few tips to offer. Son, there exist words that heal and words that hurt; and I want you to major in the first kind, the healing ones."

"Secondly, my sweetheart, there are five phrases, special to me, that I feel should be liberally sprinkled throughout the course of your life. They aren't complicated or fancy. They don't belong to scholars or gurus. They belong to everyone. They're words, Tommy, that mend, that soothe, that give life! So, I pass them on for your safe keeping and caring use. And whenever you're not sure what to say, either be quiet or offer one of the following basic phrases: "Thank you. I love you. How are you? I'm sorry. Tell me more.""

Mom went on: "Now, of course, there are going to be inappropriate times to use any of these words. However, almost universally, Tommy, these five phrases express gratitude, respect, and love—the most important freight that any language can ever carry."

Of all five phrases Mom passed on to me, her clear favorite was "thank you!" which, she quickly added, came with two conditions. First, "if you never share your gratitude, son, it'll never reach its destination. Plus, if you don't offer thanks precisely when you feel it, you won't get around to doing it later. The moment will pass. So, gratitude is ground floor, Tommy. It's life's spiritual engine; all the big virtues are motored by gratitude. Everything of worth flows from a thankful heart."

That was the main mini-lecture of my entire growing up. And I've spent the rest of my years trying to live up to it.

I think my Mom resonated with Cicero who declared that "gratitude is not only the greatest of virtues, but the parent of all the others." Unitarian Universalism wouldn't disagree. For example, service flows directly from gratitude. As we revisit the ancient Ten Commandments, that 3000-year-old set of Hebraic moral guidelines, we notice their relevance for the steering of our contemporary lives.

Ironically, the most underrated yet crucial verse in the entire chapter of Exodus isn't any specific commandment but the prologue itself: "And God spoke saying I am the Lord your God, who brought you out of the land of Egypt, out of the house of bondage!" (20:2).

In short, the entire Decalogue hinges on the saving event of the Exodus. Since Yahweh has liberated the Israelites from slavery, they're spurred to demonstrate justice and mercy. The Hebrew religion says that we do genuinely good deeds out of neither guilt nor fear, neither to impress our neighbors nor gain heaven, but we lead moral lives mainly because we hanker to say thank you to God, to the Creation, to Life itself for our very existence, for being freed from all sorts of slaveries, and for being loved ongoingly.

Conducting lives of gratitude, we remember the Sabbath day, to keep it holy; we honor our fathers and mothers; we refuse to kill, adulterate, or steal from our loves; and we won't bear false witness against or covet the possessions of our neighbors. Everything true, good, and beautiful streams directly from a soul full of thanksgiving.

Unitarian Universalist Wallace Robbins put it accurately:

Ours is a faith of moral work not because we think morality is a sufficient religion but because we know of no better way of showing our gratitude to God and our confidence in one another.

We can best say thank you to the Creation by stretching our hands and hearts in compassion. Our life purpose is to become magnanimous, literally "great-souled." Indeed, in Buddhist religion, the *bodhisattva* vows not to enter enlightenment until he or she has helped all sentient beings become enlightened.

Thanksgiving is one of the greatest of all our American holidays because it honors not military prowess but spiritual freedom. It celebrates kinship with the earth rather than victory over a human foe. It's simply more spiritual than patriotic. In fact, it's more spiritual than anything else, for religion is born and lives in a state of thankfulness. The Thanksgiving holiday is set deeply in our own theological appreciation, since the pilgrims are our spiritual forebears. When they landed in 1620, they built their community at Plymouth, Massachusetts. This congregation, First Parish Plymouth, is the oldest in our Unitarian Universalist Association, notes historian Alice Wesley.

The truth is that human gratitude is a mature human emotion, and not readily come by, for the real story of Thanksgiving Day is filled with mixed motives and results, just like our lives. We tend to romanticize our holy-days. We idealize the setting, the characters, and the virtues of the first Thanksgiving because, among other reasons, we're fearful of sullying our American image, if we confronted the muddied facts. On the contrary, I find more inspiration when acknowledging that the Pilgrims were roughly as brave and beastly as humans of most eras.

Take a good look at the Pilgrims. They were a motley handful of families who defied all good sense in seeking to settle a wilderness in winter and to plant seeds of democracy in the new world. The Pilgrims came to build a way of life and community that would furnish, as John Winthrop said, "a light unto the nations."

It was tougher than anyone could have imagined. In that first winter at Plymouth, over half of them died of starvation and exposure, including many children. They had to wonder whether the trek was really worth it after such difficulties and devastation. Yet, William Bradford wrote in his simple journal, "They knew they were pilgrims, and they summoned answerable courages!" What a marvelous phrasing of the central religious response to life: "They knew they were pilgrims, and they summoned answerable courages!"

We too are pilgrims, even if most of our journeys require not passage across actual oceans but the spanning of interior or relational gulfs. In these 21st-century times of hardship and uncertainty, you and I are constantly pressed into summoning "answerable courages" for the living of our days.

"Answerable" means possible, denoting responsibility (the ability to *respond*); it refers to the fact that the Pilgrims did what they had to do to survive the winter and settle the new land. I pay close attention to that kind of courage, because it's basically the same kind you and I are asked as Unitarian Universalists to summon for our daily adventures as freethinking mystics with hands.

Have you looked recently at some of the forgotten twists and turns of the first Thanksgiving?

The first notable irony is that the Pilgrims came to America not because of gratitude but due to ingratitude. They were dissatisfied with the conditions of life in their homeland. They were gravely discontented, and discontent marks the human spirit breaking out of the prison houses of the past. It's the human spirit doing what the spirit was made for—namely, bursting forth with new and unfettered energy.

Our Unitarian Universalist heritage has been filled with radical social reformers, who were spurred to goodness from a nagging sense of ingratitude, or what Martin Luther King, Jr. called "creative maladjustment." Dorothea Dix, Horace Mann, Susan B. Anthony, Whitney Young, and so many others in our religious ranks—from days past as well the current era—have been impelled to proclaim: "I can't, I won't abide conditions that contribute to the ills of my world!" These humanitarians were absolutely ungrateful for anything that was injurious to the soul, body, and mind of their brothers and sisters.

Whenever our present day shameless agitators for racial justice, for marriage equality, or for human rights across the world stand tall for justice and mercy, they are standing in the noble tradition of the "creatively maladjusted."

We can never underestimate the role of ingratitude in human change. If the Pilgrims had been only a lot of thankful sentimentalists, they would have never left home in the first place. Three cheers, let's hear it for discontent, dissent, even disgust—for without these motivators transformation rarely occurs.

Here's another piece of Thanksgiving ambiguity. The Pilgrims intended a new start in the moral history of the world. Yet their intentions were both noble *and* ignoble. They pursued religious freedom all right, but they came to America to worship in their own way, and to make other people do the same!

Now, don't get me wrong, I'm glad the Pilgrims landed. I'm pleased that their land has become my land. But that same landing of the Pilgrims also marks stealing territory from the Native Americans—the destruction of their religion and way of life, centuries of agony and poverty and loss and death for the natives already dwelling here. So our gladness on this day must always be tempered by a disturbing sadness.

A while back I read about a classroom of children who were assigned to write an essay about Thanksgiving. It was different than most classrooms in America, however, in that the school stood on a reservation and all of the children were members of the Chippewa tribe, a tribe found in Minnesota, Wisconsin, and Michigan. The assignment for the theme was written on the blackboard. Can you guess what it was? The words on the blackboard were: "Why we're all happy the Pilgrims landed!" Internalized oppression is a subtle, profoundly insidious, reality, isn't it?

Not only was the winter hard and harsh for our early immigrants, but their entering this land was also hard and harsh—devastating—upon the native peoples. There's a cartoon showing the Pilgrims landing in this country, and it reads, "At long last—an end to our religious persecution! Now where are those rotten, heathen Indians?"

The first Thanksgiving was a tainted one. Yet it's not much different today. Our Thanksgiving celebrations are just as checkered: filled with food and famine, family and loneliness, compassion and bigotry, greed and gratitude, all in ample measure, sometimes intermingled under the same roof. Our contemporary Thanksgivings aren't any more romantic than those of our Pilgrim forebears, when we dare to scrutinize them.

As a life-affirming religion, Unitarian Universalism claims that in spite of our brokenness and cowardice, we still possess the capacity to demonstrate thankfulness for our lives and, therewith, to share the bounty of earth with fellow travelers.

In the final analysis, thanksgiving isn't really a holiday or even a season, a fair or foul weather response; rather it's a permanent way of being in the universe. A way of starting the day, a way of ending the day, and a way of living all the moments in between.

Zen Buddhist roshis remind us to make little bows of gratitude throughout the course of the day to the wondrous world in which we're blessed to live. It's a noble and necessary practice to bow to the day, to bow to creation, to bow to the events and people of one's journey. To bow in deep gratitude for the unmerited gift of yet another day of living and loving and liberation, come what may. Bowing places both our body and soul in a bendable, supple posture.

Gratitude can actually be improved with practice, but where does one start? Well, the obvious starting point for me is surprise. I find that I grow seeds of thankfulness in my soul by making room for the unexpected, by heeding writer Alice Walker's advice: "Expect nothing. Live frugally on surprise."

Once we stop taking things for granted, our own bodies become some of the most startling discoveries of all. It never ceases to amaze me that my body both produces and destroys 15 million red blood cells every second. Fifteen million! That's nearly twice the census figure for New York City. If the blood vessels in my body lined up end to end, they would reach around the world. Yet my heart needs only one minute to pump my blood through this filigree network and back again.

It's been doing so, minute by minute, day by day, for the past 69+ years and still keeps pumping away at 100,000 heartbeats every 24 hours. Obviously, this is a matter of life and death for me, yet, even though I have no idea how it works, I'm brimming with curiosity, surprise, and gratitude. Thank you, body, thank you!

Oh, the marvels that life delivers, marvels we humans can neither fathom nor earn, marvels we can only soak in, remaining still and wordless.

In sum, whether we feel lousy or great at any given moment doesn't affect the bedrock "attitude of gratitude." Our thankful spirit is a response that transcends states of feeling. Remember Job's prayerful words: "The Lord giveth and the Lord taketh away; blessed be the name of the Lord." Now, there's the spirit of perpetual thankfulness. And we come back to the Pilgrims.

Unitarian Universalist author Peter Fleck put it aptly:

> *Sermonizers…assume that the Pilgrims were thankful for having survived. It seems to me that they were able to survive because they were thankful.*

Why should the Pilgrims have given thanks? After so much grief and loss, suffering and death? Why give thanks after a hard winter's endurance by dint of their own human effort? If anything, they probably should have had a gathering of shared commiseration for what they had been through and mutual self-congratulation for what they had accomplished. That would have been more logical, more fitting.

But no, the Pilgrims were thankful because they believed that survival isn't possible and life isn't really livable, let alone robust and beautiful, without being grateful. Through living our thankfulness, moment by moment, we claim our true humanity and bless the Creation from whence we came and to which we will ultimately return. That is what religion is all about, and that is what Unitarian Universalism, our chosen faith, aspires to become as it completes its first fifty years of existence and blazes ahead.

In summarizing this theological theme of gratitude, it's abundantly clear that there exist times to be ungrateful, times to moan and lament loud and long. Remember that's how our spiritual ancestors, the Pilgrims, arrived in America, driven by complaint. But such complaints, while necessary outbursts, ought never to undermine our bone-deep gratitude.

Whether arguing or rejoicing, the thankful person remains thankful. Whether celebrating beauty or protesting injustice, the thankful person remains thankful. Whether laughing or crying, fearful or in pain, the thankful person remains thankful. Thanksgiving isn't a passing state or an annual feast. It's a perpetual condition of the religious pilgrim.

We're lucky to be here in the first place. Lucky me, lucky you, lucky mud!

FOR REFLECTION AND DISCUSSION

1. Cicero noted that "gratitude is not only the greatest of virtues, but the parent of all the others." In what ways is this claim true in your life?

2. Unitarian Universalist theologian Galen Guengerich has claimed that the "ethic of gratitude" is central to our liberal religion. As he puts it:

   I am made up of the world I inhabit. Thus, I am responsible to nurture the people and world upon whom I wholly depend… the ethic of gratitude demands that we focus on three areas that have been an afterthought for traditional religious ethics: (1) the status of disadvantaged and marginalized people, especially women; (2) the way we treat animals and plants that provide our sustenance; and (3) the way we care for the environment.

   Discuss the core of this theological assertion and its attendant ethical challenges, as it relates to your personal and congregational life as a Unitarian Universalist.

3. Share the lessons of the original odyssey of the Pilgrims and the first Thanksgiving for the living of your present-day life as a Unitarian Universalist.

4. Specify ways in which moments of *ingratitude* or dissatisfaction have produced healthy changes in your religious journey.

COVENANT

Covenant is an agreement made between parties, not a statement by an individual to be discarded or forgotten unilaterally. A church united by a covenant is made up of people who have made commitments to one another…Joining a church should not be quite the same thing as joining the National Geographic Association.
—Conrad Wright

The religious community is essential, for alone our vision is too narrow to see all that must be seen, and our strength too limited to do all that must be done. Together, our vision widens and our strength is renewed.
—Mark Morrison-Reed

THE NATURE OF COVENANT

Covenanting means we promise loyalty to one another, as members of a chosen Unitarian Universalist congregation, not because of self-interest or advantage but because of an elemental hunger for belonging. Covenanting entails staying in regular and close intellectual and spiritual touch as we engage the theological hallmarks of our common faith. Covenanters confess that we cannot shape or articulate our progressive religion alone but reckon to do so within the caring critique and support of a beloved community. Covenanting is our "best practice," our truest way of being and doing theology as Unitarian Universalists.

It has always struck me that no one ever prays the Lord's Prayer in the first person singular: "Give *me* this day *my* daily bread." Rather it's a community petition: "Give *us* this day *our* daily bread." We are dependent for our daily bread upon one another, on hundreds of strangers whom we will never meet. I can't grow wheat; I don't package it or deliver it to myself.

There's a greater cycle of which I am but a part. Therefore, I freely desire to give back something in exchange for that. If we let each other down, our humanity withers, our flame fizzles, our covenant is broken.

As Unitarian Universalist minister Alice Blair Wesley avers:

The most precious freedom, always—a marvelous gift we choose to accept—is the freedom to enter the covenant, the freedom to promise mutuality. All other freedoms depend ultimately upon this one. The pledge of mutuality must by definition include the promise to respect the "individual religious insight" which can never go unvoiced or be bypassed or coerced without violation of the covenant of mutuality.

Covenanting refers not to a joint theology but to a shared process, not to tenets of faith but to bonds of faithfulness. Covenant specifies what we do together. Covenanting is the process and promise our Unitarian Universalist heritage must pursue at this historic passage upon turning fifty years of age. Covenanting comprises both the spirit and the substance of our continuing to stoke the blaze of our faith.

Unitarian Universalist minister Richard Fewkes, in reflecting upon our current Article II, writes:

Please note that what you have before you is a covenant, not a doctrinal catalogue of religious beliefs. A covenant, in distinction to a creed, is a voluntary agreement between parties that states the basis of their relationship, its purpose and intent, and which spells out the terms upon which the relationship will proceed. A covenant does not have the force of law, but of conscience.

Parishioners are charged to grapple with the content of THEOLOGY ABLAZE within the context of congregational life rather than solely in private reflection. At our finest, our religion is practiced upclose and personal, in soulful circles of respect.

In fact, the title of the 2009 proposed revision of Article II was specifically named "Covenant" to signify the range of bonds among congregants, local parishes, and the Unitarian Universalist Association. Our entire movement is, in the richest sense, an ever-widening cluster of covenantal ties. Covenant is the spiritual practice by which we embody the interdependent reality we affirm and promote at every level of our religious existence.

We inhabit a global web, where our economies, energy sources, and environments all interlace. Our socio-religious era is also one that necessitates "covenanting," where like-minded people join together in animated conversation and caring community. We dare not risk going it alone as a collection of freethinkers. We are summoned to be purposefully connected.

Paul wrote in the Christian scriptures: "If the trumpet gives an uncertain sound, who will arm for the battle?" (I Corinthians 14:8). Our children, youth, and adults must be spiritually "armed" for life's partisan fray. Colleague Gordon McKeeman reminds us that the derivation of the word community—although related to communion and communication—comes literally from the Latin *munio,* meaning to arm. Therefore, with the prefix *com,* meaning together, community actually happens wherever there is shared security and growth, a context of mutual assistance and vigilance.

Healthy Unitarian Universalist religious community is comprised of compassionate arms engaged in fair, firm, and friendly wrestling matches rather than bloodbaths or backstabbing. Arms huddle together in times of sorrow and swing open in periods of rejoicing. Arms reach outward in justice-building and peace-making not merely inward in narcissistic embrace.

In a genuine community arms are watchful to guard against any behavior that would endanger our covenantal bonds. Parishioners defend one another against arrogance and shallowness, outside agitators and internal saboteurs. So, whenever we strengthen our local beloved communities, we envision our work in terms of sharing our hearts and heads, our souls and arms.

As our member Unitarian Universalist societies gather across the continent, during the 50th anniversary year and beyond, to explore the theological traits delineated in this book, both actual and mystical linkages will grow among us.

What does it mean when it says in our current Article II, "we covenant to affirm and promote"? It means that in a world where fundamentalism is burgeoning, it behooves religious liberals to band together in hearty and dynamic outreach. It's precarious and ineffective to fan the flame of our free faith merely as lone wolves.

We covet the power and witness of a continental movement "affirming and promoting." Note the numerous words in our Purposes and Principles that denote explicit mutuality: *con*gregation, *com*passion, *com*munity, *con*science, *coun*sel, and *cov*enant.

Unitarian Universalists convene not primarily to discuss and debate but to "affirm and promote" the heart of our liberal and liberating theology: *affirm* as in state with fervor and clarity; and *promote*, as in publicize regularly and rigorously. Affirm and promote are not passive terms; they connote "evangelize," the art and action of spreading our blaze abroad.

Note that "covenant" is a verb at the outset of our Principles and Purposes and a noun at the conclusion. This implies that covenanting includes a blend of movement and substance, action and context.

Unitarian Universalists are often a confused lot. On the one hand, we acknowledge that our unity emanates from joint commitment to common promises; yet, on the other hand, we jostle to forge a cluster of personal beliefs and/or theological preferences that will somehow unite us. Such scrambling is doomed to failure. Why? Because we can only be who we are: an intentionally diverse lot of religious travelers who harbor a hodgepodge of affirmations...yet gather in covenant to grow the beloved community.

We appear frightened to be left out of the creedal guild of mainline religion, even though we know we don't belong there. We possess our own niche, and it's both a respectable and an honest one. As life-long Unitarian Universalist leader Earl Holt claims: "we aren't an alternative to religion, we're a religious alternative."

Unitarian Universalism has nothing to be ashamed of in practicing religion in a covenantal rather than a creedal fashion. In being united more by promises than beliefs, much is gained (our integrity for starters), and nothing major is relinquished (neither our personal convictions nor our favored theologies). All of the foundational themes saluted in this section are not to be treated as set tenets we uniformly affirm, but rather as a range of traits that spark deep and growthful dialogue, catching fire in deeds of mercy and justice.

DEMANDS OF COVENANT

Our fourth principle, "a free and responsible search for truth and meaning" stands as a pivotal and bridging principle among the sacred seven adopted in 1985. Amidst the data collected by the Commission on Appraisal from 2006 to 2009, there existed considerable interest in adding the concept of "discipline," echoing what was in our 1961 statement: "the free and disciplined search for truth." Some Unitarian Universalist respondents even preferred an earlier version adopted by the American Unitarian Association board in 1944: "discipleship to advancing truth."

Our Unitarian Universalist folds are increasingly visited by individuals and families who, among other things, desire a disciplined and demanding faith, not a free-form outfit that promulgates Jonathan Swift's "anythingarianism." Folks are asking from the git-go: What is required of me to belong to this particular outpost of Unitarian Universalism? What are the commitments I'm being asked to make?

Unitarian Universalist minister and member of the UUA Board Wayne Arnason advocates: "I've begun to wonder whether we should affirm '*accountability* to each other for practicing our principles with integrity' as a kind of eighth principle."

By all linguistic measures, being accountable and being responsible denote the same sense of spiritual meeting of our human obligations and duties. Both terms claim that we're answerable for what we do with who we are and what we possess. In recent times, particularly in our anti-oppression work as a religious movement, the term accountability has cropped up frequently and appears to indicate upping the moral ante in our behaviors.

I like the way theologian Sharon Welch phrases it in her quest to promote empowering accountability: "Another approach is conducive to social change. Rather than being asked to feel guilty and then to give up power, privileged people, 'oppressors,' are challenged to use their privilege, and thereby put it at risk, in the interest of justice." In essence, to become more accountable.

Furthermore, in the covenanting process, individuals must find common ground which means forgetting our own rigid sense of rightness. Healthy theological discourse means negotiating compromises on a regular basis. Too many folks see compromise as a sign of weakness rather than strength.

Alone I don't stand on holy ground nor do you: ground becomes holy when we move beyond our previous biases into realms we haven't yet ventured, trusting that sacred possibilities lie before us. Ground becomes holy when we migrate to a higher plateau that includes each of our visions but transcends us all. Holy ground requires deep listening and creative compromise.

Raimundo Panikkar, a priest and mystic whose father was Hindu and whose mother was Spanish Roman Catholic, used to warn folks that most conversations between religious persons quickly go astray because participants begin advocating, comparing, and defending... acting like hardened diplomats negotiating a self-serving treaty.

What Panikkar yearned for was more respect, for silence, for shared awe and openheartedness—where we wait and receive more than posture and pontificate. Remember that when Michelangelo did the Sistine Chapel, he painted both the major and the minor prophets from the Jewish heritage. And you know how you could tell them apart? Though there are cherubim at the ears of all, only the major prophets are listening!

COVENANT AND PROMISES

We are naturally promising-making, promise-breaking, and promise-restoring creatures. Our theological mission is not *orthodoxy* (shared beliefs) or even *orthopraxy* (shared rituals and practices) but what fellow commissioner Jim Casebolt has coined *orthovotumy* (shared vows), doing everything we can to sustain mature vows, and when we break them, to repair them.

I've grown to think of Unitarian Universalism as the invitation to "pledge our troth" (a striking, traditional phrase that weds both *truthfulness* and *trust*) to one another, as we forge our religious paths alone...together. Truthfulness means we'll intentionally spread no falsehoods. And trust suggests we'll commit no deliberate harm. Author Brenda Ueland claims that compassionate community entails two major virtues: "No lying and no cruelty!" Unitarian Universalism agrees.

Promises point us not only to *who* we are but primarily to *whose* we are. Promises remind us that we're beholden to one another in the "living tradition" of Unitarian Universalism. Promises awaken us to the reality that our theological quest is never merely personal but always public as well. We're spiritual kinfolk; we're colleagues, literally, "leagued together" in aspiring to embody our chosen faith, through good and bad times alike.

The core of a lasting covenantal promise is *generosity*: being liberal of time and resources, talents and respectfulness. Partnerships and congregations cannot endure, let alone thrive, without mutual magnanimity.

There is an epitaph on an English gravestone that goes to the hub of the beneficent spirit. "What I kept, I lost. What I spent, I had. What I gave, I have." Without a doubt, when our communal lives come to a final reckoning, we will realize, once and for all, that we resemble our gifts of energy, of dissent, of affection—gifts born of generosity rather than stinginess. We are not the sum of our aspirations or our affirmations, but rather the sum of our gifts.

There are three kinds of givers: the flint, the sponge, and the honeycomb. To get anything out of a flint you must hammer it. And then you harvest only chips and sparks. To get water out of sponge you must squeeze it, and the more you use pressure, the more you get. The honeycomb just overflows with its own natural sweetness. While we continually fall short, our goal in a creative and compassionate covenant is to exude the sweetness of our beings, one with another. Thriving theological tribes bank on a sufficient number of honeycombs.

You might know the story of a plain-dressed member of the Church of the Brethren (originally known as a Dunkard), accosted on the street of a Pennsylvania town by an evangelical young man who asked, "Why, brother, are you saved?" The long-bearded Dunkard didn't respond immediately. He pulled out a piece of paper and wrote on it, then handed it to the stranger. "Here," he said, "are some names and addresses of my family, neighbors, and people with whom I do business. Ask them if they think I'm a generous and accountable person—indeed, if I'm saved. I could tell you anything!"

One of the central religious notions in our progressive movement is the recognition that we are responsive and responsible beings. Both words arrive from the Latin word *spondere*, which means "to promise." Therefore, as re-sponding persons, we are committed to continually renewing our promises.

Unitarian Universalist minister David Blanchard wrote directly to the issue of covenant in his meditation manual *A Temporary State of Grace*:

> *Do more than simply keep the promises made in your vow. Do something more: keep promising. As time passes, keep promising new things, deeper things, vaster things, yet unimagined things. Promises that will be needed to fill the expanses of time and of love...keep promising.*

Nonetheless, partners, as well as congregations, are human; we fall short in the execution of our promises. Breakups occur for multiple reasons: boredom, negligence, and misbehavior. As a covenantal faith we have assumed the vow of stability. We stay awake, we stay present, and we stay faithful. At our truest, Unitarian Universalists stand ready to heal our bonds and restore our covenants through heartfelt repentance and forgiveness. We are willing to start over, forming ever-fresh and more current and workable promises, both within and beyond our congregations.

Such fidelity requires the best of our beings; it costs effort and time, it entails restraint, it summons all our resources. Fidelity dwells at the crux of covenant, our way of being and doing theology.

FOR REFLECTION AND DISCUSSION

1. Alice Blair Wesley has composed an adaptation of the
    covenant of the Pilgrims, written specifically for contem-
    porary Unitarian Universalists:
    We pledge to walk together
    in the ways of truth and affection,
    as best we know them now
    or may learn them in days to come
    that we and our children may be fulfilled
    and that we may speak to the world
    in words and actions
    of peace and goodwill.

    In what fashion does this covenant speak to your commu-
    nal pilgrimage as a present-day Unitarian Universalist?

2. Unitarian Universalist commentator Michael Durall
    claims:
    The prevailing culture in too many UU congregations is that
    churches offer programs that people attend. Parishioners are
    educated, informed, enlightened, fed, and entertained—but not
    challenged to lead lives of meaning and purpose.

    Is that statement true for you as a practicing Unitarian
    Universalist? If so, how? If not, why not?

3. The newly inaugurated President of our Unitarian Uni-
    versalist Association, Peter Morales, has written:
    All the great traditions teach us that spirituality is ultimately
    about connection—connection with self, with other humans,

with life, with the vast and powerful mystery of the cosmos. We need to take time for whatever spiritual practice helps us reconnect...a spiritual practice is something that prepares us to live transformed lives.

This statement seems to address the challenge of the covenantal community: first to connect deeply in multiple bonds, then to produce a "transformed" life as a result of the nourishment of those covenants.

How are you expressly finding time and ways to do that?

4. Our 17th-century theological ancestors from Dedham, Massachusetts are very specific in their 1637 foundational covenant. The language may appear quaint but the substance remains germane to how we behave in our congregations today. In their house meetings they spoke and acted in ways that "were humbly and with a teachable hart, not with any mind of caviling or contradicting." The record reports that all their "reasonings" were "very peaceable, loving and tender, much to edification." What from this 17th-century covenant proves useful for our own congregational code of conversation and conduct in the 21st century?

SABBATH

*But God rested on the seventh day; shall we not make definite
time for such rest in our lives?*
—Drew Loder

Slowing down could be our single most effective action to save the world.
—Donella Meadows

There has been a noticeable change in our ambience as Unitarian Universalists: we have been shifting from constant activism to more timely rest and recreation, even granting our religious professionals sabbaticals, something unheard of when I entered the ministry over four decades ago. Additionally, it is becoming a modest yet necessary practice in several of our congregations to deliver well-earned "sabbaticals" to hard-working lay leaders. Nonetheless, we have miles to go before Unitarian Universalist parish life is better balanced between bustle and renewal.

We definitely need to affirm the theological virtue of Sabbath—not merely as a weekly practice by attending Sunday worship but also as a serious spiritual discipline in our daily flow.

A personal example. I used to run upwards of 20 miles a week. I was a modest jogger, never an avid racer, although I would periodically engage in 10K events. Year by year, my runs have diminished in length and intensity, until now, I mainly walk with Carolyn every morning, play tennis regularly, and try to average 8,000–10,000 steps per day on my pedometer, which is equivalent to 4–5 miles; but I rarely run anymore. My body and soul have adjusted to a different pace of motoring in the world.

That recurrent admonition in our childhood years, "walk, don't run," has acquired fresh meaning during my homestretch years. I've actually grown a passion for walking; I sweat less, but I see more. My joints are kept well-oiled, my cardiovascular system rejoices, and a sense of calm sets in while moseying around town, which we do a lot of, since we live in the thicket of urban San Diego.

The robust spiritual life truly starts by paying heed to the fourth commandment in the Hebrew scriptures: "To remember the Sabbath, to keep it holy!" (Exodus 20:8), especially for goal-oriented, grinding Unitarian Universalists. In truth, two commandments are contained here, since we're charged not only to *remember* but also to *keep* the Sabbath…both individually and communally.

There's no single route to honoring the Sabbath in your personal or institutional life, but various paths (singing, prayer, yoga, sauntering, meditating, and so forth), and you and I must locate the source that consistently feeds our spirit.

What's overwhelmingly true is that keeping the Sabbath is a daring pursuit in a culture where busyness is equated with human value and being industrious is rewarded far more than tranquility.

Unitarian Universalists increasingly yearn, so our surveys show, to "turn up the quiet" as we age—ask any fifty year old and above, which is not only the age of our movement but also roughly the median age of our membership across the land. We hanker to be still and acknowledge that we don't own everything—even our souls; we merely inhabit them. We want to be still and permit hidden, unconscious streams to flow. We ache to be still and invite the fountain of tears to pour forth. We long to be still and allow clarity to come to the muddy pool of our oft-confused spirits.

I say "allow," because we can never produce, garner, or win the grace of being still. We can only invite or stifle its arrival.

Someone once inquired of a Zen master, who possessed great composure no matter what pressures he faced, "How do you maintain such serenity and peace?" He replied, "I never leave my place of meditation!" You see, he meditated early in the morning, and for the rest of the day carried the calm of those moments in his body and mind.

Whether we're sauntering, chanting or sitting quietly in a corner of our house, every Unitarian Universalist requires sabbatical nourishment to stay centered while moving, grounded while soaring…for the remaining hours of our remaining days. Maintaining a serene spirit isn't the sole province of Zen masters. It's the spiritual obligation of every human being.

Withdrawal and return, as historian Arnold Toynbee used to frame it, is a pattern that can be found throughout history, particularly in the lives of those who've creatively changed the course of human events. Withdrawal marks the journey into solitude, and return signals the road back into the human circle. Being solitary and solidary require an exchange of merely one letter, but both are spiritual necessities that mature pilgrims practice in rhythmic balance.

Gotama, for example, when he was twenty-nine years old, withdrew into the forest, seeking enlightenment, and when he found it, he returned among people and shared his wisdom. Immense interest surrounded the start of Jesus' ministry—40 days in the wilderness—and its close—a lonely vigil in the garden—but we forget that the Nazarene prophet took mini-Sabbaths, all his days and nights. The Christian scriptures recount Jesus withdrawing from life's tumult on a regular basis:

"And when he had sent the multitude away, Jesus went up into a mountain apart to pray; and when the evening was come, he was there alone."
—MATTHEW 14:23

As productive spiritual pilgrims, we need to discover daily mountains and wellsprings where we can go "apart to pray," or simply park ourselves, silencing our minds and replenishing our souls.

There's perhaps no four-letter term considered viler in our Unitarian Universalist lexicon than "lazy"—an epithet hurled at loafers who exasperate us, test our patience, and defy our understanding. It takes real chutzpah to be lazy by choice, but that's precisely what this theological theme orders.

Restorative sabbath challenges us to embody the cue of Lin
Yutang:

> *If you can spend a perfectly useless afternoon in a perfectly useless*
> *manner, you have learned how to live.*

Unitarian Universalists need to revision laziness as a serene kind
of unambitiousness, as the capacity to live on the periphery of life
and not always be engaged on center stage. Being lazy in all good
conscience signals the ability to empty ourselves of daily pressures,
even holy duties. It bids us to halt computing things or climbing over
people. Laziness denotes a willingness to step aside and step back in
order to reflect...to do nothing in the process of being more fully
human.

In Christian lore some folks reportedly come to Jesus and want to
know what they must do to inherit the realm of God (Mark 5:36 and
10:21). Much to their amazement and consternation, the "Prince of
Peace" responds that it won't take doing but *being* something. Not
surprisingly, most inquirers turn aside and traipse off. How would
you, as a partisan Unitarian Universalist, respond?

This much we've found to be true: when humans are trained
to observe quality moments of Sabbath every day, all the other life-
commandments seem to fall into place.

The Sabbath is not only a day denoting the absence of work; it's
far more. Honoring the Sabbath is a visible reminder that every one
of us is more than a cog in the economic and social machine, that we
have a divine right to our own bodies and minds.

For religious folks like Jews and Christians, Hindus and Moslems,
and Unitarian Universalists, Sabbath denotes a way of traversing space
and time that includes outbreaks of song and dance, restorative naps
and rituals, contemplation and conversation, smiling and breathing.
Moving at a Sabbath tempo permits us to mow the grass or vacuum
the floor not merely to accomplish a necessary task but, moreover, to
engage in a spiritual practice. There exists not only scrubbing dishes

but also relaxation—yea, potential moments of pure delight.

As expected, every Unitarian Universalist will shape Sabbaths according to her or his own preference. The scriptures remind us that the Sabbath is given to us and created for us, not the other way around. That's a handy reminder, for Sabbath-time loses its pertinence and power whenever it becomes a batch of compulsions, untrue to one's heart. The Sabbath summons us to find our own best ways to breath, smile, and relax.

During the day, every little stop brings something of one's self back to the whole, the way a bee brings nectar to its hive. The pauses in our lives add up.

Perhaps you recall the story of a South American tribe that customarily went on long marches, and all of a sudden they'd stop walking, sit down to rest for a while, and then make camp for a couple days, before going any further. They explained that they needed the rest in order for their souls to catch up with their bodies.

In your life, are you allowing space and time for your soul to catch up with your body? Moments will do. St. Exupery asks the consummate theological query: "What are you worth when motionless?"...a prickly question for "type-A" Unitarian Universalists to answer.

Wouldn't it be a shame to come to the end of life's road and not have gotten to know our inner realm better? The only sure way to do so is to spend quality moments alone in peace and repose.

Even the Hebrew God, Yahweh, takes the Sabbath personally, for in the book of Exodus we read: "In six days God made heaven and earth, and on the seventh day, the Eternal One rested and was recharged." Here the word recharged literally means "and Yahweh exhaled." Similarly, the healthy flow of our human days requires inhaling and exhaling, in cadenced measure.

Judaism sagely taught our bodies the habit of saying *no* on every seventh day. There's a rhythm in seven that the body understands, since our cells reproduce every seventh day.

This theological trait is two-pronged: authentic Sabbath-time must always be both personal and public.

First, weekly worship is prime time for Unitarian Universalists. There are many ways we are bound together as a religious community: through education and service, through caring and communion, through music and gardening, but nothing is more crucial than worshipping together. Worship occasions the heart and soul of our institutional Unitarian Universalist identity.

I know of no other hour (albeit, it's usually closer to two plus hours from arrival to departure), when we can entertain such a poignant awareness of the goods of life in all their freshness and intensity than during Sunday services.

Without such glimpses of beauty, without such gestures of tenderness and calls to compassion, without such outbursts of gratitude and humor, without the driving devotion to make of our universe a gentler, more loving place…without all the life-sustaining nourishment gathered during our Sunday mornings together, our humanity isn't very safe or strong. We burn out instead of blaze forth.

We convene on Sundays to worship in *spirit* and in *truth,* as the Christian scriptures put it: that is, to worship with both a full dose of spirit or energy and truth or integrity. We come to have life and share it more abundantly.

The Sabbath marks a day when we live with no other task than to be entirely human, in touch with the depths and heights of our very souls. The Sabbath also notes a day to celebrate harmony between humans and nature, with an afternoon stroll, relaxed lunch with buddies, or playtime in the park. If we can't find time for such spiritual replenishment, then what can we find time for?

People sometimes say: "I don't have enough time to go to Sunday worship." And my only response is: "If I dare say so, perhaps you don't have time *not* to worship on Sundays." For sabbath is time well spent, essential time, holy time, time we can ill-afford to lose. It's brief, yet potent when compared with countless other expenditures of time.

Dr. Oliver Wendell Holmes, when asked why he went to worship, replied that he had a plant called reverence which needed watering each week. Each of us has a plant—indeed, *is* a plant—that needs oodles of watering every week.

Sabbath means literally, to catch one's breath. And one of the most common complaints of our overstressed era is that so many of us are perennially out of breath, winded; hence, we desperately desire a place where we can catch our breath and rejuvenate our weary, worried, worn beings.

We crave a place where we can cease the clutter, stop and get off the train for awhile, sit down and just rest...and restore. By rest we're not talking about uninterrupted bliss. In fact, you'll often hear Unitarian Universalists say during prayer, "O Spirit of Life, give us peace *and* unrest—sufficient peace to deliver serenity *and* enough unrest to keep us spiritually awake." As one wit put it: sound religion exists both to comfort the afflicted and to afflict the comfortable. Both/and.

It's interesting to read that when Jesus invites people to rest, he does so with a certain type of folk in mind. He says: "Come to me, all who labor and are heavy laden, and I will give you rest..." The invitation is targeted to those of us who are down, scuffling a bit, perhaps oppressed. If and when we're hurting or heavy laden, Sunday worship is the place, the people, the time, just for us...to be held, sometimes even healed.

As a minister, I occasionally hear from non-attenders: "But I'm just too pooped to make the effort to go to Sunday worship service." Yet being fatigued puts one in precisely the proper state to appear. We can come plumb pooped out and just be present all morning, without any pressure or obligation other than sitting still and giving our souls time to catch up with our bodies!

Let me say more about this entire matter of catching one's breath, of better breathing, as a way of helping us staying spiritually fit the rest of the week. As a person who often succumbs to hoarseness and lives on throat lozenges, due to incessant speaking, singing, and mingling, I'm an ideal candidate to learn how to breathe more properly.

If there's one central message to heed in this theological hallmark, it's the clarion call to slowly but surely catch your breath. Any disciplined practice of conscious breathing, whether through meditation or yoga, or sitting quietly for a few daily moments in a corner of your house, has been proven to reduce stress, blood pressure, and cholesterol levels. One Harvard study showed that even nursing home patients who were in their eighties when they first began meditation felt happier, functioned better, and lived longer than non-meditators.

Why not launch every morn by reciting a simple mantra, such as that of Thich Nhat Hanh: "Breathing in, I calm my body and mind. Breathing out, I smile. Dwelling in the present moment, I know that this is the only moment." Then spend the rest of the day trying to ensoul that mantra.

Breathing, you see, is at once involuntary and voluntary, both ordinary and transformative. To breathe deeply is a religious act; for in breathing, our individual spirit partakes of the Infinite Spirit.

In conscious breathing we become aware that the air taken in is part of the world-envelope of air, which is the product of the inhalation and exhalation of all humanity and the product of the planet's animals and vegetation. We're bound in a universal experience of mutuality—needing what the plants and animals exhale, oxygen, and giving what they require, carbon dioxide. What they need and what we need are the very building blocks of the cosmos itself. Plus, we're yoked with fellow humans as well, since the same air flows in and out of everyone's lungs. In paying heed to our every breath, we participate in all-embracing compassion.

For the resilient and ever-growing theologian, teachers are found everywhere and dwell in every era. However, our most accessible and omnipresent instructor is discoverable right underneath our nose...

when we open our mouth and breathe.

We don't have to visit a sacred site, we don't have to adhere to a certain scripture, and we don't have to follow a guru. We just need to observe our breath: breathe in and breathe out, and pay attention to the breathing process. We can do this any time during the day, while waiting in line, sitting at a stoplight, or listening to music. Whatever we're doing at any given moment, we can stop a moment and observe our breath without trying to influence it. Paying heed to our breathing de-stresses us and puts our minds in a neutral, unruffled place.

And as all experts urge: we need to breathe abdominally. When we take a deep breath, our belly should thrust outward. Then, at the end of a breath, our job is to squeeze more air out of our lungs. If we practice this exercise regularly, we'll deepen and lengthen the period of exhalation until it equals our inhalation.

In sum, let's make our breathing deeper, slower, quieter, and more regular. If today we can be aware of breathing for ten seconds more than yesterday, we will have taken a measurable step toward an expanded integration of our mind and body, and, we'll be honoring and keeping the Sabbath holy.

Having every one of the 75 trillion cells in our bodies breathing more slowly and harmoniously is decisive to a healthy and holy life. And it just may be the most important religious thing we ever do.

FOR REFLECTION AND DISCUSSION

1. Unitarian Universalist minister Victoria Safford writes:
    *I understand the impulse, and I deeply sympathize (after all,
    I was finishing a muffin in my lap when my hygienic fellow
    traveler passed me on the highway), but I know that brushing
    one's teeth while you drive is bad religion. Doing almost any two
    things at once, in the same moment, is bad religion. **Rushing** is
    bad religion.*

    Name some of the ways in which rushing has proven to
    be "bad religion" in your Unitarian Universalist journey.

2. When you are stressed or out of breath during the day,
    are there times and locales where you can go "apart to
    pray" or renew? Contemplate the possibilities for seizing
    such daily Sabbaths.

3. How has Sunday worship become essential and holy Sab-
    bath time for you? And when it falls short, what are you
    willing and able to do about it?

BEAUTY

Beauty feeds us from the same source that created us. It reminds us of the shaping power that reaches through the flower stem and through our own hands.
—Scott Russell Sanders

They shouldn't call it the beauty aisle, that place in the store with all the makeup. Call it the decoration aisle. I know what beauty is. It's not in the store. It's everywhere. May it be above you, below you, and all around you.
—Meg Barnhouse

There has been no mightier tussle in our movement during the past fifty years than reclaiming the missing link in Emerson's trilogy of "truth, goodness, and beauty." Beauty, for all intents and purposes, has been considered our weak or lost cousin, veritably absent from our theological landscape. Shortly after our union in 1961, in the work of the Commission of Appraisal (1963), there was an entire section entitled "Religion and the Arts," which exclaimed:

> ...the historic weakness of the liberal church, for a variety of reasons, historical, rational and psychological, has been its suspicion of the emotive and the non-rational and even of art itself. A major purpose of our commission is to help religious liberalism understand its prejudices in these matters and to overcome them so that it can make an unreserved, creative and mature use of the arts.

Over the five decades of our consolidated existence, the verdict has become manifest: Unitarian Universalism, to become a full-service faith, will need to balance its analytical mind with an appreciative one. Full employment of both our left and right brains is required to fan our flaming chalice.

Shortly thereafter, in 1976, a comprehensive survey of Unitarian Universalist values was conducted by Robert L'H. Miller, the religious studies professor at our Tufts University. This analysis adroitly distinguished between instrumental and terminal values. In the latter category, the survey determined that "a world of beauty" was a terminal religious value, alongside "self-respect, wisdom, inner harmony, mature love and an exciting life."

Moving ahead in time, beauty was widely affirmed as a premier and unacknowledged source in our theology, reflected in the monumental input from Unitarian Universalists across the land, from 2006 to 2009, on revisions for Article II. The Reverend Richard Davis crystallized it this way:

> There is a seventh source that has not been recognized and affirmed. That source is art. This is how I would describe it: 'the living tradition that we share draws from many sources...#7 The Creative Arts: which reveal to us the face of life's beauty and joy, its enduring truth and meaning and which opens our hearts to feelings of awe and gratitude.
>
> Art and spirituality are so intertwined that they cannot be separated.

And colleague Kendyl Gibbons phrased it similarly in our collected data:

> Artistic works from various cultures compellingly express the profound dimensions of the human condition, feed our longing for beauty, summon us to reverence and nurture our individual and collective creativity.

In the final proposed revision, our Commission on Appraisal stated it thusly:

> Unitarian Universalism is informed by direct experiences of mystery and wonder, beauty and joy. It is enriched by the creative power of the arts, the guidance of reason, and the lessons of the sciences.

That was the first time since 1961, in any of our formal Unitarian

Universalist declarations, that beauty and the creative arts had made the final cut and reached a level of prominence in our theology.

What are notable attributes of beauty that qualify it as an essential virtue in our movement catching fire theologically?

First and foremost, beauty is an accessible experience to everyone who pays attention and stays awake. The Buddha, called the "awakened one," is a prime exemplar of one who found and embodied beauty. Brimming with energy, the Buddha trudged the dusty roads of India for nearly half a century, calling women and men to live the examined life. He summoned us to lean our ears both to the earth and to our heart...and to hearken. The Buddha charged humanity to wake up, moreover, to stay awake—senses wide open to both the splendor and anguish in existence.

The illustrious Spanish poet Antonio Machado echoes the same imperative in his ode to the Nazarene:

I love Jesus, who said to us:
heaven and earth will pass away.
When heaven and earth have passed away,
my word will still remain.
What was your word, Jesus?
Love? Forgiveness? Affection?
All your words were
one word: Wakeup.

Naturally, great work is often accomplished, or at least fertilized, while we're asleep or daydreaming. Yet too many of us are prone to narcotize or lull ourselves into zombiehood, when we'd do well to practice wakefulness, if we wish to experience the blessings of loveliness.

Mature theological pilgrims savor every surprise, heeding the Jewish blessing: "Blessed be the Source of Life that brings us to this moment." To bask in the comeliness of present beauty we must outgrow the grudges and glories of yesterday. If we're emotionally fixated on past experiences, we'll never surrender to living in the now.

Beauty need not be esoteric or exotic. In fact, it is visibly available everyday, if we live in a state of wide-openness.

Staying awake, we behold beauty in the here and now.

Although we tend to focus upon the special moments or works that exude beauty, the truth is that authentic, deep—not merely cosmetic—beauty permeates our days and nights. Among the senses, sight develops last, but when it does, it can grip and steer our daily destiny…lifting our souls toward the beyond.

Our human mission as reverent travelers is to behold beauty, whenever and wherever it arrives. As Thoreau reminds us: "Wisdom does not inspect, but beholds. We must look a long time before we can see." To respect another creation means to look again and again with fresh eyes, with eyes of appreciation and awe.

When the Christian scriptures report Jesus as saying, "Behold the lilies of the field," the Nazarene isn't saying, "Hey, look at those lilies over there," in some detached, smug, analytic fashion. Rather the word "behold" means showing profound regard, perceiving with a deep caring and gentleness, which suggests that things possess their own beauty and dignity apart from human beings, apart from our viewing them. Apples, volcanoes, yucca, rattlesnakes—earth's infinite panorama of flesh and bones.

As a wondering tribe of spiritual wanderers, perhaps our primary vocation is to become beholders, observing with an active gaze and level glance all that moves, or doesn't move.

We exist on earth to "behold the lilies of the field," the moon, the raccoon, the sunset, and even the tornado, for we cannot wrest beauty from the whole. Everywhere we roam in the universe we find comeliness mingled with the harsh and disturbing. And let us behold the rocks as well, for a brook without rocks has no song.

When we acknowledge that beauty dwells in the natural realm (the only realm in which humans reside), then we'll rove through existence at a measured pace. We will saunter.

The saunterer is one who strolls in measured manner, with one eye on nature, the other on soul—treating the terrain, and all therein, as sacred. As the French say, there goes a *Saint-Terrer*, a saunterer—literally a "holy-lander."

I awoke to the beauty-laden benefits of walking when I took a month-long soul-journey, by myself, several years back, in the Southern California woods, with native easterner Henry David Thoreau, as my guide…in my wilderness corner of the West.

Thoreau claimed that "it is a great art to saunter," and so it is. Sauntering poses the optimal activity of the spiritual trekker: still moving but in unrushed fashion. The saunterer is on a sacred quest—not exercise so much as exploration, less for recreation and more for re-creation. It's not the length but the depth of walk that makes it blessed.

Sauntering was not extraneous but indispensable to Thoreau's daily fare. He would walk in the woods up to four hours each day and scoffed at those who considered sauntering worthless.

Although Thoreau would tolerate walking companions, he normally trekked alone. He put it bluntly: "Ask me for a certain number of dollars if you will, but do not ask me for my afternoons." Do you and I, as active Unitarian Universalists, stroll everyday, exploring the nooks and crannies of our city or countryside? And do you prefer to saunter alone or accompanied?

Saunterers stride in reverent, appreciative gait, treating the land, every piece of it, as hallowed, touching the earth with deft hands and tender feet (there was nothing between Thoreau's soles and the soil except the skin of an animal). Saunterers awake, as is the Hindu custom, to caress the earth each morn, stroke it gently, and then apologize for treading upon it in the hours ahead.

While sauntering, we can muse about the state of the world's beauty in a leisurely manner. Or chant if we're alone—one of my favorites being the piece composed by Schlomo Carlebach, "the singing rabbi": "Return again, return again, return to the home of your soul. Return again, return again, return to the home of your soul. Return to who you are, return to what you are, return to where you are...born and reborn again..."

That chant goes straightway to the core of our Unitarian Universalist theology; for our mission is to keep returning to who we are, what we are, where we are...being born and reborn again in the process.

When we meander through this sprawling maze of a universe, may we truly behold wonders both beauteous and fierce. Our spiritual forebear Thoreau remarked: "My body is all sentient." He savored pleasure through gratification of the senses. For Henry, beauty wasn't merely in the eyes of the beholder. It permeated one's entire being.

During his afternoon excursions, Thoreau would whet his senses: the sounds of birds, the sight of the sun, the taste of wild berries, the smell of flowers, the feel of the marsh. "We can never have enough of nature," he rhapsodized.

One could find Thoreau standing in the swamp up to this chin, drenching his body in the opulent "juices" of the bog, yet keeping his head, the reflective organ, above it all. This way, both his instinctive and intellectual natures were equally stimulated: a prudent menu for Unitarian Universalists to savor as we forge, or should I say, *forage* our futures.

Thoreau was not a sensually indulgent person, deficient in moral pursuits. Rather, for Henry David, employing our senses was a spiritual exercise. In experiencing nature's splendor up close, he encountered the holy, the multifarious beauty of the universe.

Thoreau waxed mystical about his sensuous activities. He referred to hearing "beyond the range of sound" and seeing "beyond the verge of sight." Henry went so far as to say that he could "see, smell, taste...feel that everlasting Something." God, he felt, could be apprehended by "divine germs called the senses." Thoreau was a naturalistic philosopher, an ecological mystic—a zany, incorrigible blend. He was on an expedition to find and sustain the unfathomable magnificence of the universe. For Thoreau, the fully sensuous and the wholly spiritual person were one and the same.

Naturalist Louis Agassiz was once asked how he planned to spend his upcoming summer. "Why, crawling across the backyard on my stomach and observing insect life, blades of grass, the pebbles and the earth," he replied. "Then, what will do you do with the rest of the time?" his questioner continued. "It's going to take me the whole summer to get halfway across the yard," Agassiz exclaimed.

While we are perhaps not as disciplined, let alone compulsive, as brother Louis, it remains our joyous duty, performed daily, to behold all the brilliance of this sprawling cosmos, beauty both awe-inspiring and ferocious.

May you and I internalize the ancient Celtic imagination that welcomed nature, divinity, and human existence as equal partners in one unified ecosphere…every bit of it rampant with soulful beauty.

Finally, a progressive faith celebrates the virtue of beauty in our own human creations and interactions.

Where did our human urge for creativity begin? Whence is its source? Contemporary cosmologist Brian Swimme relates how primal for human survival was our insistent drive for creativity. Our ancestors discovered fire in Africa over a million years ago, then set out on a great journey, arriving in EuroAsia. Alas, the ice age broke out, and they were compelled to hole up in caves for thousands of years. What did they do during this epoch? Did they whine and wither? No, instead their inner spirits spurred them to become astoundingly innovative and resourceful.

Progressive theologian Matthew Fox continues the story:

They put their imaginations to work. They learned how to prepare hides, sew warm outfits, hunt animals for food and clothing, and how to tell tales around the campfire and entertain themselves. In short, this is where our creativity came to birth.

Hence, our human capacity for inventiveness has ancient origins and continues to display itself through infinite expressions. Beauty is resplendent in the visual and visceral arts of dance, painting, sculpture, weaving, song, and architecture. Unitarian Universalist mystical humanist Kenneth Patton acknowledged that "the arts are the voices of humanity...peculiarly the language of religion."

In our current society, it has been noted that, at the age of five, about 90% of the population measures "high creativity." By seven, the figure has dropped to 10%, and when we reach adulthood, the number is staggeringly low: 2%. Why? Our creativity seems to be thwarted or diminished not by external force so much as criticism and innuendo. Countless adults have forgotten the magnificence of our inherent creative potential, when it comes time to beautify either our drab daily lives or our scruffy congregational buildings and unkempt grounds.

We can rekindle our original aptitude for beauty by holding in abeyance our analytic skills while bringing to the fore our appreciative ones. At core, beauty yearns to be experienced not over-scrutinized. Beauty often lies concealed, waiting to unfold and be disclosed—never fully caught—in its own peculiar way.

An art director friend refuses to pin descriptive labels on the original works in her gallery. Why? So that every visitor will experience these irrepeatable creations of beauty: first-hand, soul to soul. Martha is encouraging viewers to have what Jewish theologian Martin Buber called an I–Thou rather than an I–It experience.

Indeed, can we encounter an artistic creation, first and foremost, as a subject rather than an object? Subject to subject?

In our theological formation and deepening, beauty can take our breath away at the same time that it stimulates our mind and infuses our entire being with soulful quickening.

Our awareness is sharpened after viewing a Van Gogh painting or listening to a Beethoven sonata. Zen artists and craftspeople will often declare in the midst of something exquisite that they feel "received" or "embraced"...or as Plato said, "the inner and outer become as one" in the presence of beauty.

Not only is our perception heightened, but experiencing beauty often inspires us to create beauty of some sort, whether or not we're conventional or trained artists. When our hearts are imbued with beauty, we hanker for additional beauty in the world; we even yearn to contribute ourselves, however modestly, toward the beautification of the planet.

We begin to acknowledge, then internalize, our primary religious vocation as creators not destroyers. We vow, as our lives edge closer toward completion, to leave behind gifts of splendor and loveliness. Our creative response need not be a painting or a dance; it may be some caring, wonder-filled deed...magnificent to the core.

Beauty can be found and created in the midst of tragedy and injustice as well. Thoreau spoke of "severe beauty," by which I assume he meant that a moment or exchange is often abrasive and harsh, but still beautiful. Beauty at its most authentic can flourish in the throes of travail and travesty. Elaine Scarry in her book *On Beauty and Being Just* insinuates that "when beauty opens our hearts, our capacity to care for what is just and true enlarges."

Beholding or creating beauty lights our inner fire. It sets our souls ablaze. Beauty can generate the capacity, in human beings, to become bolder, better selves. Artistic pleasure doesn't necessarily produce a more responsible citizen, but the potential is present. Our mission is to embody Plotinus's sage phrase: "Those who behold beauty become themselves beautiful."

The word "fair" refers to something lovely but also to something just; for fairness yokes the worlds of beauty and justice. Unitarian Universalist Edward Harris professes: "Fair people keep their commitments, give fair gifts and forgive fairly. Try love as fairness. Life isn't fair, but love can be." So can beauty.

Emerson's trilogy of theological virtues—truth, goodness, and beauty—are vividly interweaving in our consciousness and conduct, as Unitarian Universalism reaches its golden anniversary and dances forward. For each virtue banks upon and kindles the other.

Deeper beauty harbors the promise of occasioning sounder truth and broader goodness in our religious lives, personally and communally.

REFLECTION AND DISCUSSION

1   Unitarian Universalist minister Elizabeth Lerner has written:
    Plato said that the good and the beautiful were inherently related, almost interchangeable. What is true and beautiful are good.

    Ponder and share.

2. In what ways have you found beauty present in your social justice efforts to eradicate the ugliness of the world?

3. *Each of us is an artist whose task it is to shape life into some semblance of the pattern we dream about.*
    The molding is not of self alone, but of shared tomorrow and times we shall never see. So, let us be about our task.
    The materials are very precious and perishable.
    —Arthur Graham *73 Voices,* 1972

In what ways do you consider what you do as a religious person to be "artistic" or "creative"?

4. Do you feel that when you are creating something original, perhaps attractive, that you are truly "sharing in the divine power of creation," to use Unitarian Universalist theologian Jack Hayward's phrase?

Please amplify.

5. *For me, the energy I experience in the process of creating a work of art is clearly the same energy I've experienced in mystical moments of spiritual insight or relationship. Creativity is core to my Unitarian Universalist theology.*
—Linda Weaver Horton

Is this the case for you? If so, share examples.

EVIL

Both the capacity for brutality and the capacity for love exist in all
of our hearts. A belief in our innocence is not an option.
We must find a place that can know the reality of both.
—William Sinkford

Evil is the capacity, within us and among us, to break sacred bonds with
our own souls, with one another, and with the holy. Furthermore, it is the
willingness to excuse or justify this damage, to deny it, or to call it virtue.
—Victoria Safford

Most religions focus on the inherent badness of humankind: we fell, we have fallen, and we will continue to fall. In contrast to the deeply pessimistic view that Martin Luther and John Calvin—and the churches they founded—have taken of human nature, Unitarian Universalists have been consistently optimistic. Sometimes, too much so.

In fact, we've been soft on sin and evasive with evil. Naturally, we've observed that people sometimes behave badly or do downright wicked things, but our steadfast focus has been on the human potentiality for good, the improvability, even the perfectibility of humanity. The faith of our liberal religious movement has riveted on the progress of the human race, "onward and upward forever."

The 20th century has been sobering to our romantic liberalism. Progress, it turned out, wasn't automatic; plus, some of our own progress has often been at the expense of other people, usually the disenfranchised and marginalized. The impulse to lie, to hurt, to kill has not been civilized out of us. There is indeed a propensity not only to live well but also to live dreadfully. Particularly, since World War II, our religion has become a more chastened one.

When I entered the Unitarian Universalist fold and was grilled before the Ministerial Fellowship Committee in Seattle in 1970, I remember being stopped in my tracks by one of the veteran and highly respected ministerial questioners, who said: "Tom, you seem like an able and amiable fellow. How do you deal with the evil in your personal and public lives?" All I recall is that the acuity of his question outstripped the profundity of my answer.

From that moment forward I've been ultrasensitive to the checkered nature of our humanity, starting with my own. And, so has our movement. Our theological quandary is this: if we're neither going onward and upward forever, nor tumbling backwards indefinitely, what keeps us from getting stuck, struggling to a standstill, or, at best, slithering sideways?

Our progressive religion has been acknowledging, in the last fifty years, that "nothing human is alien to our nature." We're still squeamish about facing up to our own demonic nature, evidenced by the fact that in hymn #205, "Amazing Grace," we allow folks to substitute, with impunity, "soul" for "wretch." But we're shifting.

In 1975, at my first UUMA (Unitarian Universalist Ministers' Association) Convocation in the Poconos, the preponderance of working papers on humanness stood in favor of our basic goodness. There were but a few on human treachery. However, on Convo's closing day, our communal attitude had altered. Our final verdict read that the human condition was inherently neutral with vast potentialities for embodying both good and evil:

> Our range of human behavior is ambiguous, complex and varied. Persons are capable of deep caring and destructive aggression. Our humanness must be defined to include us in our moments of the bestial and the sublime. We live in tension.

One visual summary of the week stands out in my memory. A colleague had drawn a circle surrounded by three words: "holiness, whollyness, and holeliness." How's that for our emerging trinitarian analysis of human nature!

What we shared in the Poconos was reinforced by what we were experiencing in Vietnam: our own grandeur and wickedness, ugliness and compassion on full display.

In any case, our optimism has been chastened, our cheerfulness qualified in the decades since merger. Nonetheless, we Unitarian Universalists won't ever apologize for being inveterate hopers. We still believe that it's possible to grow beyond tragedies, make spiritual comebacks, endure our plights, and, from time to time, even prevail.

In exploring this core theological theme, I want to accent the unflushable demons, the fact that evil is unconquerable and that wickedness comes with the territory of being alive. My assessment is that we can struggle and pray as hard as possible and evidences of evil, from which we cannot be delivered, still remain. Evil lives on before, during, and after we battle it—personal as well as systemic evil.

REFLECTIONS ON EVIL

There exists a tremendous temptation to spot or fight evil as if it is something totally outside oneself. In our current Article II, we promote a noble sentiment that runs:

> *"Words and deeds of prophetic women and men which challenge us to confront powers and structures of evil with justice, compassion, and the transforming power of love."*

That's an accurate description both of society's condition and our religious mandate, but it's a 100% half-truth. Article II doesn't recognize our own complicity in the evils we abhor. It imagines evil existing solely outside without recognizing the evil within ourselves and our movement.

Twenty-five years later, in our revised Article II (2009), the Commission on Appraisal recommended the following addition, mentioning for the first time since consolidation our own culpability in the perpetration of evil:

> *Capable of both good and evil, at times we are in need of forgiveness and reconciliation. When we fall short of living up to this covenant, we will*

begin again in love, repair the relationship, and recommit to the promises we have made.

Unitarian Universalist minister Richard Gilbert echoes this same outlook in his volume *The Prophetic Imperative*, a classic for kindling our flaming chalice:

Our potential for creativity is matched by our propensity for destruction... the line between good and evil runs right through the middle of each human heart.

Unquestionably, we have grown to the place of confessing more readily our own collusion in the evils of the cosmos. For the truth is clear: you and I, as well-intentioned Unitarian Universalists, have been known to wreak havoc at home and work, in our congregations, throughout society, and to the earth itself.

Most religious liberals don't commit felonious crimes. We don't steal cars or use the mails to defraud, embezzle company funds, or mug elderly people. Insofar as the law defines morality, we're fairly moral people. However, as we know, the law doesn't define morality. Evils and sins exist, to which the writ of the law does not run. We know the canker in ourselves.

We spot it in our small malices and our petty lies, in our angers, selfishness, and unworthy fears. We know it in our hypocrisy and jealousy and greed, in the minute brutalities that we commit, in our overweening pride and slothfulness. In the picayune angers that partners vent on each other, in the bullying of children by parents and vice versa, in the rivalries and vendettas within our organizations, including our congregations. In this panorama of daily evil, we see the shadow of all the murders and rapes and holocausts that have ever been or ever will be.

We humans have a tendency to locate evil in special, external spots where it can be placated and controlled. We do everything imaginable to avoid looking at the evil in our own souls. This is the great moral of Unitarian Herman Melville's *Moby Dick*, the specific tragedy of a person driven to confine all evil to the being of a mammoth white whale. The result is that Ahab, the one-legged fanatic, pulls down around his shoulders the lives of almost all with whom he comes in contact.

Now there are those who will say: "Well, while Unitarian Universalism can't conquer all evil, surely we can withhold our consent to it." Sounds reasonable, but that's precisely the shallow optimism we've been outgrowing in the past fifty years. The problem of evil is far more intractable than our most impressive resistance or retaliation.

Furthermore, the presence of evil is finally not only ineradicable, it's also inexplicable. There are countless explanations for why evil exists, but ultimately we must confess that we know not whence it cometh and why.

One of our sterling religious education curricula units, developed during the early decades following merger, was entitled "Why Do Bad Things Happen?" Our children were exposed to cross-cultural/religious samplings of the range of human responses to misfortune and suffering. Why do bad things happen has been a theological query befuddling folks from the beginnings of human life. And it's also a question children really ask.

The curriculum explores various answers concerning why bad things happen: because people or gods did something wrong in the very beginning; because we were bad in a past life we lived, we're being punished in this life; because of wrong thinking; because of evil spirits or the Devil; because we upset the harmony of the universe; because we're bad in this life and God is punishing us; because of an evil force fighting a good force; because of fate; because that's just the way the world is; and, finally, we don't know the ultimate answer and will always be searching and wondering.

This curriculum has been an impressive way of letting our children know early on that there's no single, conclusive answer to the tough theological enigmas of life but rather there exist innumerable hunches worth exploring, including their very own.

A mature Unitarian Universalism invites our children to recognize that evil isn't a problem to be solved so much as a reality to be faced. We want our children to be comfortable moving amid the imponderables of existence. We want them to know that they can't expect a guarantee that life will always be safe or fair. We want them to understand that bad things do happen—including bad stuff of their own doing—despite all human efforts to the contrary. These lessons are crucial in the theological development of our offspring, indeed of us all.

How desperately we upbeat, life-affirming religionists would relish both understanding *and* flushing evil once and for all. However, we humans can do neither completely.

The Hindus have a much subtler understanding of the nature of good and evil than have our Western religions, where we tend toward absolute dichotomies. The Hindus recognize that nothing is all good or all evil; everything in existence is a mixture of both. Our aim, although not necessarily our accomplishment, therefore, must be to let the good predominate.

This is all reflected in the marvelous myth of Narakarasura on whose birthday Divali, the great fall festival of India, is celebrated. Does it seem strange to celebrate the triumph of good over evil on the birthday of an evil demon? In Hindu lore, Narakarasura was an evil demon, but was the son of the great preserver-god, Vishnu. Narakarasura was by no means all bad. He did much good in his life, and for a long while the good prevailed.

However, he became an increasingly evil influence, and when the evil began to outweigh the good, Vishnu decreed that he must die. "But," protested Narakarasura, "don't the scriptures say that good follows good as evil follows evil?" "Yes," said Vishnu, "that is correct." "Then what do I get for the good I have done?" asked Narakarasura. "What do you think you should get?" asked Vishnu. "I think," said

Narakarasura slyly, "that when you celebrate the triumph of good over evil, you should do it on *my* birthday!"

That's why the Hindu festival of Divali falls on the birthday of an evil demon. Divali reminds us that, in the long run, our best solution is to proclaim a truce, an end to dualism, and welcome the warring factions into the human commonwealth.

As Unitarian Universalists, we will continue to do what we can and must in the ongoing struggle with evil. Struggle is central to fanning our flame. We won't end evil, but we can diminish our participation in it. We can confess when and where we're involved in evil—socially, economically, politically, spiritually, and environmentally—and alter our behavior to support mercy, justice, sustainability, and peace.

A turning point of spiritual growth arrives when we make sufficient peace with our wild and wooly natures, when we recognize as Unitarian Universalist lay author Peter Fleck puts it "the blessings of imperfection."

I remember asking a religious education class of fifth graders, early in my career as a Minister of Education in the late 1960s, the following question: "If all the good people in the world were red, and all the bad people were green, what color would you be?" And 10-year-old Jeannie thought mightily for a moment, then her face brightened, and she replied: "Reverend Tom, I'd be streaky and so would you!" And a little child shall lead us.

In his book *The Medussa and the Snail* biologist Lewis Thomas observes that we humans "are built to make mistakes, we're coded for error," that is, for being imperfect. We learn primarily by trial and error, not by trial and triumph. Progress requires error. This principle doesn't only apply to humans. It permeates the animal realm too. It's the very stuff of evolution. Take the amphibians. The first one that crawled out of the water onto the land didn't do so because its feet were so strong, but because its gills were so weak. The imperfection of its gills made that first amphibian into an animal of a higher order.

Ben Franklin used to say that he had created about 200 inventions, but that since each success first required an average of 15 failures, he boasted that he had to his credit over 3000 failures.

Mistakes are our human way of doing something different, perhaps creatively new. When we do only those things that please us—that are safe and unfrightening—after awhile, fewer and fewer things please us. Over time, our circle of options shrinks, until we're prisoners in tiny manicured gardens of our own making contented and dull.

Hence, theological maturity calls us to combat perfection. While singing the praises of imperfection, a liberal—make that liberating—theology would exhort us to be good not pure, to be whole not flawless, to keep evolving all our days and nights.

Unitarian Universalism proclaims that perfection is an unrealizable goal, even when you think of it in terms of eons and eons. Gutzon Borglum, the sculptor who created the tremendous Mount Rushmore memorial, was once asked if he considered his work perfect in detail. "Not today," he replied. "The nose of Washington is an inch too long. It's better that way, though. It'll erode to be approximately right in perhaps 10,000 years."

Do you know that it's only imperfect heartbeats that keep us alive? Cardiologists are discovering that the heart approaches a perfect symmetry and balance…only a few hours before we die. As we live and love and cry and dance, our hearts always contain a slightly irregular rhythm.

Perfectionism isn't only an unreachable goal; it's an undesirable one as well. I happen to find people who strut about, like the Pharisees in Christian scriptures, thanking God they're not like other folks to be both boring and obnoxious. Religion for too long has suffocated from what some wit called "the passionate pursuit of passionless perfection."

Unitarian Universalist comic Steve Allen used to proclaim: "I'm loyal to a fault. That is, I've got a great many faults, and I'm loyal to every one of them." Mistakes are our human way of doing something different, perhaps creatively new. Jazz musicians declare that our job is to make our mistakes mean something in the overall stream of a musical piece. Indeed, the most striking evidence of life anywhere is growth, and growing entails making bundles of mistakes.

Here's the bottom line: we're both good and evil. I've been saluting the evil side, but the truth is we're good, good enough, just as we are, and while we need to negotiate improvements along the way and reduce the evil we perpetrate, we'll never approximate perfection, so let's drop any and all efforts to do so. We're placed on earth, during this single and wondrous lifespan, to be whole persons, defects and all. We're neither immaculately conceived nor impeccably developed creatures and never will be. Yet we humans have everything at our disposal to live gratifying lives for ourselves and all living entities.

Unitarian Universalist theology is progressively impelled to say that existence, including our very humanity, is neither all good nor all bad. It is simply all. And always will be. Turning fifty and catching fire theologically, we're sounding more and more like Job:

> *Naked I came from my mother's womb, and naked shall I return. The Lord gave and the Lord has taken away; blessed be the name of the Lord. (Job 1:21)*

Interpreted, that means good and evil exist, and it's still worthwhile, make that blessed, to be alive.

FOR REFLECTION AND DISCUSSION

1. In serving as a member of the Unitarian Universalist Trauma Response Ministry in New York City, right after the September 11th (2001) attacks, minister Rosemary Bray McNatt mused:

    I am afraid we have consistently underestimated the people and the systems we opposed, and overestimated our own skill, our own willingness, and our own resilience. I am afraid that we have settled for cheap grace in a very expensive world...None of us can ever really be innocent again, and frankly, innocence is overrated. But we can be givers and receivers of a more demanding love and a more focused power, starting with one another in the religious communities that shelter us and support our lives.

    Consider and comment upon this statement for the living of your personal, congregational, and societal lives.

2. *The Humanist Manifesto III (1983) clearly states: "We are committed to treating each person as having inherent worth and dignity." It does not say that all people have inherent worth and dignity. Clearly they do not. As William Schulz points out, people have "to be assigned worth...and taught to behave with dignity." This is our responsibility.*
    —James Carroll Simms (excerpt from a *UU World* letter)

    In light of our evolving theology of evil, how would you respond to this combined statement of Simms and Schulz, both card-carrying, contemporary Unitarian Universalists?

3. Lois Fahs Timmins, the daughter of Sophia Lyon Fahs, our most notable religious educator, relates the story of her own experience growing up in our religious education program:

   We spent 95% of our time studying good people doing good things, and skipped very lightly over the bad parts of humanity... Consequently, because of my education, I grew up ignorant about bad human behavior, incompetent to observe it accurately, unskilled in how to respond to it, and ashamed of talking about evil.

   Is that still the case in our religious education programs? If you were in charge, how would you design a religious education curriculum, with respect to the good and evil in human beings?

GOD

How do you prove God? How do you prove love? It can only be proven by the
evidence of its presence, by witnessing acts that convey the assurance that lets
one feel loved. One feels God…and then one knows.
—Marni Harmony

If I used the word God this week, I don't commit myself to use it next week.
Nor do I contradict myself if, late the same Sunday, I say gods or Void or
Goddess or (that old humanist standby) Spirit of Life.
—Dan Hotchkiss

My life-journey has been one extended wrestling match with God—starting with an early mindless embrace to categorical rejection, then gradually yet resolutely proceeding toward my current status as a questioning believer or trustful agnostic. I'm a theological hybrid who chooses to juggle live paradoxes concerning the Holy. I dwell at peace with Walt Whitman's claim: "Do I contradict myself? Yes, I contain multitudes!" I imagine that innumerable Unitarian Universalists, when pressed, would admit to being hybrids as well.

Without presuming to encapsulate the overall Unitarian Universalist theological climate, I detect a palpable enthusiasm (literally, "god-filledness") within our contemporary fold. Let me elaborate.

A couple decades ago when poet May Sarton addressed the Unitarian Church in Brattleboro, Vermont, she remarked that "the kind, intelligent people gathered in a big room looking out on pine trees did not really want to think about God, His absence (many of my poems speak of that) or His presence." Sarton's pointed observation no longer holds certain for Unitarian Universalism as we turn fifty years of age and mosey ahead into our sixth decade as a movement.

Nowadays, newcomers are entering our gates hungry for both spiritual affiliation and discipline, particularly the younger generations. Most are unabashedly seeking some sense of the transcendent.

As Unitarian Universalist minister Fred Muir reminds us: "Younger and newer people expect a language of reverence when they enter our ranks, simply one free of dogma."

A new member in my own parish recently opined: "I originally came to this congregation to seek God, but I quickly became occupied on various committees, and soon I lost the time and energy to look for the Holy. In retrospect, I'm sorry it happened that way. I seem to have suffered a huge spiritual loss, and I want to get back on the theological track!" Parishioners are finding the time and pressing the issue now—bursting forth from cocoons of theological shyness, apathy, or blatant resistance.

Modern-day Unitarian Universalists are engrossed in covenant circles and study groups, feeding their spirits through doing *theology*: engaging in a form of mapmaking where the mystery of *theos* is represented by means of a *logos* or word picture. Congregants are choosing to become intentional, oft-serious, passionate "practicing theologians" themselves rather than merely turning the job over to the hired, in-resident religious professionals.

Furthermore, witness the extensive interest concerning deity in our larger society. Steve Waldman, co-founder of *beliefnet.com,* remarking on the most popular topics on the Internet, says: "God is right up there with sex!" The same is true in the printed word as well, with a spate of recent volumes either rebuking or advocating the presence of God in human existence…in either case, consciously wrestling with "divinity."

The Infinite One has been getting more pro-and-con ink today than in several decades, oft from the unlikely pens of established physicists or adventurous literati. Plenty of Unitarian Universalist sermonizers and commentators have chimed in as well. There even exists contemporary medical research that makes the case for a sixth human sense that intuitively perceives the divine. God may be on the human brain, declare some scientists. Perhaps we're hardwired to be theologians.

God is presumably bemused by the current avalanche of chatter about Him/Her/It. Is this theological fervor due to social unrest, spiritual appetite, psychic loneliness, or just what, especially in our own Unitarian Universalist ranks? I would venture all of those reasons plus countless others.

In any case, we must be cautious never to confuse verbiage about God with proximity to God. *The Upanishads* (Hindu scriptures) send brash metaphysicians reeling when they caution: "Those who think that God is not comprehended, by them God is comprehended; but those who think that God is comprehended, know God not."

Whereas there exist mounds of words from both apologists and detractors today, there's precious little, spoken or composed, that applauds critical piety, trustful uncertainty, and skeptical believing as complementary attitudes in the theological quest. That's where Unitarian Universalism shines, for, at our most superb, we celebrate an unheralded yet distinct approach to the question of an Ultimate Being.

Along with Jacob, the epitaph of countless Unitarian Universalists could gladly read: "You have wrestled with beings divine and human" (Genesis 32:29). We've been known to emerge from many a theological skirmish limping yet graced with a new name such as the one Jacob acquired: "Israel"—literally, "the one who struggles with God." From our perspective, being a bona fide godwrestler comprises a reputable pursuit and holy bargain. We freethinking mystics would second Simone Weil's sentiment: "One can never wrestle enough with God, if one does so out of pure regard for truth."

The 21st century demands our healthiest grasp, however flawed and unfinished, of the human–divine dynamic.

Being riders of paradoxes is our peculiar niche as liberal religionists. We seem to pitch tent and stoke our flaming chalices in the creases between mysticism and humanism, theism and naturalism, believing and doubting, devotion and skepticism. At our most stout and resourceful, Unitarian Universalists are spiritually ambidextrous, defining ourselves both from below and above. We're a reasonable religion with numinous sensibilities—in short, we're theological crossbreeds. Colleague Frances West puts it sagely: "The humanist and the theist live in me, each sometimes puzzled by the presence of the other, but willing to keep talking. So may it continue."

There's a danger in either extreme. Arid humanism can trap us in the mundane and material, making us oblivious to transrational (note I didn't say irrational) nudges. On the other hand, unbridled theism can swallow humans in the supernal ether, when our paramount job is to make this precious earth more beautiful and just.

God-fearing or mystical humanism is a principle theological paradox Unitarian Universalists must harness, then ride. Some do it sidesaddle, tentatively; others with both hands to the reins, galloping full-bore ahead. Regardless, it can provide a spirited jaunt.

As Unitarian Universalism turns fifty and blazes ahead theologically, we embrace being fully rational, fully spiritual, and fully compassionate—heeding Ezekiel's imperative "to go into the gaps." We deem it not merely tolerable, but desirable, as theological nonconformists to live well amidst the intractable qualms and nasty confusions at the heart of Reality.

Speaking of gaps, I'm reminded of our family excursion to the Sistine Chapel in Rome during a sabbatical. My mind's eye remains riveted upon the dazzling panel in Michelangelo's ceiling mural depicting Adam and God. Adam raises an arm in the direction of the Infinite One, whose extremity, in turn, stabs down toward the dewy creature. Index fingers on both hands reach toward the other but do not touch. Everything trembles in midair between these outstretched fingers of humanity and divinity tirelessly striving to connect, perhaps bond. And so it goes. In that zone where we stretch but do not grasp one another is precisely where the bulk of our existence is lived as Unitarian Universalist theologians.

Who really wants reality tidily wrapped up? Who covets convictions set in stone? Lots of people to be sure, but not Unitarian Universalists, at least not theologically. Being riders of paradoxes isn't a dire position of last resort but our first choice. It's the way we desire to walk and talk, live and die during our sojourn on this planet. It's the way our flame is kindled and stoked.

When we examine the credentials of the signers of the Humanist Manifesto back in 1933, two things stand out. First, most of the 34 were card-carrying Unitarian and/or Universalist ministers. Second, while the designers were neither secularists nor supernaturalists, they exuded an obvious fondness for the sacred. Unlike the orthodox theists of their day, they didn't worship an omnipotent, patriarchal figure, high in the sky. Nonetheless, they were conspicuously reverent travelers. They handled holy things with feeling. They were utterly open to the divine circulating through this earthly trek.

These thorough-going humanists dared to talk of God, indeed, comfortably so, but in collaborative, naturalist terms. They considered some sort of partnership between heaven and earth to be our sacred summons. As Unitarian signer Burdette Backus put it:

Whenever we are helping humanity to be at its best, we are worshipping God...we are the children of a creative and dynamic universe, and its restless energy is at work within us to carry forward the work of creation. This is something of what I mean when I say that I believe in God...God is not an idea to be believed in; God is work to be done in the world.

The Humanist worldview was amplified with an additional manifesto in 1973, then another in 2003. The central theme of all three manifestos is the elaboration of a philosophy and value system that doesn't necessarily include belief in any personal deity or "higher power." It was intrepidly stated in the manifesto of 1973: "No deity will save us; we must save ourselves. We are responsible for what we are and for what we will be."

Our Unitarian Universalist spiritual ancestors and contemporaries have struggled to extend religion beyond narrow humanism and doctrinaire theism. They've been both hard-headed and soft-hearted theologians, refusing to harm anyone with their view of either humanity or divinity. We've inherited a legacy of seekers who are grounded in the soil of this planet, whether meditating upon the heavens or protesting earthly wrongs. That's still our summons as conscientious theologians in 2011.

It's the manifest strength of present-day Unitarian Universalism, as we wrestle with God, that our adherents can honestly assume the positions of affirmatist, agnostic, and atheist—at different junctures in our journey, or even concurrently—and still be considered honorable religious questors.

When the three A's (atheism, agnosticism, and affirmatism) are clasped in resourceful tension, our Unitarian Universalist identity becomes hale and hearty—for each attitude brings an indispensable gift to the theological table, furnishing a cogent system of checks and balances.

Atheism is a purifying influence, burning away obsolete or abhorrent renditions of the divine. True prophets invariably spend the bulk of their time interfering with and raging against puerile notions of the Eternal.

Atheism proves most valuable as a clarifying, cleansing vehicle and least useful when stubborn or combative. *Protest* marks a progressive attitude that not only rejects certain viewpoints but, moreover, "testifies on behalf of" what we hold to be true. Atheism is beneficial when employed in service of religious wisdom rather than as an outright negation of it.

Being an honest atheist places one in good religious company the world over. There are nontheistic as well as theistic strands of Hinduism. Such pilgrims are also consonant with the philosophy of Theravada Buddhism, one of the major world religions, where there exists no single, uniform concept of a deity. Buddha himself warned that speculation about either the nature of deity or an afterlife not only was futile but also tended not to edification.

As for the Zen Buddhists, when one famous Roshi was asked,

"What does Zen say about God," he remained silent.

The high religions of Asia do not acknowledge a personal absolute, yet consider the world to be unmistakably numinous. In China, Confucianism is essentially atheist in that it concentrates on rules of behavior for the conduct of human life but has little to say about deity as a personal entity. It challenges earthlings to live in harmony with the way of duty rather than worship a supernal being.

Jainism, another great religion born in India, possesses no notion of a creator god, yet remains an uncommonly ethical faith, whose aspiration is to free the soul from bondage to matter through ascetic discipline.

Atheism at its healthiest—dare I say, at its holiest—provides a critical, purifying role in the pursuit of reasonable religion.

Agnosticism supplies the essential gift of measured indecision, challenging earthlings to handle the sacred lightly without forcing it into formulas, to "live in the questions" (Rilke), rather than yielding to either certitude or apathy.

Agnosticism—the permanent suspension of belief based on incomplete knowledge—marks the human condition. We can't escape the existential state of partial wisdom. Certitude will never be within our grasp. "A definite maybe" was the phrase cartoonist Walt Kelly used when answering what he considered the really big questions.

As proper agnostics, Unitarian Universalists don't possess the luxury of freezing our minds or tethering our spirits. We keep on keeping on, engaged in a lifelong theological adventure. We refuse to recline in premature ignorance. Our minds and souls remain ablaze.

The term agnostic, from the Greek *a-gnostos*, translates as "not knowing" and specifically refers to one who remarks, "I do not know." The Sanskrit antecedent of the Greek contained additional emotional overtones: "to stand in awe before the unknown." Standing in awe means more than merely being ignorant, nonchalant, or dumbstruck. It denotes active reverence. Indisputably, one can be a reverent agnostic, singing with the psalmist, "Great is the Lord, and greatly to be praised; his greatness is unsearchable."

There is a time in the theological sojourn to voice our affirmations with clarity and cogency. A season also exists to show the courage of our confusions. Furthermore, part of the religious quest impels us to surrender to what the Buddhists call *sunyata*: emptiness or void, a reality that cannot be pinned down as this or that. Emptiness is emptiness, the void is void, and is to be experienced, even celebrated, as such.

The agnostic proudly identifies with sacred journeyers such as the Muslim who speaks of a quaking heart and a stuttering voice in the presence of God, and St. Anselm of Canterbury, the Christian theologian of the Middle Ages, who posited *fides quaerens intellectum*... namely, "faith in search of understanding." These spiritual travelers exemplified a reverent agnosticism.

Huston Smith, a world religions specialist and frequent presenter in Unitarian Universalist circles, has playfully remarked: "A human trying to understand God is like a dog contemplating humans. They know something about the other, but not everything." Such is the plight of the agnostic—sometimes perturbed and perturbing, but more often than not, aglow with sufficient calm. Admitting that we possess but partial knowledge keeps our egos in check, our souls lit, and our minds maturing...theologically.

Affirmatism unflinchingly insists upon the inherent sacredness of existence, announcing "the lurking places of God" (Thoreau), especially surprising locales of holy portent.

When focusing on where to look for God in the crazy tangle of the cosmic web, it's seductive to fixate on familiar and flamboyant haunts, such as natural beauty, sexual communion, musical epiphanies, truth-speaking, and deeds of goodness. While conceding the richness of well-trod avenues to Divine Presence, the challenge of Unitarian Universalism remains to stalk the Holy in fresh hangouts, such as service, laughter, materiality, turmoil, quietude, and surrender…a few of my own favorite lurking-places of God.

Presumably the key for a transformative theologian is to remain wide-open to fresh sightings of the divine in our daily existence, remembering, as Rainer Maria Rilke suggests, to think of God as a *direction* rather than an object. One of our prominent contemporary Unitarian Universalist essayists, Nancy Shaffer, counsels in a similar vein: "May our list of names for the Holy not ever be finished; and may we hear God chuckling with us as we find still more."

Two of our most prominent 20th-century Unitarian Universalist theologians Charles Hartshorne and Henry Nelson Wieman were proclaimers of this serendipitous view of the divine. Hartshorne, who maintained a vigorous mind to the end of his 103 years, was influenced deeply both by his father, a practicing theologian, and by his mother, who inspired him with a simple statement that he never forgot. "Charles," she told him, when he was a boy, "life is big, life is big." Consequently, Hartshorne continually expounded a theology that was expansive in scope and vast in spirit.

Hartshorne concluded that God breaks into human experience through the truly novel and creative. Wieman developed a philosophy of naturalistic theism where God is understood to be a power inherent in the universe that "persuades" or "lures" all living things forward toward their ultimate fulfillment. He named that power "Creative Interchange"—the universal force that, when enjoined, utterly changes human beings. Therefore, to participate in the radically open, interdependent, transformative venture called Unitarian Universalism meant, to these process theologians, linking in faithful partnership with Creativity.

Whatever the nature of our individual wrestling matches with God, Blake's admonition obtains: "Without contraries, there is no progression." Healthy atheism produces a more inventive agnostic, while affirmatism impels us to be more supple atheists and agnostics. Holding paradoxes in sincere stretch keeps both suspicious and gullible proclivities from running amok.

While entertaining the singular wisdom of all three approaches, Unitarian Universalists are motivated to proceed cautiously along the soulful path, for each interpretation harbors its own shadows as well. The atheist is susceptible to narrowness of soul and horizon. The agnostic is vulnerable to "the brutality of indiscriminate skepticism" (Unitarian Herman Melville). And the affirmatist can unwittingly become a sanctimonious crusader.

Holding to the critical gifts of our atheism, agnosticism, and affirmatism, we avow God as wholeheartedly as proves reasonable to each Unitarian Universalist seeker. And unless we succumb to premature hardening of the spiritual arteries, we'll likely argue with heaven all the way home. The good news intrinsic to our life-affirming religion is that, as Thomas Carlyle remarked: "Life is one long quarrel with God, but we make up in the end."

Well, to be painstakingly honest, some of us will reconcile and some of us may never do so. For others, the divine–human connection will remain annoyingly half-baked, perhaps partially broken. The best any of us earthlings can promise is to keep our wrestling with God current, honest, and respectful.

FOR REFLECTION AND DISCUSSION

1. In what specific ways would you claim to be an atheist, an agnostic, and an affirmatist? If you prefer another self-declared theological identity, please share what it is.

2. Does the phrase "theological hybridism" relate to your spiritual posture in any fashion? If so, describe and discuss.

3. Dana Greeley, the first President of our merged Association, wrote:

    I cannot think of God as a person. But I can think of God as energy and light and love, both in me and around me, and present a thousand billion miles away. The universe is too wonderful not to have a cohesive and purposeful power behind it. It cannot be an accident.

    Comment and discuss.

4. Amplify upon when and where you seem to find the divine, the holy, God or Goddess in your daily existence.

5. Describe the ways in which your Unitarian Universalist congregation has created opportunities for respectful conversation concerning God. If it remains uncomfortable to talk about God in your parish, what might you and others do about that situation?

FAITHFULNESS

God gives different gifts, different kinds of faith to different people.
Therefore, we dare not try to change another person's faith. It is God's gift
to them...Francis David knew that faith cannot be given by bishops, neither
can it be taken away by dictators.
—Carl Scovel

Belief comes from an Indo-European root that means to love and has the fla-
vor of trust. Somehow the core of religion seems to be a profound trust, and
that is laid in the heart and grows from love.
—Kenneth Collier

FAITH

When conventional religions talk about faith, they're referring to either: (1) belief in the traditional doctrines of a specific religion; or (2) the firm belief in something for which there is no proof. On both scores, Unitarian Universalists beg to differ. For us, faith is deeper than belief or doctrine. Faith is the energizing spirit that gives birth to our convictions, which lie deeper than our anxiety and stretch higher than our comprehension.

A spate of books have arrived recently announcing religion's demise, volumes such as *The End of Faith* (*Religion, Terror and the Future of Reason*) by Sam Harris. These authors properly deride the dangers and absurdities of organized religion. However, they never demolish the virtue of faithfulness, at least not in our eyes, since, for the most part, they're razing straw-figures.

Genuine faith is that confidence which allows, indeed implores, us to keep on moving forward even when we see partially, know incompletely, and act imperfectly. Faith liberates us to pursue precarious and flawed living without either the illusion of omnipotence or stifling despair. When we're faithful (full of faith), we often become devoted and dependable pilgrims.

In religious circles we've improperly translated *credo* to mean "I believe" when it actually means "I give my loyalty, my heart, my faithfulness to." Belief implies intellectual assent; faith grips one's entire being. Credo, in its original sense, has to do with our core affirmations that result in firm commitments, not just warm feelings, leaping surmises, or noble sentiments.

As Unitarian Universalists, avoiding the treacherous extremes of gullibility and cynicism, we aspire to maintain an attitude of faith. We embrace a faith that enables us to face head-on tragedy or disaster, then be spiritually fortified to rebuild our lives. We harbor faith that, however limited by poverty or health, mind or material resources, people can think honestly and live nobly. We have faith that folks can, not that they always will.

We hold faith that the universe is webbed, organic, one, unified, and to be treated as such. We don't know that proposition for sure nor can we prove it in any definitive fashion, although there's ample evidence. Unity-of-life is more a perception than a certainty. What makes it more than just an idle assertion or viewpoint is our willingness to bank our lives on it. In point of fact, faith is not something we posit or possess so much as something we practice. That's why it leads to faithfulness.

When we hold something on faith, we bet our lives on it. We take leaps of faith, albeit reasonable and compassionate ones. That process constitutes our religion. It takes time, a whole lifetime.

Put another way, Unitarian Universalists are skeptical, while skirting cynicism. What's the difference? Skepticism aids us in pruning and clarifying our faith, while cynicism leads to spiritual treason. There's doubt that leads to creative dissent or skepticism and doubt that results in debilitating denial or cynicism. In short, liberal religionists are comfortable being doubting believers, wherein we can still be decisive without turning dogmatic.

Skepticism is a precision tool that prunes out the dead wood from the trees of our faith. Yet if trees are clipped ruthlessly, instead

of intelligently, they'll bear little fruit. They can even die. Overprun-
ing is the result of cynicism. We are a dogged lot, holding on to hard-
won claims while remaining open to novel insights. Our theological
mission is to be faithful to ourselves, to the human community, and
to the universe and all therein: maintaining fidelity and loyalty to the
entire crew of living entities on this spacecraft.

Furthermore, our espoused values and virtues must prove reasonable to us. While we may affirm principles that go *beyond* our
reason, they're summarily dropped if going *counter* to our reason. In
short, we make the distinction between the transrational or mystical
and the irrational or dubious.

The rationale for labeling this theological theme "faithfulness"
is that we're a covenantal religion that majors in people making
pledges and promises to one another. We wish to be resolute in our
affection and conscientious in our duties: in short, faithful.

Novelist Philip Roth in *Portnoy's Complaint* renders a poignant
passage where Portnoy ends up saying in effect: "May I never hurt
someone else with my view of God!" Alas, religion has comprised one
of the most fiercely dogmatic and bigoted—indeed, hurtful—realms
of human intercourse, and our job as followers of the open mind
is to produce a safer, saner globe for everyone: doubting believers,
nonbelievers, and, even inflexible believers.

Believing in the inherent worth and dignity of every person
means that, on the whole, people possess sufficient capacity of mind
and heart to make our own good decisions rather than turning our
souls over to some guru, however bright or charming. The Buddha
put it plainly: "Be a lamp unto yourself."

Here's the litmus test: beware of anyone who fascinates, capti-
vates, or overwhelms us. Remember: Unitarian Universalism isn't
exempt from such a temptation; for pedagogues can sport a new age
look or be housed in an ultraprogressive guise.

My point is simple: fellow humans can serve as useful guides but
can never be the governors of our personal destinies. Only we are

responsible for shaping our singular character and course, by wisely processing all the animate and inanimate stuff, human and divine resources, circulating in this cosmos.

As people of the open mind, we simply can't affirm whatever we'd like, for we're a people of faithfulness not fantasies, mystery not sorcery. We can affirm only what our minds in consort with our hearts and consciences will allow us, indeed authorize us, to affirm.

We live beyond reason and despite doubt. We live by faith. Faith is integral to every central bond of our human existence: be it communion with self, neighbor, nature, or God. In all these covenantal bonds, we proceed deliberately but confidently, despite partial wisdom and flawed vision. We advance by faith. Such faith means that, despite the nagging insecurities and doubts of our existence, we believe that this world is bathed in working miracles.

As religious pilgrims committed to faithfulness, we know that we dare not travel alone. We build beloved communities, garnering companions with whom we can demonstrate the courage of both our convictions and our confusions…and with whom we can persistently serve, without ever expecting to save, the larger world.

TRUST

Many therapists would claim, and I would agree, that the basic task of all religion is to reaffirm the first relationship of trust between parent and child: namely, the original assurance that somebody is present for and tied with me, without whom I cannot live.

We can never experience too much trust, too early. Little ones need all the sustaining support they can receive from the moment they burst into this magnificent yet frightening scene called life. During our Unitarian Universalist child celebrations, our purpose isn't to save babies from purgatory, let alone hell, but to give each child the best running start possible on this earth. We concede our babies' "vulnerable requests for warmth and affection, for trust and honesty." We let our offspring know that not only their parents are glad they're alive, so is an entire congregation.

Our three San Diego grandchildren—Trevor, 15; Corinne, 13; and Owen, 8—are blessedly surrounded with many trustworthy, loving hands, beginning with their devoted parents and circling forth through solid schools and a supportive Unitarian Universalist congregation. Carolyn and I possess the unsurpassed joy of merely adding our ingredients to the nurture of these grandchildren.

Almost every Wednesday, since Trevor was born, we've had one of the grandkids with us for the entire day. Not long ago, we closed out our time with Owen—our final San Diego grandbaby—before he trekked off to kindergarten.

I'll never forget the little stylized ritual that Trevor and I enjoyed, when he was perhaps three or so. Late in the afternoon, we'd go outdoors, and with him on my shoulder, we'd peek over his family's fence into the backyard of a certain neighbor, scouting about for new and old objects or whatever grabbed our attention. Then we'd play with a rubber ball or engage in some physical activity. When it grew nearly dark, we'd gaze skyward to see what might be going on in the heavens.

One time, we spotted the moon and some stars and were staring away, quietly. I gave his tiny back a circling rub; then, I felt his little hand return the favor. No words were spoken or necessary. Loving, I was loved back. Caressed, Trevor kept the gift moving. It's what we call trust.

Kids need such connections of embodied trust from birth or their spirits shrivel. And, yes, we adults never grow too old for back rubs as well.

Let me relate another childhood incident of trust, an exchange I had as a ten-year-old newspaper carrier. I'm sure our son, Russ, experienced something similar when he delivered papers as well on his trusty Schwinn.

As Mrs. Taylor grew increasingly blind, she came to the place where she could no longer see to make accurate change when I came to her home to collect. Perhaps you remember the days when we delivered daily newspapers by foot and bicycle rather than by car and when we collected at the end of the month in person.

Anyway, on that unforgettable Saturday morning Mrs. Taylor drew her leather pocketbook from her purse, handed it to me and said: "Tommy, I can't see very well any more; please help yourself to whatever I owe you, plus a quarter tip." As I opened the purse, with a snap on top, I was suddenly struck with far more than money. I was struck with what a wonderful thing it is to be trusted, utterly trusted!

By definition then, trust is neither intellectual certitude nor impulsive faith. It's even more than confidence. Trust is derived from the German word "trost," meaning *comfort*, implying an instinctive, unquestioning reliance upon something or someone. Sort of like Trevor gently rubbing my back and my rubbing his, or Mrs. Taylor opening her purse and her heart to me. Trust happens whenever we embrace another person without pressure or strings attached.

Trust is a profound spiritual affirmation; it becomes our core way of seeing and sizing up the world. The trusting person claims that it's right and good to be alive, for *me* to be alive, right *here* and *now*.

When I trust my inner self, I can grow to become the person I'm meant to become. And when I trust you, I'm able to allow you to share life's journey with me. I'm able to give and receive generously. I'm able to be intimate. Trust is crucial to a stable and enduring devotional bond, be it between family members, partners, work associates, or members of a congregation. The Beloved Community is an impossibility without a sufficient supply of ongoing trust.

Another parallel exists. In rock climbing, there's a step called the "commitment move." You're tied to the ropes, and there's a moment you have to let go of solid ground to move to the next higher place. It's a scary step. Why? Because you must trust what you're tied to more than what you're standing on.

To keep our flaming chalice ablaze, Unitarian Universalists need to remember that we're not involved in some independent trek but enmeshed in an interdependent adventure. We're tethered in sacred trust, within and among congregations, for all the days and nights we shoulder this valued venture called Unitarian Universalism.

We're yoked not only to all current Unitarian Universalists across the globe; we're also tied inextricably to countless sisters and brother in our illustrious free faith heritage who've gone before us as well as all those "freethinking mystics with hands" coming on ahead. Truly knowing, then fully trusting, "whose" we are is central to our spiritual evolution.

We're fastened to a whole lot—events and deeds, as well as people. Can you feel the tug? Are you willing to yank and be yanked purposefully and compassionately, all the way home, as a partisan Unitarian Universalist compadre?

Trust means that we won't ever intentionally be harmed by another; yet trust also means that we'll be positively critiqued and gently challenged, when necessary. Whenever we're filled with trust, we can blurt out: "I'm surrounded and sustained by support even when I seem to be slipping or sinking." Philip Booth's poem epitomizes trust when it says: "Lie gently and wide to the light-year stars. Lie back and the sea will hold you." Booth is pointing to what Christianity has called the loving arms of Jesus or what our Universalist faith means when it encourages us to "rest assured," knowing that everyone everywhere resides in the trustworthy embrace of a spirit of eternal love.

One doesn't have to practice a conventional religion or even to believe in any particular conception of God to be whole. What's critical to becoming a whole person, indeed a holy pilgrim, is whether or not we harbor an attitude of bedrock trust in response to ourselves and others, indeed the entire Creation itself. At core, are we fearful or are we trusting? Are we filled with faith or bedeviled by pessimism and suspicion? Are we ablaze with gladness or awash with despond? Unitarian Universalism is far from being a perfect religion. We're marked by ample warts and biases, but when we remain true to our mission, we're a life-affirming rather than a life-denying people. We major in hope not despair, trust over dread, and we place love at the heart of our every choice.

It's our clear charge to create a good earth rather than wait around for a flawless heaven. While realizing the inestimable value of boundary-setting and establishing clear-cut noes in life, we choose to be an affirming flame that will shine the way for those we know and those we'll never meet. We choose to become a living Yes, each in our own, inimitable fashion.

When Moses struck the Dead Sea with his wand, nothing happened. The sea only opened when the first person plunged in. When that first person took the plunge, said Yes to life (*L'Chaim*) with his very body and soul, then, and only then, did the Dead Sea open forth.

Oh, that tiny but majestic word: *Yes*, the mightiest word in the lexicon of any language. Yes is unquestionably the key word of our life-affirming, this-worldly, faithful religion. Yes, I can be that; yes, I will do that; yes, you can count on me to be present and responsible. Unitarian Universalists hold tenaciously to the conviction that no matter how bruised, betrayed, or burned our spirit may be, you and I can begin to experience and deliver assurance and confidence in safe, secure, steady doses…starting in our own chosen religious home.

Yes *and* trust are yoked in the robust religious journey. People who are trusters give themselves over to friends or partners or religious shareholders without giving themselves away. In trusting, we learn how to negotiate surrender yet bypass subjugation. Inherent in trust is a willingness to roam beyond the familiar and comfortable into foreign territories of bold surrender.

To trust someone/something, either human or divine, won't require certainty. While adequate evidence must be present, there's never final proof. We can't conclusively prove our trustworthiness to anyone, even our dearest comrades or fellow congregants. If we could, we'd be referring to something other than trust.

Trust, the real article, is the union of some data, some gamble, some buoyancy, some grace, some risk, and ample release. In matters of friendship, family, and faith, where trust is sorely tested, the power of our love is in direct proportion to the fountain of our trust. The religious odyssey is finally about being faithful, saying Yes, pledging our trust while wandering this earth. For a sense of unshakable trust in the Creation *and* in one another surely makes love achievable and death endurable.

Gordon McKeeman poetically phrases the core of our gospel:

> *Trust yourself to the world.*
> *It will possess you in the end.*
> *Let it have you living, that it may cradle you dead.*

FOR REFLECTION AND DISCUSSION

1. One of our veteran ministers, Christine Robinson, has noted:

    The theology of doubt is the underlying theology of Unitarian Universalism…it's a theology which keeps us from self-righteousness, but not action. So let's cherish our doubts. They not only lead to larger truth, but they make us wise, keep us humble, and allow us to live together in love.

    What do you think?

2. Nestled in our Unitarian founder King John Sigismund's edict is the trenchant phrase: "for faith is the gift of God," which means that no congregation, no guru, no government can enforce the reception of a certain faith. It is a gift that claims us, then we claim it...a process requiring both grace and assent.

    Ponder and comment.

3. When our Commission on Appraisal was wrestling with the question of how we can best embody our faith in the world as a possible study topic, it led to yet another query:
    If you had never heard of Unitarian Universalism, how would you be different from the you that you are?

    Related is the perennial query: "If you were on trial for being a Unitarian Universalism, would there be enough evidence to convict you?"

    Please address both questions and any others they might spark.

4. The Hebrew word for faith, *bitachon*, really means trust, hence the profound connection between authentic faith and trust. In all the bonds of faithfulness in our theological journey, a modicum of surrender (not submission) is required. We must learn how to give ourselves over to another person or reality without giving ourselves away. Or what Wendy Wright calls: "the art of learning to free fall." How do we do that?

INTERDEPENDENCE

*If, recognizing the interdependence of all life, we strive to build community,
the strength we gather will be our salvation. If you are black and I am white,
it will not matter...if we join spirits as brothers and sisters, the pain of our
aloneness will be lessened, and that does matter.*
—Marjorie Bowens-Wheatley

*Each of us needs a clubhouse, a place where we can be at home, where we
can gather with other dreamers and adventurers. A home, a church, or a
bench in the city park can be a clubhouse. The people in a real clubhouse do
not ask us to adapt so much as to dream, not of the world as it is, but of the
world as it should be.*
—Jane Mauldin

The romantic myths of rugged individualism and the separateness of things are being systematically debunked by contemporary thinkers, including Unitarian Universalists. Interdependence is perhaps the chief and inescapable insight of our epoch. David Bumbaugh, who was a fledgling Universalist minister at time of consolidation in 1961 and has served as minister and professor for all five decades of our associational existence, phrases it in this manner:

> *We believe that in this interconnected existence the well-being of one cannot be separated from the well-being of the whole, that ultimately we all spring from the same source and all journey to the same ultimate destiny.*

John Ruskin Clark, late 20th-century Unitarian Universalist theologian, describes us as integral partners in "the great living system." Less than a century ago, Einstein considered the universe a static, unchanging system, no larger than the cloud of stars that we now know to be our own galaxy. Today we realize that the cosmos is expanding rapidly and contains at least 50 billion galaxies, each with

100 billion or more stars. The universe is an exquisitely living system of which we humans are neither extraneous nor central to the web but integral parts in its evolutionary flow.

Kurt Vonnegut, erstwhile Unitarian Universalist, used to whimsically talk about "the Great Big Everything." Our Purposes and Principles document names it "the interdependent web." Call it what we will, the universe bespeaks inescapable kinship. We humans share the chemistry of all the nonhumans among which we live. Everything that lives on earth is made of the same stuff.

The era of interdependence is being fully ushered in by the evidence of both science and spirituality. The role of biology, physics, and chemistry is striking and persuasive in all this. So is that of religion.

Mature theology is declaring that we're born through partnership and nourished by relationships from our early to our final days. Rampant individualism forgets and corrupts this original bond and produces desolate, lonely people. The dawning truth is that we're not self-sufficient creatures. We are built for intimacy, for linking, and for love. We avoid nourishing bonds at great peril to ourselves and our globe.

Religious virtues are relational by nature. Our supreme invitation is to love and be loved—hardly achievable in seclusion. When we dream alone it's only a dream, but when we dream together it can be the beginning of a reality. Faith, compassion, mercy, and hope are all undeniably communal experiences. Even our solitude is prelude to dialogue.

We praise, give thanks, are filled with awe not in a vacuum, not in some narcissistic frenzy but in affinity with another: a human, a god, an event or object, an animal—realities that transcend yet include us.

20th-century Jewish theologian Martin Buber was convinced that "I become through my relation to the Thou; as I become I, I say Thou...All real living is meeting." Buber would often state, "I believe—rather, I mean, I meet…" for he knew that the heart of theological growth was association, communion, dialogue, meeting—meeting self, meeting neighbor, meeting nature, meeting divine mystery.

By meeting, Buber meant rigorous, resourceful engagement with others, not quick, glib acquaintanceship. The German word he employed for "meeting" was *begegnung* which translates as "encounter." Meeting is the most profound and daring movement we humans negotiate while alive. It demands our whole being. It's rugged, restorative, and religious. It embodies our interdependence.

Therefore, global unity is a biological fact and a religious aspiration. Humans need not make the universe one, so much as acknowledge its unity. We didn't create the ecosystem; our job is to live according to its inherent guidelines.

Solidarity is an option that is ours to affirm and actualize. The universe indeed is one and interdependent. It started that way, and our relentless human quest is to conserve that oneness.

Unitarian Universalists have a pivotal role to play in the realization of an interdependent world. Why? Because our heritage aspires to speak with power and pertinence to the vision of global consciousness. Interdependence is one of our chief theological virtues. Listen to the way a member of our fold, Bill Gagnon, midway through our fifty years of evolution, poured new wine into our theological wineskins:

> *Unitarian now stands not only for the oneness of God, but for the unitary view of all life, the merging of the sacred and secular into a single substance, every particle of which is sacred…It celebrates the unitary character of the human family, rejoicing that no matter what our race or faith or condition, we are all one people, belonging to the single family of humanity.*

> *Universalism has grown beyond the idea of universal salvation to embrace the concept of the universality of truth…It also desires the one*

universal spirit of compassionate and all-redeeming love, which has the power to inspire, judge, encourage and ultimately to gather our separated and warring nations into one world fellowship of the free.

Thus have the Unitarian and Universalist theological heresies grown up and been transformed into the broad and philosophical foundation for Unitarian Universalism, a New World faith which is inclusive in spirit, comprehensive in character, and uniting in influence.

As we commemorate our 50th anniversary in 2011, Unitarian Universalism resoundingly salutes a spiritual and social, physical and moral reality that is interdependent, indivisible, one. Our 16th-century forebear Francis David put it tersely: "*Egy Az Isten,*" which translates as "God is One." All else is footnote to this fundamental theological theme.

However, depicting the huge, mystifying, and wondrous eco-system in communal terms carries little relevance unless we shape our daily lives in earthly communities and partnerships. The key to staying ablaze is not merely positing but actually living the interdependent web, at every level and moment in our lives. As colleague Jan Christian phrases it: "Spiritual growth must always exhibit signs of spiritual maturity."

Although the vote was close and somewhat contentious, one of the major theological shifts in Unitarian Universalist consciousness was the adoption of the sixth source in 1995, namely, "spiritual teachings of Earth-centered traditions which celebrate the sacred circle of life and instruct us to live in harmony with the rhythms of nature." In matter of fact, this 6th source has expanded and granted substance to our seventh principle.

Earth-centered religion reinforces two essentials of our evolving Unitarian Universalist theology: the interconnectedness and the blessedness of the Creation. At core, paganism also charges us to honor the spiritual significance of seasonal changes. For example, the celebration of the arrival of winter is not only about the shift in weather, but it salutes those periods in our lives when we're stripped bare and must regrow our faith.

ALL LIVING BEINGS

Just as this planet is not the physical center of the universe,
our species is not the center of this planet.
—John Millspaugh

In the proposed revision of Article II, placed before the 2009 General Assembly in Salt Lake City, our movement crept closer yet wasn't quite prepared to include the inherent worth and dignity of "all living entities" in our premier confessional document. This remains a challenge for future theological revivals in our ranks.

At different times in human history those in political or religious power have denied "soul" to entire classes of beings whom those in power sought to control. Women, it was once said, had no soul. Slaves were deemed to be without soul. And now, we perpetuate that practice whenever we treat ourselves as conscious subjects and all other animals as inert objects, hence without enduring value or stature.

The very word animal comes from a Latin root that means soul. To ancient thinkers, soul was the mysterious force that gave life and breath to a myriad of the earth's creatures...but later theologians restricted the possession of a soul to human beings.

At long last, we're beginning to realize that all oppressions are interrelated and, moreover, that when one living reality is ignored, rendered disposable, or destroyed, the entire cosmos wails. Considering them to be inferior creatures, we humans have sometimes engaged in remorseless mistreatment, slavery, experimentation, yea, devastation of animals.

As Unitarian Universalists we have come to recognize that there's only one big law we have to obey during our stay on earth, and that law is respectfulness. We're summoned to treat everything we meet with respect: the earth, the animals, the plants, the sky, and other people. Everything. Our seventh principle, "Respect for the interdependent web of all existence of which we are a part," bespeaks the expanse of our moral responsibility.

Consequently, in 2011, a theological case is ardently being made for full-fledged recognition of all beings. Animals, like humans, are creatures with an inherent worth and dignity and must be reverenced precisely because they cannot speak for themselves. Animals, as well as plants, embody the tracks of goodness amidst the stuff of the cosmos.

Unitarian Universalist minister, Gary Kowalski, puts it compellingly in his trenchant volume, *The Souls of Animals*:

Animals are not our property or chattel, but our peers and fellows travelers. Like us, they have their own likes and dislikes, fears and fixations. They have plans and purposes as important to them as ours are to us. Animals not only have biologies; they also have biographies. When we treat them as if they were mere biological machines, we injure both their nature and our own. They are our spiritual colleagues and emotional companions. We know this to be true less through debate than through direct experience.

Naturally, not all animals are social or altruistic, all the time, but neither are human beings. Every species has the capacity to do destructive things. Yet as our hymn #323 entitled "Break Not the Circle" states:

Break not the circle of enabling love where people grow, forgiven and forgiving, break not that circle, make it wider still, till it includes, embraces all the living.

STEWARDSHIP

The Earth may be saved for human habitation, or not,
but what will you do?
—Mary Wellemeyer

We humans are entrusted to be stewards (literally "keepers of the hall") or caretakers of the earth's well-being. The seventh principle, "respect for the interdependent web of all existence of which we are a part," has been considered foremost by professional and lay theologians among us, ever since its adoption 25+ years ago. In fact, many Unitarian Universalists still contend that the seventh should be the first principle not the final one, since all our other principles emanate from this foundational commitment to being honorable stewards of the well-being of the cosmos.

The Unitarian Universalist Ministry for Earth, an independent affiliate organization of the Unitarian Universalist Association, phrases our overall mission compellingly:

We envision a world in which all people make reverence, gratitude, and care for the living Earth central to their lives.

Our purpose is to inspire, facilitate and support personal, congregational, and denominational practices that honor and sustain the Earth and all beings.

Environmental justice is the human affirmation of our place within the interdependent web of all existence. It recognizes the inherent value of all species, and acknowledges our human responsibility to seek a sustainable balance between the rights of nature and human rights.

We two-legged beings can certainly launch our ministry to the earth by affirming our *relatedness* with all reality: animals are our brothers and sisters; wells are sacred sites; rivers and streams are the outpouring of earth's emotionality.

We are related to and are a product of nature. We are of the soil, of the sea, of the air...created of the same matter, inextricably interdependent. We are dependent upon one another—literally, we all hang together. Hence, we are summoned to heed the biblical call: "For thou shalt be in league with the stones of the field, and the beasts of the field shall be at peace with thee" (Job 5:23).

Beyond affirming our relatedness to the entire ecosystem, beyond displaying respect for all living things, there is the call for repentance.

We are now realizing the organic view, namely, that we are part of an entire web, and if part is broken or torn, the whole shudders. As wanton, almost compulsive, despoilers, our initial religious response must be one of *repentance.* This doesn't mandate incessant breast-beating; repentance simply entails a willingness to turn ones life around. In fact, many are those among us who can pound ourselves with remorse; few are brave enough actually to change, to make restitution, to reconnect with the universe.

A lay leader in one of my recent interim ministries, when tweaking our principles, produced a relevant addendum to our seventh principle:

> ...*reverence for the interdependent web of all existence of which we are a part, **supported by responsible stewardship of a sustainable environment.***

Charles' amendments are slight but significant in strengthening the seventh principle's call for comprehensive stewardship. A sustainable future isn't just a manageable present.

In the Garden of Eden myth, we were given the imperative to tend it, "to till and keep it," to be its caretakers. Life itself was deeded to human beings under the requirement that we remain obedient to its basic laws and prove responsible for creation's well-being. Tilling means more than having a green thumb. Some of us don't own green thumbs, but we're hardly exempt from the caretaking of earth. I used to plant gardens on our Iowan property, a land with ground as lush and fertile as exists anywhere in America. I learned always to keep the empty seed packages. Sometimes they were just the right size for storing my crop! Tilling entails cultivating an evergreen sprit. We must be persistent stewards, even if not successful planters.

Accordingly, we're summoned to use the basic tools at our disposal as accountable humans—all the tools needed to till and tend earth's elements. The tools of technology, the tools of economics, the tools of politics, and especially the tools of the religious spirit—a spirit born in wonder, filled with gratitude, sparked by relatedness, respect, repentance, and responsibility...and reverence, for we cannot sustain for long that which we do not revere.

Each act of compassion for the natural world, each measure of conservation, each decision against dirtying the air, land, or water—these are gifts of the highest order, gifts back to the Infinite Love that brought us into being and nourishes our every step. We cannot do the perfect thing; yet we can approximate deeds that are helpful not harmful.

We are unable to comprehend fully the earth and all its precarious rhythms and equities in the very moment in which we are required to act. We simply respond with exceeding care and tenderness. We ask and answer with our lives: "What can the planet best do through me at this particular juncture of my earthly stay?"

One more R word: *relish*. There's an apt and powerful line in the novel by John Barth entitled *Tidewater Tales*:

> *You need not love the world...you need not even approve of it, but relish it you must.*

Yes, that's it. The world, and all therein, is often brutish and ugly, deceitful and violent. We humans are certainly prime contributors to the cumulative nastiness. Nonetheless, it's likely to be the only universe we'll ever enjoy close up, so it remains our spiritual summons to become its proud and persistent relishers, both ardent servants and savorers all our days and nights. Isn't that what our naturalist forebear Henry David Thoreau meant when he urged us "to live deep and suck out all the marrow of life"?

Painting by Owen Chapman

"The world is a great joy. The two hands are children's hands holding up the world that they love. The night and the stars represent a calm that the children want. The light is from the parents. Children need their help to make the world calm."—OWEN CHAPMAN

FOR REFLECTION AND DISCUSSION

1. Mary Midgley has penned wise words worth discussing:

    To find the universe meaningful is not to decode an extra, cryptic message hidden behind it, but simply to find some continuity between its patterns and those of our own lives—enough continuity to confirm that our presence here makes sense. The point is not that this world belongs to us, but that we belong to it. We only need to see it as ordered in a way that makes our presence here intelligible to us.

2. Our own Sophia Fahs uses the phrase "Universal Living Unity," while religious nonconformist Stephen Hawking talks about the "Grand Unified Theory." What words do you prefer to delineate the "interdependent web" and our role in it?

3. *For me, the seventh principle implies a respect for all of creation, including animal life. I would like to see the seventh principle re-written to read something like "respect for the interdependent web of all existence, of which we are a part, including the animal life we share our planet with…"*
    —Manish Mishra

    Weigh in with your own thoughts concerning how we might best state both principles one and seven, as we wrestle ongoingly with a theology that embraces all reality.

4. Judy Moores, representing the UU Ministry for Earth, has recommended the following:

    I would suggest that we begin to refer to our planet as "Earth, Our Deep-Home-Place" to mean the unique location in the Universe that is our ancestral home, our home, and the only home that we will ever have… a place deserving of reverence, gratitude, wonder, love and care. Deep, home, place—all simple words that we have used for centuries and perhaps, millennia.

    Share your comments in group conversation.

PEACE AND NONVIOLENCE

How do we find inner peace? We don't. Peace is a gift. We cannot seek it directly. Rather, peace is the by-product of living life well.
—Will Saunders

Peace and justice require as much or more sacrifice as war, and until we are willing to sacrifice for peace and justice and until we understand that our own well-being is tied up with the well-being of others, our sacrifice will be for war and not for peace.
—Jan Christian

Peace, salaam, shalom...now and until we create it.
—Wendy Bartel

In 1866 in Waterloo, New York, Memorial Day was officially born. Legend has it that the town women gathered in a labor of love and sorrow to create floral wreathes, which the townspeople then carried in solemn procession and placed on the graves of Civil War soldiers, both Blue and Gray, North and South.

The intent of this event, which was first called Decoration Day, was to mourn and remember *all* those soldiers, without distinguishing among them, in an attempt to surpass differences of allegiance as well as to emphasize the horror and loss of war for everyone. It was very similar in purpose to Unitarian Julia Ward Howe's peace-focused Mother's Day Proclamation of 1870.

The meaning of Memorial Day has shifted from healing and reconciliation to today's celebration of war and might, replete with parades rather than processions, fireworks, picnics, and parties rather than solemn services of prayer.

As a religion committed to peace-making and justice-building, we don't quarrel with the conventional understanding that war memories were for the purpose of honoring those who lost their lives in service to their country, as well as for all those scarred by war, the walking wounded...including families of the aforementioned soldiers. Yet Unitarian Universalists, of whatever patriotic persuasion, would broaden our memories of war to stand in alignment with the originators of Memorial Day.

We would envision it as a day of somber reflection and reconciliation, wherein we might profitably address difficult moral questions such as: What is worth dying or killing for? How do we defend what we value? Who are the victims and who are the victors of military combat?

Unitarian Universalists won't arrive at a consensus on these moral issues, whether on Memorial Day weekend or ever, but as responsible patriots and religious questers, we can't avoid dealing with them.

At the core of Memorial Day must be communal mourning not unrelenting celebration, a time of silence more than earsplitting noise. Our young need to recognize that armed conflict is always a tragic last resort, that the memories of war must always contain the seeds of peace, and that those seeds should be tended faithfully by every last patriot.

Since the formation of the Unitarian Universalist Association in 1961, there have been both general and specific resolutions fostering peace throughout the world. We've established our own Peace Network, been active in the Conscientious Objection to War effort, and have been deeply enmeshed in movements ranging from Beyond War to Nuclear Freeze, throughout the course of these past five decades. Recently we've seen an increase in the number of Unitarian Universalist ministers serving as chaplains in the armed forces. Yet violence and war are still endemic within our hearts, our congregations, and in the greater world. We have neither failed nor been successful. Our efforts have been checkered.

The substance of my version of an evolving theology of peace and nonviolence arrives in the form of a letter I wrote to a Unitarian

Universalist marine some years back.

I address it to all Unitarian Universalists willing to wrestle soulfully with issues of internal, interpersonal, and international peacemaking.

First, some background. A Unitarian Universalist acquaintance from the East Coast had a son in the Marine Corps based at Camp Pendleton, an hour north of the site of our San Diego congregation. This young man went UA ("unexplained absence") after experiencing extreme upset in response to something he saw at the camp.

In the throes of considerable personal hell, Bruce (not his real name) returned to the Marines, still confused, and according to his father, in need of ministerial support. There was no fellow recruit, officer, or chaplain at the Camp who could hear, let alone, appreciate, his raw anguish. So I was invited to counsel with him. My visit proved helpful to Bruce as well as transformative for me.

Bruce was a reserved yet muscular 19-year-old who for seven years had dreamed of becoming a Marine and following in the footsteps of both his uncle and cousin. He was among the top achievers during basic training, so when he jumped camp, it startled everyone, including his buddies. I think he surprised himself as well.

Bruce was a brave young man saddled with a tormented spirit. He still enjoyed the drama and grandeur of Marinehood but had grown to loathe the system. He appreciated the discipline of military life, yet he'd learned an irrevocable truth about himself: he was aggressive alright, but not prone to violence. Bruce simply couldn't kill, in any way, shape, or form.

Bruce confided that he'd always been an emotionally expressive young man, crying openly as a child and youth. Now his inner feelings were stuffed under the standard regimen of the Marines. Just prior to joining the Marines, Bruce was joyfully involved with a group of preschoolers as an assistant teacher. In fact, he said that he had but two pressing goals for the future and, now, neither of them was being a career Marine.

The first dream was to own and manage a gym, with special emphasis on bodybuilding; his second mission in life was to teach preschool children again. Somehow Bruce hoped to blend these visions in one adult life. As a Unitarian Universalist minister of some 43 years standing, I don't recall hearing a 19-year-old male express either of those specific desires, let alone both of them together. But there was no doubt in my mind that Bruce was the kind of guy who would realize his dreams.

He told me that the preschool children were like little trees that he was summoned to cultivate, prune, and nourish. Now in the Marines he was being trained to cut down similar, if older, trees, and his heart was utterly torn in half. He couldn't just stand up and quit the Marines, because he was the kind of guy who honored commitments; plus, to get out of his military contract at this stage would require extreme measures. Although trapped in severe conscience-pain, Bruce vowed neither to commit suicide nor assault anybody.

I reminded Bruce that quitting the Marines was complicated, to be sure, but quitting on his soul, an even tougher move, was ultimately at stake. I asked him to remember the trees: the little ones he was tending back in Michigan, the foreign trees he was being trained to cut down, and the ever-growing tree he represented himself. I gave him my phone numbers, lest he ever need me again, whatever decision he made.

When I got back to my car, I found myself quivering with deep tears for both red-blooded Marines and nonviolent ministers, and for all those conflicted with elements of the warrior and the peace-maker clashing in our consciences.

I was reminded of the wisdom of that hard-nosed pacifist, A. J. Muste, who wrote in 1965 that "those who go into war having seriously thought their way to a decision are on a higher moral level than the smug pacifists who have little notion of the fierce ambiguities the decision involves!"

So I wrote him a heartfelt letter.

DEAR BRUCE,

I want you to know that our lengthy conversation on February 8th was a powerful one for me. And what follows may say more about me than be useful for you, but it's the best my soul can muster.

From a young age on I've been motored by a peaceful, accommodating personality. Cops and robbers never held much fascination for me. I can't ever remember desiring a Red Ryder rifle for Christmas, although there was a period in my life when I was enthralled with water pistols. And the only time I ever handled or shot a real gun was in a Boy Scout drill during a camp-out. I not only flunked the exercise physically but emotionally as well. I came away from that experience fearful that shooting at tin cans might be a warm-up exercise for shooting at animals or humans. And I remember feeling weird, because other scouts seemed to get a real "bang" out of firing guns.

Even when I played sports, which I did with fervor and excellence (I'm reminded, Bruce, of your passion for wrestling and weight-lifting), my prime drawback was lack of aggressiveness at "crunch-time." My natural meekness would fade into a kind of unwanted passivity. In a nutshell, I seemed "too gentle to live among the wolves," let alone run with them.

Oh, by the way, Bruce, none of my close male relatives were war veterans, and due to age and academic status, I always managed to avert conscription. I was too immature, perhaps cowardly as well, to obtain "conscientious objector" status, although that was clearly what I believed and who I was. No wonder I became such a devoted CO counselor during the Vietnam War, Bruce, helping braver ones than I pursue what my conscience had sidestepped.

Peace activist Walter Wink describes himself thusly: "I don't see myself as a pacifist. I see myself rather as a violent person trying to become nonviolent." On the contrary, Bruce, I view myself as a cowardly type, a sanitized pacifist if you will, struggling the road toward becoming genuinely nonviolent as well. Wink and I dwell at different spots on the continuum; nonetheless, both of us require more creative aggression to reach our mutual destination of forceful nonviolence. How would you review yourself in this regard?

Bruce, let me say, first off, that your resistance to taking another person's life is at the heart of nonviolence. By refusing to kill human beings you're proclaiming the supreme worth of every single individual, not only your compatriots but also our enemies as well. To kill is perhaps the height of arrogance; for it means playing God, who alone gives life, and who entrusts it to us to cherish and develop, as a gift received with grateful love. Like those trees you've been talking about.

As Unitarians you and I believe in the sacred dignity of every human *unit*. As Universalists we contend that transformation is *universally* accessible to everyone or to no one. And the only salvation worth having must always include brothers and sisters, known and foreign, buddies and foes.

More confession, Bruce. Being tranquil by temperament and conciliatory by conviction, I've had considerable spiritual difficulty in becoming a more tough-minded, stouthearted peacemaker. I can all too easily become a smug, self-righteous ideologue, mouthing peaceful platitudes yet far removed from the raging battles of reality. Sometimes, my resistance to clear-cut, obstinate evils has been so passive that no one even noticed I was resisting, because I wasn't. I was wearing cowardice in disguise.

What I'm urging in a nutshell, Bruce, is for folks like you and me to be brave, not spineless…to become aggressive but not violent.

While we're at it, Bruce let's wrestle a bit with another thorny concept that the Marines talk a lot about, namely, being a *warrior*. The term warrior is sullied, perhaps irredeemable, what with its history of paid soldiers whose sole mission is to find and destroy the opposition. Usually in our modern world, when the word warrior is uttered, war is spoken as well.

Yet in current women's and men's sacred literature, a compelling interpretation of the warrior archetype denotes those individuals who are protectors of righteousness, boundary-setters, and guardians of goodness. For example, Greenpeace, the activist coalition of environmentalists, insistently promotes its mission as tough "Rainbow Warriors."

Warrior energy, at its healthiest, aggressively pushes toward humane possibilities. Yet if disconnected from compassion, the warrior can easily be driven by a zeal for cruelty. The shadow side is exemplified in any governmental, religious, business, or military enterprise that employs its power to abuse and destroy life.

On the one hand, I stand ready to retire the concept of "warrior" until we've shown a sincere willingness, for example, to dismantle nuclear weapons worldwide. On the other hand, I know, Bruce, that in my efforts to approximate justice and combat wrongs I could use greater guts, more aggressiveness.

There's another twisting truth on my heart. It's tempting to place all the so-called "good guys" in the non-military camp, yet I want you to know that, in your own heritage of Unitarian Universalism, there have been brave champions within our American military establishment. Did you know that the Secretary of Defense under President Bill Clinton, Republican Bill Cohen from Maine, is an active Unitarian Universalist layman? Cohen happens to be a very introspective man who writes poetry and, yes, worked hard to master the mysteries of the Pentagon. Cohen reminds us that in Chinese culture, the generals and warriors, as well as political leaders, were often poets.

What I'm driving at, Bruce, is that it's naive to stereotype military leaders as being violence-mongers. Some are and some aren't. And to complicate matters, I've known my share of public pacifists who were physically abusive at home.

Again I confess, my friend, that truth is stubbornly complex, yet I beckon you to dwell in its messy midst, as you valiantly sculpt a life of holy and kindly aggression.

Aggression isn't an ugly word at root. It literally means taking action—moving forward toward a person, a posture, a principle, or an event. It means eluding the grasp of lethargy or fright and advancing toward our goal. We need to aggress what we value: to move toward someone in respect; to move away from apathy and toward courage; to move against something in resistance.

Of course, Bruce, there will be subtle dangers to dodge. Our respect dare not breed docility. Our courage cannot slide into foolhardiness. Our resistance must avoid recklessness. Nonetheless, aggression is the ground floor, animating energy that undergirds all, brave, forward moving deeds of peace and nonviolence. Mohandas Gandhi talked about committing "aggressive civil disobedience" and Martin Luther King, Jr. chose to engage in "militant nonviolence."

Justice and peace are never enterprises for the dispassionate of spirit or sluggish of body. They require joyful decisiveness and aggressive advocacy. I know this to be true: without aggression, courage chickens out, love turns inept, generosity loses heart, and righteousness shrivels. Remember the Bible blesses the peace-makers, not the peace-enthusiasts.

Nonviolence invites you and me to find creative alternatives beyond violence, to seize the moral initiative, to assert your own dignity as a human being, to discover inner resources of power you didn't know you had, to break the cycle of humiliation with ridicule or humor, to refuse to submit or to accept the inferior position, to expose the injustice of the dominator system, to be willing to suffer rather than retaliate, to force the oppressor to see you in a new light, to be willing to undergo the penalty of breaking unjust laws. There's nothing soft or feeble about any of those actions, Bruce, is there?

Furthermore, my friend, there will be situations that are crushingly tragic, where nothing we can possibly do will help. Holding hands and singing "Give peace a chance" sometimes doesn't stop warlords from stealing food from starving babies. There exist woeful binds when the violent and the nonviolent alike are forced to suffer the agony of irrelevance and may themselves reside among the victims.

There's nothing magical about nonviolence. It requires courage, self-discipline, and a well-integrated spirituality. It entails a willingness to learn from our enemies. It demands the ability to desire their safety as well as our own, to love the part in them that tries to hurt others, even while we refuse to cooperate with it.

No matter how nonviolent we purport to be in theory or practice, Bruce, you and I must never envision violence as if it were something arising outside ourselves. We must confess our complicity in the very web of violence we abhor. So, beware, Bruce, of the sin of pride, as you struggle with your conscience to stay in or leave the Marines.

In closing, Bruce, your final allegiance must be paid not to the Marines or to our shared religious heritage of Unitarian Universalism or even to your parents, but to an innermost voice that impels you to stay truthful to yourself and in loving alignment with the greater Creation. You must pay heed to your conscience.

Freedom of conscience is a deceptively radical notion signaling that neither homeland nor deity comes first in our lives, but our conscience does. Naturally, Bruce, our human consciences do not operate in a vacuum. They need to be clarified by the loving critique of fellow truth-seekers. We must decide for ourselves what to believe and do, but never solely by ourselves.

Conscience is a human phenomenon, all too human. It not only leads us to meaning; it can also lead us astray. Our consciences err, are fallible. We need to take ourselves seriously, our world seriously too, but not too seriously.

And, above all, my friend, be patient with and kind to yourself, knowing that there's no decision that you can ever make—however honest, brave, and compassionate—that will prove pure or pain-free. Your soul-brother...

—REV. TOM

I wish I knew what happened to Bruce, you might be curious too, but, you know what…that's not the point of our mentoring encounters and soulful exchanges in life. Our job isn't to reap certain results or garner personal gratification; our job is simply to listen deeply, then speak our truths in love.

I was blessed that my path ever crossed with that of Bruce.

FOR REFLECTION AND DISCUSSION

1. How do you deal with the tendencies to violence and abuse in your own soul and behavior?

2. In what ways is your local congregation actively supportive of and involved in actions for peace and nonviolence in your greater community? Everything qualifies, from a victims of sexual abuse circle to a PFLAG program to a deployment blues support group. Be creative in recalling and claiming the ways your parish serves peace and nonviolence for all ages.

3. What do the terms "aggression," "warrior," and "militant nonviolence" mean to you? Interpret them as well as find other phrases of comparable meaning for doing the work of peace and nonviolence.

4. Does your congregation have a Covenant of Right Relationship that determines how you pledge to behave with one another? If so, share it or shape it.

5. Do you have a conflict resolution team in your congregation? How do you deal with difficult and disruptive folks in your parish?

6. What would you like to say, in addition to or in place of, my words to Bruce?

GRACE

We receive fragments of holiness, glimpses of eternity, brief moments of in-sight. Let us gather them up for the precious gifts that they are and, renewed by their grace, move boldly into the unknown.
—Sara York

I am not fussy about forms or spiritual geography. Whether helps comes from the outside or inside, by praying or willing, is not important. What is impor-tant is that help can come!
—Greta Crosby

GIFT OF GRACE

To speak of grace is to say that our lives are finally not our own, that we're not only recipients of an existence we didn't create, but also throughout our whole earthly travels we're granted gifts we don't deserve. To be sure, we're crucial participants in the crafting of our singular destinies; we are surely the stokers of our singular flaming chalices.

Yet grace reminds us that we're even more those whose lives are crafted by human and divine forces beyond our creation and control, often comprehension. In some Middle Eastern languages, the word for "rain" and "grace" are the same, suggesting invisible gifts falling on our ground, enriching the soil of our souls.

In contemporary Unitarian Universalist circles, one finds the perennial query "Who am I?" being gradually complemented by its partner questions: "Whose am I?" and "To whom do I belong and to what am I beholden?" An ablaze theology dares to address all these interlocking matters.

There may be no more slippery and unnerving theological concept for Unitarian Universalists to address than "grace". Slip-pery, because grace is a blessing beyond our grasp and unnerving, because grace is beyond our achievement. To complicate matters, grace appears too mystical for our rational side and too passive for our activist bent.

Nonetheless, this most ticklish theological virtue has been gaining coinage in our realm. Check out the number of sermons by Unitarian Universalists preached, in our recent history, upon the human and divine attributes of grace.

First, we will address *grace* as a theological category–its source, location, and nature. There also exists *graciousness,* the ethical response to the spiritual gift. Then there's being *grace-ful,* an essentially aesthetic experience. I will briefly comment on the saving grace of humor. I've chosen to close this chapter with reflections upon grace's spiritual kin: humility.

For classic Christianity, the source of grace appears rather clear-cut. An omnipotent God breaks into human life and saves us from transgression and alienation. Grace is an expiatory act of divine intervention. *Amazing Grace,* the title of the popular traditional hymn, states it unequivocally:

> *Amazing Grace! How sweet the sound,*
> *That saved a wretch like me!*
> *I once was lost, but now am found,*
> *Was blind, but now I see.*

The movement of conventional grace is vertical, dynamic, and redemptive.

For Unitarian Universalists, the sense of a transcendent deity may reverberate too much like a triple-deckered universe: heaven, earth, and hell. God seems more attractive and understandable to liberal religionists as an immanent power–a source of divine nudging and nurturing from within the soul. This viewpoint claims that God or grace emerges from the innermost regions of self or nature, rather than descending from the outermost stretches of the cosmos.

Unitarian Universalism tends to affirm that the Infinite Spirit operates alongside and through us while not being identified with us. The human and divine are partnering religious forces–separate but supportive.

Wherever grace comes from, our emerging conviction is that grace, in fact, does arrive, usually by surprise and rarely on cue. The location and source of grace matter little in comparison to the import of grace's presence. Springs of strength and replenishment, goading and healing can and do enter our human existence.

Such grace, both startling and sustaining, is not of our doing. Oh, we humans can prepare our hearts for its receptivity, but we cannot program grace. We can visit where grace has struck others, yet we cannot promise its appearance nor control its stay. We can relax attentively, pray diligently, and meditate regularly, except we cannot manufacture grace. Grace, in one fashion or another, creates us, or re-creates us…endowing earthlings with renewed spark. Grace is the incessant prompt that there is a sheer and utter blessedness to our existence.

Believing in grace is especially hard for productive, self-govern-ing types like Unitarian Universalists. Opening our souls to the gift of grace is a prime example of where we've struggled to grow up theologically in the past fifty years. Progressive religionists have clas-sically claimed to be able to do just about everything we want to do, and if we can't do it now, we'll accomplish it someday, and if that's impossible, then no one else will be able to do it either.

Our self-assured stance mirrors the lyric line in the Billie Hol-liday song:

The possible we'll do now; the impossible will take a little longer.

Such conceit simply stifles the flow of grace. Overweening self-reliance can also lead to an arid rationality that cuts and slices up mystery into bits of palatable and manageable data. All in all, resistance to grace proves to be an immeasurable loss.

However, if we're able to make a distinction between being self-possessed, which is a desirable pursuit, and being self-sufficient, which is unattainable, then we can navigate lives exposed to the presence of grace.

Personally, I'm a theological hybrid–a naturalistic theist or a mystical humanist–one who finds grace extraordinarily difficult to define or describe yet a spiritual explorer who periodically feels and welcomes its presence.

What about the nature of grace, the movements of grace? To speak of grace, first of all, is to say that the things most worth expecting are the things that are unexpected. Our explicit anticipations will be fulfilled or disappointed. But the unforeseen encounters, those things that come to us as amazement, full of grace...those are frequently the very moments that groom us for additional surprises.

A stranger walks into our life, and a friendship blossoms.

A piece of music is first heard by the chance spinning of a radio dial or because someone happened to play that piece and not another and it becomes an instrument of healing in subsequent times of ailment or despond.

Grace dumbfounds us in modest ways and hidden places.

We are accepted by the Infinite Spirit, by life–you supply the name–but the reality remains. The grace-filled person believes that he or she is unconditionally worthwhile, accepted not provisionally or because of what we might yet accomplish...rather accepted from the very ground of our being.

Remember the story of the Prodigal Son in the Christian scriptures. The younger son seeks an early inheritance, goes off and squanders it in loose living. Then he sheepishly, even ashamedly, returns, asking for forgiveness, but expecting his just desserts.

Instead, his father rushes out to greet him, and note that the text says, "when he was yet at a distance", (both emotionally and physically), rejoices in son's return and sets the village to celebration. "Let us eat and make merry; for this my son was dead, and is alive again; he was lost, and is found."

The son is accepted not because of any demonstrated worthiness, rather is summarily forgiven, upheld, and accepted for who he is. Just accepted, no questions asked and no justification required. Such is the way of acceptance, of a loving Universalist God, of grace.

Grace may also come in the presence of adversity or through the guise of admonition. We make a patently wrong decision and have to pay a price, or we invest too much reliance in a person or cause and are disappointed, even burned. Or there is a great loss; how can we call that grace? There exists a line beyond which I, at least, cannot. I refuse to call the death of a child anything but tragic. I will not name collective evil, whether holocaust or war, a sign of grace. Nonetheless there are some dislocations and travail through which, while grace may initially appear as a stern and painful teacher, it ultimately produces a healing, restorative result.

Living in a state of grace is to have the joy which dwells inside us touched, triggered, and released. Having our cups filling up, we overflow. For the graced person there is no other way to respond to unmerited love, favor and mercy than to be gracious and graceful.

BEING GRACIOUS

Being gracious is the ethical response to being loved–beyond our deserving, beyond our anticipation, beyond our anything. I said response not repayment. For grace is never repaid in full, only responded to in part. As J.B. says in Archibald MacLeish's play, "we got the earth for nothing." The gracious response is to give in return, give back to the blessed creation, everything we have and are, all the way home and count not the cost.

The moment of grace we bestow or is bestowed upon us is what makes the religious tussle really worth it. I think of the story told by Unitarian Universalist religious educator, Til Evans, about a gracious interaction between two children in her R.E. program. She calls it a *hallelujah* story. Indeed it is.

> *Chloe was 1½ years old with dark hair and a solemn face. She came into a gathering service one morning and said she didn't need to wear a dia-*

per anymore. Everyone gave her a "rah, rah." She sat down next to Blythe who was two–a blond, frail looking, and rather contained child. Blythe had a pacifier in her mouth. At one point, Chloe leaned over to Blythe, took the pacifier out of her mouth very delicately, and leaned forward and kissed her on the mouth. Then she put the pacifier back in Blythe's mouth. No word was spoken.

This is where humility enters the equation.

Humility and all its etymological kin–humanness, humor, humus, and humaneness—are rooted in the sensibility of grace. As our 7th principle reminds, we are neither the whole of nor extraneous to Creation but a critical cog. This is our glorious challenge and sobering admonition. It's foolish either to grovel as lackeys before the Most High or conspire to storm the heavens. Things work best when we humans accompany God, filled with a spirit of grace and humility, inching together toward the co-creation of a more just and beautiful cosmos.

The sources section of our Unitarian Universalist Principles and Purposes astutely warns against "idolatries of the mind and spirit." The fundamental attitude of humility enables us to counter the allure of self-veneration. In the last analysis, humility beckons us to define ourselves in terms of human duties and yearnings, strengths and frailties.

We aren't the center of the universe, no matter how bloated our egos might grow. Humans are integral contributors, to be sure, even co-partners in the ongoing cosmic flow, but we didn't start creation, our record is checkered at sustaining it, and we won't likely end it. We're mid-streamers, earthlings who have emerged from the dirt–the humus–and shall return to the dirt. That's our story, a noble yet humble one.

With the sacred interval that's entrusted to each of us, Unitarian Universalism urges its adherents never to betray the magnificence of our humanity. It exhorts us to live our days with overflowing humaneness and bellies bursting with humor, heeding Micah's spiritual requirements for incarnating a robust and resourceful religious life: "What does the Eternal require from you…but to do justice, and to love kindness and to walk humbly with your God?" (6:8)

The book of the Hebrew prophet Micah marks a defining moment in the evolution of religion: migrating from animal sacrifice to human service, from ritual worship to social righteousness. If we pay heed to Micah's three imperatives of justice, kindness, and humility, then our theological house will stand in sound condition.

Micah contends that these interlinking ethical demands appear from beyond our ego or imagination. They emanate from the Eternal, from Yahweh, from the Creation. They aren't intriguing, optional challenges we've dreamed up. They're what is expected, make that required, during our earthly adventure. They are transcendent claims upon human life. They constitute our depth theology as Unitarian Universalists.

The first imperative is "to do justice." Not to think or visualize justice but to do some justice every waking day of our lives, not merely when we feel like it. Justice entails mending a broken world by making sure that what belongs to people gets to them: be it freedom, dignity, or resources.

As progressive theologian Matthew Fox reflects:

Injustice is a rupture in the universe, an affront to cosmic wholeness, an invitation to chaos, an unraveling of the ropes that bind the universe as whole. It is by justice that we bring together the broken, neglected, cut-off, impoverished parts of the universe to render them whole again.

And what does God require of us but to do justice, then "to love kindness." In Jewish tradition it's voiced explicitly in an old proverb: "the highest form of wisdom is kindness." No footnotes or amendments need be made. Kindness is the final determiner of the merit of one's existence.

That's what social responsibility constitutes, at its highest common denominator: kindness. Those who are kind know they are kin. All else is footnote. When in doubt, be kind; when frightened, risk kindness; when bitter, speak kindly. As the eminent philosopher Aldous Huxley voiced: "It's a bit embarrassing to have been concerned with the human problem all one's life and find at the end that one has no more to offer by the way of advice than this—'Try to be a little kinder.'" Or similarly phrased by one of our ministers Sean Dennison:

> *What would happen if we decided that kindness was more important than proving ourselves knowledgeable, smart, or right?*

Kindness enhances both the giver and the receiver...especially when it arrives unbidden or occurs without news coverage. A moment of kindness, no matter how modest or small, is never wasted.

Micah continues. "What does the Eternal require of you, but to do justice, and to love kindness and to walk humbly with your God?"

We need humility, because arrogance builds walls not bridges, between individuals or clans. We need humility, given that brash egos hanker for personal credit rather than shared accomplishment. We need humility, since, although human beings are marvelous works of art, we're neither the Infinite One nor the centerpiece of creation.

As religious pilgrims we're committed to being shameless agitators for justice and kindness. We're also dedicated to walking humbly with ourselves, with our neighbors, and with all living things. Additionally, we're called neither to walk in front of God in haughtiness nor behind in servility but alongside as bona fide partners in the interdependent web of all existence. Note that Micah directs us to walk humbly with *our* God, not somebody else's.

Remember walking humbly doesn't allow us to wander off into apathy or laziness. Just because we humans can't do everything, it doesn't mean we can't do the things that we're peculiarly gifted and charged to accomplish.

Being filled with grace, being accepted to the hilt, we hunger to show compassion…to rejoice, leap and dance our delight. We yearn to be graceful along with being gracious.

GRACEFUL LIVING

But as we're not always gracious, so also we're not always graceful. We're clumsy, we wobble, and we stumble over just about everything including our own two feet or single, earnest heart.

Being graceful connotes both inner and outer beauty, attractiveness of appearance and loveliness of movement. These qualities are neither to be spurned nor worshipped, merely appreciated in their multifarious shapes and styles.

Years back, our family saw Twyla Tharp, the modern dance troupe. They were exceptional dancers who performed intricate and exquisite, stylized and expressive movements. But they didn't embody aesthetic perfection. They made noticeable mistakes and were occasionally uninspiring.

Twyla Tharp dancers are graceful but human. They dance not for perfection, or even for performance, rather they dance primarily to pay witness to the belief that, as Alan Watts, stated, "In the very heart of God there is that colossal gaiety which is represented in the symbol of the angelic choirs encircling the presence of God in an eternal candle of ecstasy."

There are ample lessons from the art of dancing that are applicable for growing theologically.

Dancers declare us that our minds and bodies are animated by inner joy. Dancers remind us that true grit often unclenches its teeth and grows wings, and an unfettered spirit soars. Dancers unveil the intrinsic value of the playful, the whimsical, and the "unnamed immensity within us" (Jean Erdman). Dancers declare that life is bathed in mirth and graced with zaniness.

Dancers remind one and all that depth theology is not about drab toil or bitter struggle but truly a sporting proposition, an interplay of opposites, a cosmic dance…with everyone lured from the sidelines squarely onto the dance floor, shifting with each and every dance: be it jitter-bug, reel, contra, waltz, or rock-and-roll. Dancers nudge us to stay in expressive motion, to twist and turn, bounce and sway in visceral celebration of life's unstinting graciousness.

Dancers remind us not to fuss and feud, as our congregations are prone to do, about who's leading or following in the ministerial dance. For we're all summoned straightway into the dance; we're all spiritually equipped to master the twin arts of leadership and fol-lowership. In the final analysis, what matters is the dance itself, what matters is that the gambol known as partnered ministry swirls on in creative circles of compassion and delight.

And when grace fails to come our way, or when our efforts to be gracious to others fall flat, or our movements of heart or body seem utterly graceless...then we must turn yet again to that saving grace: humor.

THE SAVING GRACE

The "saving grace of humor" doesn't primarily reference the ability to be funny, though that certainly is a blessing. Zaniness is one of the grandest things we humans ever manage during our earthly stint. A sense of humor, as a saving grace, has more to do with seeing things in proper proportion or having a sound perspective on self and existence.

It means an ability to laugh *at* and *with* ourselves. It signals the willingness to be cut down to size and emerge liberated rather than decimated. Humor is a leveling experience, when we're smug and an uplifting one when we're wounded. We've been fooled. We're less or more than we thought we were. Love is trickier or more tragic than bargained for. Humor reminds us of all that while it goes about cleansing, then restoring, our spiritual system.

There's the Apache myth where the Creator grants human beings the ability to run, talk, and to look. But the Eternal One was not satisfied until earthlings were graced with the capacity to chuckle.

Only then did God say, "Now, now you are fit to live!"

Assuredly, laughter is at the heart of the gracious spirit. Laughter: the resultant explosion when the gap of incongruity is perceived between what is and what could or should be. Laughter: the blessing that restores sanity and reduces humanity to size. Laughter: the affectionate needling that purifies our spiritual systems. Laughter: an acknowledgment of the ridiculous that dwells just inside the shell of our dignity. Laughter: a voluntary way of granting our brains an oxygen bath.

The alternative to humor is arrogance, idolatry, sometimes violence. Inquisitions, heresy trials, witch-hunts, holy wars are sufficient testimony to the stark presence of sanctity without humor.

We Unitarian Universalists are frail, yet graced, creatures, on the road toward being gracious, oft-flowing with gracefulness. We carry forth and we carry on, laughing heartily or nervously, laughing because we're unmasked and laughing with profound joy for, despite everything, we know one sure thing: we're loved, "rest assured".

A gift of grace.

FOR REFLECTION AND DISCUSSION

1. How do you frame grace as a theological virtue: its source, locale, and nature?

2. Comment on the challenge to be gracious in today's oft-harsh and bitter world? How do you manage this ethical art in the midst of a congregational battle?

3. In what ways do you consider yourself to be a graceful or awkward person? Can one grow in gracefulness?

4. What role does humor play in your religious life: personally and congregationally?

5. There is false and genuine humility. Distinguish between them.

6. Forrest Church claims that there are two founding principles of our progressive faith: "humility and openness". What do you think he means?

EMBODIMENT

If they are going to pin Unitarian Universalism on me, they will have to be able to show that I have participated in and supported a Unitarian Universalist church. That is the only way to be sure. Beliefs, no matter how noble, must be embodied in a living institution or they will have no convicting power.
—Robert Walsh

Theology is not something we do just with our heads. We must also use our hearts and guts, as well as our hands and feet.
—Paul Rasor

THEOLOGY ABLAZE is saluting theological virtues that signal our spiritual maturation as a movement during the past 50 years. What exactly is a virtue? Literally, *virtue* in Latin means "power"; hence, to be a virtuous person is to enact your given power, to live as one whose affirmations become actions. You become, as one theologian phrases it, a "resultist."

Unitarian Universalism is a reasonable faith, a responsibly free faith, an experiential faith, a hopeful faith, but there's no more crucial designation than that of being an "embodied" faith. All of our religious sentiments and principles are useless unless translated into acts of compassion. Our forebears phrased it variously as "truth stands in order to goodness," and "may our words ever become flesh."

Unitarian Universalism has long heralded "deeds rather than creeds," but we're acknowledging this angle more than ever. As *Embracing Our Theological Diversity* (2005) states: "We are dedicated to making our theology manifest in the larger world. Unitarian Universalists are summoned to become theologically informed prophetic servants, wherever we are planted. Our ways of action will be different, but our commitment is universal and unbending. In the Unitarian Universalist way of being and doing religion, faith and ethics are unified."

Indeed, the Social Responsibility department of the UUA was renamed Faith in Action a few years back, to denote that fusion. Heed the words of its former director Bill Gardiner:

Our faith is determined by the choices and commitments we make in life. When I want to see how to live a life of faith I think of those from our Unitarian Universalist tradition who have lived faithful lives. I remember abolitionists like Frances Watkins Harper and Theodore Parker. I recall those who organized the women's right to vote, like Susan. B. Anthony and Samuel May. I remember those who, like Jim Stoll, have been leaders in the quest for the rights of bisexual, gay, lesbian, and transgender people. And I honor the memory of Jim Reeb and Viola Liuzzo who were martyred in the civil rights struggle.

As Unitarian Universalists we second the Buddhists' unyielding commitment to "engaged spirituality" and the Jewish summons to *tikkun olam* or "repairing the brokenness of the creation." We stand in the direct lineage of the prophetic imperative of Jesus to be perpetual peace-makers and justice-builders. No one has phrased it more vividly than the African-American preacher who charged religious devotees to "tangibilitate" their faith.

Christian activist William Sloane Coffin adds his perspective:

Brother Socrates had it wrong; it's not the unexamined but finally the uncommitted life that isn't worth living. And Descartes was mistaken too: "I think therefore I am," nonsense. "I love, therefore I am.

Love isn't an emotion or even an intention, but a policy, a vow, a behavior. It must be embodied to become real. Love exists only in action. It crackles, sparks, is ablaze. Our religion is realized when we live by successive approximations of truth, goodness, and beauty.

Our brains are important, but only when they are connected to healthy consciences. Authentic religion, while often starting in our heads, must travel through our hearts, then be enacted through our hands. Native American elders are fond of saying "the greatest distance in the world is the 14 inches from our minds to our hearts." I would add that you need to travel another foot or so, from the heart to the hands, then farther down to our heels.

To make our lives matter, to embody our faith, we must employ our hands to the utmost. Our hands are summoned to be shaken in friendship, extended in resistance, spread in loving embrace, folded in prayer, aroused to clapping, and unfurled to welcome the alien and enfold the needy. In an embodied faith, our hands are reaching out in service, holding firm in resistance, clasping others in comfort, getting dirty in messy social causes.

However, it's tempting to try to "handle" every cause and crisis, rush out to save the world rather than serve people. It's seductive to become swallowed up in righteous indignation without nourishing our own spirits.

As religious progressives we need to avoid either extreme: excessive inwardness or frenzied outwardness. We are mystical activists, and as such, aspire to touch all points of the human circle: the world within, the world without, the world above, and the world beneath where dragons are roaming.

Unitarian Universalist history is teeming with revolutionaries whose justice work was grounded in a mature, ever-evolving spirituality—from Dorothea Dix's groundbreaking work in mental health reform to Whitney Young's intrepid stands for racial equality. The fact is that authentic prophets in our heritage have regularly attended worship and engaged in spiritual practices. Why? So their activism might not grow thin and useless. Their external actions were fortified by persistent interior renewal.

The medieval poet Kabir mused: "Suppose you scrub your ethical skin until it shines, but inside there exists no music, then what?" On the other hand, suppose your soul is flooded with song, but the music never translates into compassion. Either way, our lives, and all those whom we touch or could touch, are impoverished. When our flame is fanned, Unitarian Universalism is the crucible for forging celebratory compassion and soulful service.

If and when a judgment day arrives, the focus won't be on our brilliant or noble thoughts, or even the range of our mystical epiphanies, but upon our bold and courageous acts of joy-sharing, peace-making, and justice-building. Embodiment will be the litmus test of our earthly sojourn.

Here's a telling example from our Unitarian heritage. William Ellery Channing practiced rigorous spiritual disciplines throughout his life, yet his personal piety was maintained for one reason alone: to effect social change. He dedicated the substance of his ministerial life not only to informing hearts and transforming souls but also to reforming the structures of society.

Channing's causes ranged from child labor to alcoholism, slavery to juvenile delinquency. He was also deeply concerned for both prisoners and the poor. Flawed, Channing was. Even reluctant at times. Yet Channing agreed with Emerson that "ideas are tangible things to be lived." So he lived freedom, lived justice, lived mercy, however imperfectly. That continues to be our foremost mission as an ever-evolving 50-year-old movement, aspiring to stay ablaze.

What's exemplary about Channing was his willingness to develop as a prophetic presence. Perhaps his foremost growth as minister occurred with respect to his anti-slavery work. He had been so impressed by Lydia Maria Child's viewpoints on slavery that, despite ill health, Channing walked a couple miles to her place to discuss the issue. After a three-hour conversation, William Ellery credited Child with goading his conscience to speak out on the question, even if not as zealously as Child desired. Never a full-bore abolitionist, Channing pushed to bring an end to slavery in his "calm, self-controlled, benevolent" way.

In the final analysis, Channing's views on slavery proved too drastic for the alienated Unitarian conservatives and too tepid for the radical abolitionists. He was a moderate with courage, what progressive theologian Jack Mendelsohn called "a civilized controversialist." Channing preached week after week to stodgy, stubborn Bostonians nudging the most recalcitrant toward "cheerful, vigorous, beneficent action of each for all."

SOCIAL JUSTICE CRITERIA

There are a 1000 worthy causes clamoring for our money, effort, and time as Unitarian Universalists. We have to make smart and sensitive choices, individually, then band together in effective task forces within our congregations. Some causes won't mesh with our peculiar talents, interests, or needs. Others will suck us dry, quickly. Still others might prove a waste of time for the participants.

The anguish of the world remains overwhelming. How can we constructively and compassionately choose to do social justice? Here are some proven guidelines.

First, a particular cause may not be the greatest need, but it must be a pressing and engaging one for each of us. Our involvement can't be compulsive; it must be chosen. Unless you and I feel good, even gratified, about our choices of engaged spirituality, we will frazzle, grow resentful, be rendered powerless. No project needs us if our soul isn't in it. We need to choose involvements where we're likely to receive enlightened self-interest and commensurate joy.

Since Unitarian Universalists aren't beholden to the salvation-by-merits racket, we don't need to martyr ourselves with an overload of do-gooding. All we have to manage is asking ourselves, at every juncture: what's the smallest change I can make to produce the biggest difference?

A word of caution. Sometimes our social action involvement says more about our own needs than those of the people we're assisting. We strut about, sporting an unacknowledged "messiah complex." We're off to rescue somebody.

On the contrary, ever-growing prophets are willing to move on, move back, and move over. They are ready to move *on* from a perennial cause to another more urgent one, to move *back* from someone who once needed them but no longer does, to move *over* for someone else to take their job as helper. Negotiating these various movements requires both a sense of self-confidence and a willingness to admit our dispensability.

Secondly, it's prudent to pursue justice work that not only meshes with our desires but also with our capacities. Saul Alinsky, the professional community organizer, used to say repeatedly: "Tactics is doing what you can with what you have." That advice resounds for individuals as well as groups.

Unitarian Universalists can't be all things to all people. We're a religious minority, and as such we can't manage everything; but we can do some things. We need to pick what those missions might be. We have been particularly effective on the issue of "marriage equality" in recent times, because it reinforces our historically grounded and theologically core message of "standing on the side of love." It also squares with our capability.

It's rarely a question of our progressive faith being morally flabby or unsympathetic. Unitarian Universalists, for the most part, are dead earnest about bettering this world during their lifetimes. "Our consciences," Mark Twain quipped, "sometimes take up more room than all the rest of our insides."

Our quandary is promoting too many resolutions, with too few facts undergirding them, with too little time to debate the pros and cons, and with too few teeth in them, once we've endorsed them. The result is too little notice. Hence, we need to be more discerning in our selections.

Our Association has realized in its fifty years as a movement that there exist three distinct yet related elements for the prophetically motivated person or congregation: (1) social education, (2) social service, and (3) social action. Every Unitarian Universalist committed to social compassion will likely be involved in all three areas.

However, whereas we may be educated about many causes and supporting several service needs, we would do well to choose but a couple social action endeavors which we can shoulder with conviction and agency.

Furthermore, embodied social action contains liberal, conservative, and radical components. First, it's *liberal* because it aspires to be generous of alternatives for prophetic duty. Additionally, it's open to different perspectives and actions being honored, not just tolerated, in our coalitions of compassion.

Our approach attempts to be *conservative* as well, since we're inveterate institutionalists. Unitarian Universalism is zealously committed to conserving our deepest values and visions.

Third, our social action perspective is *radical*, because it literally travels to the root of a social problem rather than dabbling about in surface analysis and reaction. True radicals are neither fast nor rash but thorough and plodding.

We must also be socially attentive to the agonies of the outside world, while remaining respectful toward our fellow faith-partners, with whom we may disagree on either ends or means. We dare not censure or mistreat our own Unitarian Universalist sisters and brothers, all in the name of holy crusades. Writer–activist Alice Walker says: "When Martin (Martin Luther King, Jr.) talked about agitating nonviolently, I imagine he meant to start at home." Yes, right at home: in our families, workplaces, and congregations.

We need to prophet with pride: "I am personally confident that my action is right for me and good for my neighbor." Theologically mature persons also prophet with humility: "My action is more and no less than my action. It may not be yours. I cannot equate my compassionate gambles with the goals of the gods. I will not pontificate from pulpits or committees or resolutions or anywhere else. I will venture my principles, and I will listen in love to the prophet in every person."

False prophets, and we've had our share of them since our Association was formed in 1961, deal in absolutes: "You aren't moral if, you aren't religious unless, you shouldn't belong to our parish, because this is how you vote..." Beware of the false and arrogant prophet. They exist everywhere, including inside our own hearts.

BODY THEOLOGY

Some words specifically on body theology.

We contend that the religious journey must evoke the entirety of our beings—an enlightened mind, a venturing spirit, an awakened conscience, a sensitive heart, a cultivated soul, and a healthy, robust body. Ordinarily, Unitarian Universalists spend the bulk of our energy and time dwelling in our minds and rarely coming to our senses. We, like James Joyce's character Mr. Duffy, too often end up living "a few blocks away from our body!"

"And the Word became flesh and dwelt (literally *tabernacled*) in our midst," wrote John in the Christian scriptures (1:14). A faith-claim declaring that the Eternal One that covenanted with Moses, argued with Gideon, struggled within Jeremiah...that this same Spirit had returned, incarnating a fresh and robust love in the birth of the Nazarene.

When the dust of existence settles, the litmus test for all religious pilgrims is *embodiment*: the charge to resemble our preachments... starting within our own bodies then spreading to touch, even transform, far-flung corners of our globe.

As members of Western culture we've inherited dualisms, namely that the spirit is held to be essentially different from and superior to the body even as its counterpart, and that the patriarchal male is believed to be essentially different from and better than a female. As Unitarian Universalists we've been working to combat these pernicious dualisms.

Body theology is a welcome corrective to an overspiritualized religion. It takes seriously our raw physicality as an occasion of revelation. After all, our bodies are the physical bases from which we explore and engage the universe. Embodiment marks a theology of earth and wind, water and fire. It begins with the concrete not with doctrine. It emphasizes our hungers, instincts, and passions. Embodiment accents the fleshly experiences of existence: the smell of coffee, the warm touch of friends, sweating, bodies violated and torn apart in war, the scent of a honeysuckle, or the sharp blast of a winter storm.

With the fleshly experiences of existence, our bodies have profound stories and wisdom to impart. There exists frightening evidence that anti-body, anti-touch, anti-sensual attitudes are strongly correlated with high levels of adult violence of all kinds.

As this essay on embodiment unfolds, I am reminded of a Nepalese body prayer introduced to me by ministerial sister Orlanda Brugnola. My homespun version of this ancient ritual unveils the break of my every morn, keeping me on an embodied track. It's all about reaching within and beyond in balanced aspiration. This prayer aspires to stretch every limb of the embodied self. I invite you to make your own amendments to my routine. For surely that's the way of ripened theological growth.

Upon rising from bed, I plant my feet firmly on the floor, usually following a jaunt to the bathroom. After finding my body's center of gravity, I slightly bend my knees and cup my hands in a receptive mode, right above the navel. I affirm my very being with words such as: "*I am a child of the universe. I belong here. It's good for me to be alive.*"

Then my hands lift, barely touching, fully stretched to the sky in prayerful gesture, and I continue speaking outloud: "*I thank You God for most this amazing day*" (E. E. Cummings), or similar words of bone-deep gratitude.

When my arms reach their apex, I open wide my hands and shape them into a chalice to welcome all the manifold gifts, both challenges and comforts, to be delivered on this irrepeatable day. My words pour forth: "*Into my hands are received today's delights and difficulties, sorrows and joys.*" Then slowly, in circling fashion, I draw my extended hands back to the beginning position, while assertively uttering: "*I promise to spread these blessings to every living entity that I greet this precious day.*"

I repeat this ritual, perhaps three or four times, to stretch my being in ample measure. After performing this bodily exercise, the day consistently tastes better.

In summary, Unitarian Universalism is increasingly attentive to four areas of body theology.

First, we all receive a body. We may like it or despise it, but it will be ours for the duration of this earthly sojourn. Therefore, we must be vigilant, then self-governing, in the face of societal pressure to shape our body in the image of media-driven standards. Our steadfast mission stands: to be the best version of our own singular bodies rather than a second-rate version of somebody else.

We're beckoned to take better care of our given bodies or engage in what one might call "temple maintenance." We don't just have bodies; we are our bodies. We'll end up either commodities or temples, depending on how we envision and treat the bodies we were given. Our body then, while fragile and flawed, is a good gift, to be both enjoyed and carefully maintained.

Second, we're beginning to relate to the earth as one body to another. It's no wonder that etymologically and actually, central theological virtues, such as humaneness, humor, and humility, all come from *humus*, the soil. These virtues are exemplified, whenever we ground ourselves in that fellow body called earth.

Third, we're honoring love as the central principle in our sexual sharing. Our bodies are restless for intimacy, hungering for the physical and spiritual embrace of others. A mature body theology practices the ethics of honesty, caring, and respectfulness.

Carter Heyward, an astute lesbian theologian, seconds this sentiment:

To say I love you is to say that you are not mine, but rather your own. To love you is to advocate your rights, your space, your self, and to struggle with you, rather than against you, in our learning to claim our power in the world. To say "I love you" means: let the revolution begin!

Finally, our bodies, which are made of the earth, will ultimately return to the earth; we travel from dust to dust. In a well-rounded body theology, we're willing to embrace our physical end, our mortality. Whatever one's particular view of immortality, reincarnation, or resurrection might be, "until we consent to die, we cannot fully live" (W. H. Auden). Until we acknowledge death not as a defeat but as a natural and proper destiny for our humanity, we cannot truly begin to dance and drum...embodying life's swirl and throb to the utmost.

FOR REFLECTION AND DISCUSSION

1. Give instances of when and where you "embody" your theological convictions...whether at home, during work or worship, and through community service.

2. In light of the historic witness of William Ellery Channing, how would you describe your social activism ministry? Are you a "reluctant radical" or an "engaged mystic" or just what?

3. Unitarian Universalist theologian Sara York has remarked:

   Let us consider what it is that fills us with a passion for goodness, a passion for justice, a passion for beauty, a passion for truth. The kind of passion which motivated Theodore Parker...

   What, indeed is it that calls us to make ourselves, and this fragile planet, whole?

   What justice causes seem to claim your deepest passion right now? In what ways are your resources and energy going there?

4. What's the smallest shift you can negotiate in your life to produce the biggest difference with respect to social change?

5. Comment upon how each of the four qualities referenced for a mature "body theology" fit your own life.

SUFFERING

Unitarian Universalism has been called a fair weather faith, beneficial to its adherents on sunny days, but not helpful when the days are overcast.
—William Murry

As with sin and evil, our liberal religion must address suffering to be a full-fledged faith. To be theologically ablaze, Unitarian Universalism must squarely face the underbelly of existence.

Albert Camus, in his novel *The Fall,* writes about the dungeon cell in the Middle Ages called the "little-ease which wasn't high enough to stand up in or wide enough to lie down in. One had to take on an awkward manner and live on the diagonal. Sleep was a collapse and waking a squatting." There is dis-ease, un-ease, and little-ease in being human. It hurts to be alive.

Life's marked by three recurring themes: anticipated loss, loss itself, and grieving over loss. Our very origin begins with loss. We're profoundly separated from the protective womb, disconnected from the heartbeat of the cosmos, thrust into an uncertain and often harsh world. This birth trauma marks the beginning of a journey that ends with the loss of life itself.

Currently, we're stuck, without resolution, in the "worst financial catastrophe since the Great Depression." To be sure, we can raise our prophetic voices to rail against the values and policies that brought us here, generate awareness and advocate for change, and promote generosity to alleviate present suffering. Additionally, Unitarian Universalists, across the land, have huddled together to share our confusion, anxiety, and counsel.

However, this theological theme would have us view the larger picture of both the human condition and social reality, so that we might make our losses matter.

Our losses are legion and daily. Lost time. Lost limbs. Lost momentum. Lost memory. Lost faith. Lost friends. Lost jobs. Lost loves.

Lost hair. Lost innocence. Lost children. Lost money. Lost energy. Lost dreams (what I call "the nevers": I guess I'm never going to be head of the firm, never going to have children of my own, never going to be a great writer or recognized activist, etc.). On and on mounts the lousy litany of losses—some necessary yet others infuriatingly ill-timed.

You name it, we humans have lost it during our lifetimes. Many pray for a way to make sure that we'll not lose again. But God grants that privilege to no one.

Remember Buddha's classic answer to a mother who had lost her child. According to legend, he said that to be healed, she needed only a mustard-seed from a household that had never known sorrow. The woman journeyed from home to home, all over the region, never discovering a family ignorant of grief. Instead, in the paradoxical manner of myths and oracles, she found some semblance of truth, compassion, kinship, and rebirth.

And so it goes. Unexpected deaths strike, job situations fall flat, unsettling partnership breaks occur, untimely moves are required, and long-held beliefs fail us. That losses will assault our cozy comfortable lives is inevitable; what we do with those losses is up to us. That choice is sometimes a matter of hope or despair. Hence, the key question in our theological search is simply this: can we build an altar from the broken fragments of our hearts? Are we brave enough to do so?

Religions that try to rationalize or justify suffering aren't very convincing to Unitarian Universalists. The basic root of the word "suffering" means "to feel sharply or keenly." Fundamentally, we believe our human duty is to encounter and endure suffering rather than explain it. There are imponderables in being alive, and suffering is one of them. Pain comes with the territory of being a vulnerable, responsive human being.

Life entails growing accustomed to the unpredictable and unjust experiences of suffering. However, religious progressives aren't fatalists. We're not willing to lie down and be steamrolled by suffering.

There are three things we can do with pain/suffering, and two of them are bad. We can pass the pain along, we can stuff it, or we can transform it. The object of life is to transform pain, and we can do that if we don't succumb to three other pitfalls: denial, comparison-making, and self-pity or whining.

First, denial. There are crises we'd really rather ignore and suppress, so we do just that. Our partnership isn't really crumbling; it's just coasting. Our family doesn't need outside help; we just need to care more about one another. However, sometimes love isn't enough. We tell our children that grandma has gone to sleep, mainly to protect our own unwillingness to accept the permanent loss of loved ones, let alone face our own death.

Where can we turn during a loss if we don't even admit that there is one? If we turn anger, hurt, or guilt in against ourselves, we compound the suffering. If we repress, we invariably depress. The converse is also true: "Blessed are they who mourn, for they shall be comforted!" Comfort, deep comfort, comes from generous mourning.

It's natural to sugar-coat anguish, but we must keep in mind that most people who suffer severe losses retain permanent scars, no matter how much theology or therapy they imbibe. Some who have experienced grievous losses say they never again feel quite up to par. They experience a sense of chronic sorrow, bone-deep sadness. That's just the way life works.

We moderns are told to follow our bliss; we would do well also to follow our pain—sit and soak in it as a prelude to growing to the other side. Ric Masten, popular UU minister, poet, and troubadour, in his classic song "Let It Be a Dance" (#311 in *Singing the Living Tradition*) relates: "Let the sun shine, let it rain; share the laughter, bear the pain, and round and round we go again. Let it be a dance." Ric would sometimes stop the song midstream and say: "that is, *bare*... b-a-r-e...the pain", emphasizing the value of human willingness to reveal the open sores of our lives.

"And Jesus wept" is the shortest verse in the Christian scriptures, yet what a mighty sentiment. Understandably, the Nazarene was distraught over the rotten behavior of his people, of Jerusalem, but instead of resorting to macho behavior such as ranting and railing, or marshaling a political or military response, Jesus was moved to tears. He wept. Jesus suffered.

Sometimes falling to pieces is the only way to patch our psyches back to together again. Theologically mature pilgrims spend time crying...letting our tears pour forth and fertilize the ground. We avoid aridity, drying up; we hanker instead to stay moist and keep our juices flowing. As our colleague Clarke Wells declared:

It's time we assert that it's OK to live with grief as a permanent companion. To be fully human is to live with a concourse of emotions, including life's joys and sorrows irremediably entwined. Some hurts haunt a lifetime. Let's stop worrying whether we've passed the grief test. Nobody does.

Earlier in my ministry I used to equate sadness with dolefulness. I now know better. Today I trust grieving to be a sign of theological vitality. Being woundable and feeling sad come with the condition of being fully awake. Sad people aren't desperate; while acknowledging the thorns, they keep on mulching rose gardens.

With Shantideva, the Buddhist saint, we can say "let all sorrows ripen in me." We help sorrows ripen by passing them directly through our bodies and hearts, making good compost of all that fierce grief. None of us can truly afford to waste our pain.

In addition to denial, a second futile strategy is comparing our loss with those of others, usually measuring ours against the ten worst tragedies of all time. Of course, there are always people who have ostensibly suffered more or less than we have. Yet such comparisons bring only temporary or pseudo-relief.

Also, there's a clear distinction between being uncomfortable and having a broken heart. The difference was brought home poignantly in Alice Hoffman's novel *At Risk*, in a dialogue between Polly, the mother of a child dying of AIDS, and Betty, the mother who refuses to let her son have contact with the dying child's brother. "This breaks my heart," Betty whispers. "No, no!" Polly tells her. "It makes you uncomfortable. My son's dying breaks my heart!" Polly feels a sharpness and size of anguish not possibly experienced by Betty in this novel.

No matter how theologically sophisticated we might grow, none of us can climb inside another's heart. We have no idea how devastating or perhaps how relieving the loss of a certain pet or relative might in fact be. We have no business, then, evaluating the seriousness of another's hurt—our job is to be present, listen, and care. Why? Because down deep, we don't want other people rating our losses or judging the seriousness of our suffering. We need from others what they need from us: ears and arms!

"How do you feel about it?" be it retirement or divorce, is a more respectful reaction than, "Oh, I'm so sorry" or "I know exactly how you feel" or "Gee, you must be relieved." Our most compassionate responses are open-ended: "How are you doing?" Then, to follow, as appropriate, with a caring question like: "Is there something I can be or do for you?"

So, denial and comparisons are unhelpful and self-pity is fruitless in coping with loss. It's clearly more comforting to feel "put upon" or unfairly treated than it is to deal directly with the disappointments we all face. Yet, no matter how the fates may seem to conspire, we still make or forsake our own singular destinies.

Jesus didn't stand for self-pitying sorts, as evidenced when he said to more than one person: "Come on, rise, take up your pallet and walk." Sometimes that's a cruel command, if we can't possibly make it out of the pool by ourselves. At other times, it's precisely the kick in the rear that self-pitying folks require.

At some stage in our journeys, we grow up and recognize that we live in an imperfect world. We will never be fully healed from our given infirmities and deformities. We won't recover to utter normalcy from a devastating disappointment. That fractured bond or bone is as whole as it will ever be.

So many tragedies result from an unfinished, evolving world rather than from the will or action of God. God doesn't start earthquakes or administer blindness. Any infinite, loving Spirit worth its salt weeps along with us in the throes of natural or inexplicable disasters. The process theologians among us recognize the Eternal Source to be all-loving while not all-powerful.

Consequently, humans will never make total sense out of the mystery of suffering. In addition to calling upon Divine Love to companion us through our losses, we need to summon the loving resources of other human beings. It is both spiritually obtuse and immature to try to bear our losses alone.

Often when we lose something or someone, we hide out, we narrow our souls and draw ourselves tighter and tighter, trying to feel secure but actually cutting off a major source of our strength and support: other sufferers. We all belong to "the fellowship of pain," Schweitzer's phrase for the largest unofficial organization in the universe. As we are bound together in sorrow, so can we be bound together in healing.

Our third Principle—"acceptance of one another and encouragement to spiritual growth in our congregations"—contains an intertwined charge to both comfort and challenge fellow pilgrims. In the bosom of a beloved community, Unitarian Universalists, first and foremost, accept one another as we are, in our various and sundry life-situations. However, we don't merely console and embrace one another; we actively challenge one another to grow. This is the way the *Embracing Our Theological Diversity* report phrased it:

> *Additionally, Unitarian Universalism is an encouraging instead of a despairing religion. When our days are dreary and crises bedevil us, spiritual kin step forward to lift us up or push us forward by offering affection and comfort.*

Acceptance affirms people where we are and *encouragement* propels us toward whom we might become. This constitutes the rhythm of our Unitarian Universalist theology of solace amidst suffering.

Did you know that the word *care* finds its roots in the Gothic "kara," which means lament? Therefore, the basic role of a friend or companion or caregiver is to become someone with whom you can grieve, experience sorrow, and share support. It is especially useful to locate those who have felt sorrow themselves, not simply in general, but sorrow similar to yours. That's why Alcoholics Anonymous works for recovering alcoholics. That's why "Parents of Murdered Children" succeeds for that grieving group. That's why a group of single mothers isn't served well by having a partnered father in the room or vice versa.

Our mission as practicing theologians is to be strong enough to deliver care and weak enough to receive care. We're called to be caregivers not caretakers. We can't resolve or take care of another person's concerns; we can only give steady and appropriate care in the face of stress, sorrow, and suffering. As it says in our Principles and Purposes, "we promise to one another our mutual trust and support." We can be trustworthy supporters but not rescuers.

Furthermore, the theological concept of *compassion* is wisely referenced twice in our current Article II. The word compassion isn't fancy. It means just what it says: *suffering with*. It denotes participation in the anguish of our brother or sister.

When somebody else is in pain, though we may not be able to relieve it, we don't withdraw. We make room in our heart for their pain. We stay soft, present, our hand in theirs, perhaps our mouth shut, sharing their pain without closing around it.

Compassionate people know deep in our souls that we can never really find true peace and joy for ourselves until there's peace and joy for others. Genuine compassion also denotes the agility to support another without getting mired in their crisis. There's nothing worse than helper and helped succumbing together.

As colleague Brandy Lovely phrases it:
We all know misery loves company. But if everyone joins in the misery, then who will relieve the situation? Compassion is the faculty by which we acknowledge another's agony, without joining it.

It's imperative to remember that compassion is for plodders, the persistent, the patient, not the quick, the flashy, and the impulsive of spirit. Compassion requires commitment for the long haul. This becomes clear, when we realize that the word compassion can also be read as *com-patience,* because the words passion and patience find their rootage in the same Latin word, *pati.*

Love is patient, as St. Paul reminds us. It hangs tough. It endures. I like the way Unitarian Oliver Wendell Holmes expressed it: "The physician's task is to cure rarely, relieve often, and comfort always." That's our role as parishioners and pastors too.

Comfort literally means to "place our strength alongside" another person. That's doable; we can put our strength next to the weakness of another in need—on the phone, through a note, or in person. As caregivers we're willing to show up, stand alongside, and tender our strength. We do this, despite our own frailties, since, lest we forget, all Unitarian Universalists are "wounded healers."

Our Western tendency remains to be industrious do-gooders who exclaim: "Don't just stand there, do something." On the contrary, the Buddha would counsel: "Don't just do something, stand there." Comfort and be available, stand tall, stand strong, stand next to your neighbor with hands and heart outstretched.

Unitarian Universalist religious educator and minister, Elizabeth Strong, illustrates the call to be a comforter with the following inspirational exchange. A little girl was coming home and explained to concerned parents that she had encountered her friend who had broken her favorite doll on the sidewalk. "And you stopped to help her pick up the pieces?" her father inquired. "Oh no, Dad, I stopped and helped her cry!"

God and groups, while absolutely essential, don't fully cure us of our ills. We're cared about and comforted but not cured. Some pain invariably remains. Outside support, be it in the form of humans or a higher power or a formidable blend of both, gives us the energy and skill, forgiveness and hope to grow on...not beyond our pain but *through* it. And we can regain our equilibrium despite an oft-constant, deep heartache.

Unitarian Universalists often ask whether or not we would choose a life void of suffering. Generally, our answers run this way: even if we were given the opportunity for unadulterated bliss, we'd turn it down. I guess that's why the conventional notion of "heaven" has never really thrilled us.

Our theology contends that if we cut off despair, we cut off hope. Joy loses its edge without the presence of its partner sorrow. As Unitarian forebear Theodore Parker sagely put it: "When I look over my life, I find no disappointment and no sorrow I could afford to lose..."

We can't transcend suffering; however, we can sometimes transform it. The purpose of a theologically deepening existence is to manage comebacks, to be born again and again and again, or as the Zen poet phrases it: "Such is life: seven times down and eight times up!" Our human dignity lies neither in innocence nor in despondency but in new beginnings, in being scarred and healed a thousand times, in becoming seasoned, gnarled persons.

The story is told of a monk who lived in a monastery high on a mountain. One day he descended to the village below and a peasant ran up to him and said, "Oh, father, surely yours must be the best of all lives, living so close to God. Tell me, what do you do up there?" After a thoughtful pause, the monk replied, "What do we do? Well, I'll tell you. We fall down and get up. Then we fall down and get up. Then we fall down and get up. That's pretty much what our lives look like—how about yours?"

May we be understanding, for there are folks needing to avoid some pain right now. May we be encouraging, for there are others needing to face and deal with pain. May we be tough, for there are still others needing to be challenged to stop wallowing in pain. And may we be gentle, for there are those trying to endure some pain and attain sufficient courage.

Life is truly about building an altar from the broken fragments of our hearts.

FOR REFLECTION AND DISCUSSION

1. Give some examples of how you have built an altar from the broken fragments of your heart. Tell your story and listen to the stories of fellow Unitarian Universalists.

2. In your congregational existence, how are you balancing the rhythm of accepting folks as they are, while encouraging them to become the best they might become?

3. Unitarian Universalist theologian Ken Collier says: *Compassion is not an action but a recognition, a knowing, a way of being with another. It is not my work to fix you; it is my work to nurture you.*

    Ponder and discuss.

4. Relate incidents of when you have suffered from "compassion-fatigue" in caring for the hurts and sorrows of others.

5. How do you deal with chronic pain and ineradicable suffering in your own life and in the lives of other people?

6. Seasoned Unitarian Universalist religious educator Joan Goodwin wrote:

   I have to accept the fact that my life is fed by the destruction of other life, but I do not bear that burden lightly. I live to be worthy of the sacrifice and to nourish other lives with mine. I affirm the natural order as unitary, universal, and full of meaning—tragic as well as joyous.

Respond.

7. Do you resonate with our comeback theology, which, along with the Zen Buddhists claims: "Seven times down, eight times up!"? Describe some of the comebacks you've negotiated in your journey. Then listen to the tales of comrades.

THE SACRED

The sacred is present and available to us wherever we look or are willing to find it. If we remain open and expectant—watching out of the corners of our eyes, keeping our ears cocked, putting away all preconceived ideas—our lives will emanate the sacred.
—Abhi Janamanchi

The earth traditions say that all is holy, the body, the mind, the imagination, birth, sex, death—and that the stuff of the sacred is all around us, right here, right now, in the material world. Divinity is immanent in nature; it is within you as well as without. You don't have to die to get the good stuff—which doesn't mean that other worlds besides the material do not exist.
—Margot Adler

As a religion that emphasizes the here and now, we have always located the sacred within this natural realm, certainly in the past half-century when progressive theology has become an "earthly affair" in the fullest sense of the phrase. Unitarian Universalism holds this lifetime to be the only one we can know and this earth the only one we will share...at least with any certitude. Therefore, we strive to explore the magnificent epiphanies of our life cycle from birth until death.

Our 19th-century Unitarian forebear Henry David Thoreau was a devout panentheist, who believed that God was discoverable in the midst of living realities and inanimate objects. For Thoreau, the universe was ablaze with evidences of holiness:

My profession is to be always on the alert to find God in nature, to know his lurking-places, to attend all the oratorios, the opera, in nature.

Transcendentalist brother Ralph Waldo Emerson reinforced this posture:

God does not speak prose, but communicates with us by hints, omens,
inferences, and dark resemblances in objects around us.

Unitarian Universalists are clearly at home in this universe, feeling connected to and an integral part of the cosmos. Unitarian pioneer Margaret Fuller was said to have declared in the 19th century:
"I accept the Universe!" To which a Unitarian friend responded, "By
gad, she'd better!"

And from our Unitarian Universalist shared history, post-1961,
the *Embracing Our Theological Diversity* report (2005) reinforces the
theological leanings of our transcendentalist forebears when it
reveals that "religious naturalism" is the fastest growing theological
identification among us (90%).

When a pamphlet, called *The Sacred*, was written in 2007, our
at-homeness in this world was abundantly evident. All authors, albeit
from distinct perspectives, were comfortable in experiencing the
sacred in flowers and birds, trauma and ecstasy.

In the last decade, an affiliate organization has been established
called *Unitarian Universalist Religious Naturalists,* joining the ranks of
Unitarian Universalists for Jewish Awareness, the Process Theology
Network, Unitarian Universalist Christians, HUUmanists, Unitarian
Universalist Buddhists, and the Coven of Unitarian Universalist
Pagans, as well as other theological kinship circles. The cornerstone
statement of UU Religious Naturalists embodies the core of this
evolving theological hallmark on sacrality:

We find our sources of meaning within the natural world, where hu-
mans are understood to be emergent from and hence a part of nature. The
natural world and its emergent manifestations in human creativity and
community are the focus of our immersion, wonder, and reverence, and
our common naturalistic orientation generates our shared sense of place,
gratitude and joy.

SACRED IN THE COMMONPLACE

Unitarian Universalism contends that every relationship, insight, or event is a potential carrier of the sacred. The Hindus talk about the *Upaguru*—the teacher that dwells next to you. We second that attitude.

Our religion is disclosed not only in the peaks or valleys of existence but moreover on the plains. Popular rhetoric to the contrary, we must "sweat the small stuff," or at least pay close heed to it, for modest things often carry immense beauty and power. Every episode and exchange, however mundane, can prove sacramental.

Not only is the sacred found in the ordinary for us, we also contend that the deepest validation of our faith emerges from how we handle the average and the routines of everyday life. We resonate with the Zen Buddhist who claims that our quest for ultimate wisdom is usually doomed, because we tend to look in obscure places for what lies in broad daylight. Yunmen, when asked to give some sage statement for the enlightenment of his monks, replied in the most ordinary terms: "pulling a plough in the morning and carrying a rake home in the evening." Or as one Unitarian Universalist reports: "Nothing happens next. This is it."

During the middle of the day, when my energy's flagging, I'll often engage in a restorative practice. The words are mine yet soaked in Buddhist sensibility: "I breathe in energy, I breathe out fatigue. My body breathes, my spirit breathes, and my heart breathes. I am awake, joyfully awake. Right now is precious, right now is all I possess." This mantra works better for me if I get up and walk around in mindful meditation, rather than staying seated.

In the Unitarian Universalist way of religion, we recommend not a closing of the eyes, wherein we await some dazzling psychic state or ecstatic trance, but rather an opening of our eyes, our hearts, and our minds to the full reality that stands plainly before and within us. The most holy resides in our very midst.

Religion never manifests itself in some pure state, separate from the messy complexities of our actual lives. The special genius of our faith may just be to transform the little, everyday annoyances and delights, what Emerson called "the emphatic trifles of our days," into something marvelous. Not just endure or overcome, but transform, them, whenever possible.

Our lives are ultimately a mosaic of minor parts—dishwashing, transporting children, mending clothes, taking walks, answering doorbells, visiting the sick, paying bills, breaking bread with family, answering e-mails, talking with friends, and performing a hundred such commonplace tasks. How we play our roles in this daily drama registers the expanse of our joy and the fire of our theology.

Unitarian Universalist educator Edith Hunter used to remark: "Perhaps we should realize that our need is not to find something to believe but rather to discover what our lives indicate that we believe right now." Growing-up people become vitally aware of our actual expenditures of time, feelings, money, and energy so that our religion becomes conscious and planned rather than implicit and haphazard.

Unitarian Universalist religion can be felt in our hands and seen on our faces. We openly say: if you want to know our hurts, hopes, and commitments—our core *religion*—what literally binds us together again and again—then follow us around any day of the week. Observe how we respond to the animals, friends, challenges that cross our path. Notice our check stubs as well as the appointments on our calendar.

In paying attention to us, not merely when we're on public display or good behavior, you will catch the genuine spirit and substance of our religion.

SACRED IN THE NOW
We live in no other time but the present. Understanding this is
as close as we can get to understanding eternal life.
Perhaps, after all, I have enough time...
—Jane Mauldin

There isn't any more important human task than becoming better friends with time; but to do so, certain myths that cause us unnecessary frustration and grief must be exploded.

The first myth has to do with today's veritable nostalgia craze: people keep harkening back to the good old days when kids were polite, streets were safe, America was boss, men were men and women were women, hamburger was 50 cents a pound and even considered healthy for your diet. This mentality is by no means limited to people over fifty. An English professor assures me that one chief identifying characteristic of her new students is nostalgia.

Whether we're 17 or 77, whenever we look over our shoulder, it's typically to a happier, less complicated time. Such wishful thinking is understandable, since it's downright scary to live in today's world and even bleaker to envision the years ahead for our children's children. In some alluring sense, we're all tempted to scurry back to a more innocent, serener past.

Part of the appeal of the radical religious right is their enticement to yank us back to a time that existed before today's freer and more open society when you and I are called to render tough personal choices. For folks with a rigid moral agenda, nostalgia isn't some parlor game. They harbor high hopes of a major social victory where old, simplistic, exclusionary virtues will be crowned anew.

The truth is that any conceivable personal and political yesteryear is gone, forever. We can recall the past, we must learn from it, but we can't return to it, let alone live in it. Some broken relationships cannot be mended. Certain dreams are gone forever.

A fiery, robust theology charges us to live fully in the present moment, being utterly accountable in the *now*, the only moment we truly possess.

The Russian novelist Leo Tolstoy goes to the heart of living in the here and now. When asked: "What is the best time to do each thing?" he replied: "In the present moment." When pushed: "Who are the most important people to work with?" he retorted: "Those right with you." And finally: "What is the most important thing to do at all times?" Tolstoy unflinchingly answered: "Make the person in front of you happy!" These three responses composed Tolstoy's formula for joyous and fulfilled living.

Unitarian Universalism is wary of the one-minute obsession sweeping our land. There exist books on being a one-minute manager, a one-minute mother or father, a one-minute meditator. Or how about this one: "The 59-second employee: or how to stay one second ahead of your one-minute manager!"

Who are we kidding with all this one-minute appeal? Good parenting, good loving, good work, good learning, good community-building, good theology...most everything we call good in our lives takes a whole lot more time than a matter of minutes. In fact, our interest isn't in being a one-minute person, but in being a *more-minutes* one. Quickness rarely brings thickness to one's spiritual journey. The good life takes time—ample, caring, rigorous time. In fact, the good life takes all the time we've got...a lifetime if I'm not mistaken!

The ironic twist is that most of us, most of the time, have enough time to enjoy everything we love. We don't need to rush. Life isn't a race. The Zen mantra that holds our religion in balanced stead is: "Hasten slowly, hasten slowly!" We've got to keep moving, but purposefully...with intentionality. Why, the butterfly counts not months but moments and has time enough.

Modern society's compulsion to save time is summed up in computer guru (as well as generous philanthropist) Bill Gates' statement: "I don't go to church, because it's an inefficient use of time." In one sense, Gates is right: singing and reflection, touching and being touched, being stirred to moral action and plumbing spiritual depth are technologically inefficient activities, yet not *ineffective* ones. We can survive without religious community, but we can't live fully without one, and abundant life rather than mere survival, actually finding and spreading meaning, is the point of being placed on earth.

While worship may not save time, it surely replenishes our souls with essential doses of peace and purpose. A beloved community exists to help us learn how to *savor* rather than merely save time…how to savor all our moments—be they glad, mad, or sad moments—to convert everything we feel or experience into a whole life of which we can be proud, a life that's both beautiful and compassionate.

On to the third myth, that perennial cliché: "Time will heal all wounds." Like all generalizations, this statement possesses a kernel of wisdom. Yet any healing process, be it of broken bones or broken bonds, can prove acutely obstinate. For example, when parents and their adult children fail to mend fences and go into a hardened silence, time will hardly heal the breach. Similarly, the sheer march of time may lessen some of the pain from a damaged congregational clash, but the wounds often recede rather than mend. Frankly, healing, when possible, usually comes to the fair-minded, the forgiving, and the fortunate.

Time per se is neutral, as Martin Luther King, Jr. noted in his classic statement from the Birmingham jail:

There is a strangely irrational notion that there is something in the very flow of time that will inevitably cure all ills. Actually time can be used either destructively or constructively. Human progress never rolls in on the wheels of inevitability. It comes through the tireless efforts and persistent work of people willing to be co-workers with the Creation.

King's words are not only relevant for the work of racial justice, but also prove insightful for every personal, social, and spiritual struggle in which Unitarian Universalists are engaged. Time is neutral; it's what we *do* with our time that matters.

One final myth messes us up. Too many hold the romantic notion that there's an endless supply of time. Again, there's some truth in this perspective. Plus, there are those in our religious fold who believe in reincarnation—the position that enables one to entertain an eternal flow of second chances. The irony still persists: "millions of people long for immortality who don't have the slightest notion of what to do with themselves on a rainy Sunday afternoon."

Maybe we are indeed as immortal as time. Perhaps we will reincarnate endlessly, but we don't really know, do we? So, as long as we're walking this earth, we need to continue to hold the belief that time is both precious and short: too brief to do everything we'd like to do yet long enough to accomplish the truly important stuff.

Our life will prove long enough to make the world a bit lovelier for our having been here. And we know that even youngsters who die tragically and prematurely often bless the world in unbelievable ways.

Certainly, our lives are remarkably brief, given the universal scale of time. If the estimated age of the cosmos were shortened to seventy-two years, a human life would take about ten seconds. However look at time the other way. Each day is a minor eternity of over 86,000 seconds. During each second, the number of distinct molecular functions going on within our human body is comparable to the number of seconds in the estimated age of the cosmos. A few seconds are long enough for a revolutionary idea, a baby's conception, a decisive vote, a wounding insult, a beautiful creation, a loving embrace.

Our Unitarian Universalist faith majors in living in the here and now, rather than waiting around for the hereafter; it encourages us to see our lives as infinitely precious and infinitely long…certainly long enough. Unitarian Universalist minstrel, Ric Masten, dying of prostate cancer, in one of his moments of utter frustration and rage, raised his fist to the heavens and cried: "Okay, God, this is my worst mess, right, and, by the way, tell me: how much time do I have?" An answer filtered his way: "Enough, Ric, enough time to be and do and say some things you still need to be and do and say!"

Religions have always spoken about *redeeming* time. As a bona fide senior citizen, I think I finally get what that theological phrase means. We tend to be concerned with loading up our time, but religion says: "Wait a minute! That's not it. The purpose of life is to redeem time. Lots of people save and fill time; your mission is to savor and fulfill time."

We *fill* time through driven activity, by staying mindlessly occupied or by being extremely efficient. We *fulfill* time by making the very most of our moments—giving back excellence and thanks, love and joy to the Infinite Spirit that brought us into being. In filling time, we're prone to self-absorption. In fulfilling time, we serve purposes beyond our own egos, meanings that outlast our lives.

Our times, do they not, desperately need to be redeemed. For there exist worlds within and worlds without that need to be transformed. There are people waiting to be respected, people staring at us in need, other people we've forgotten, people we don't yet know, and people right next to us…all sorts of people waiting to love and be loved.

Time's a gift. Each day of our journey is unearned. None of our moments are guaranteed. Hence, we're summoned to be grateful for every extension we receive upon waking in the morning. I can't think of a finer daily prayer than something heartfelt like this: "Thank you God, thank you Life…just plain thanks for yet another day of living and loving, come what may."

THE SACRED DWELLS WITHIN

In our theology, the primary religious authority is our own personal experience. This is cause not for hubris but for humility.

Jewish scholars note that Abraham's journey launches with Yahweh urging him to "go forth" (Genesis 12:1), alternately translated as "go to yourself." This same phrase is mentioned only twice in the entire Hebrew canon, once at the start of Abraham's quest, then again at the close of his journey when he has become an elder, still trekking in search of self.

The sacred is lodged in the corners of our own beings and must be fostered there, first and foremost. As the ancient sage Marcus

Aurelius phrased it in his immortal *Meditations*: "Very little is needed to make a happy life. It is all within yourselves, in your way of thinking." Perhaps not all, but an adequate supply of it. We are charged to nurture the heart of holiness within our own interior castles. As the biblical parable reminds: "Behold, the realm of God is within you" (Luke 17: 20–12).

It was over one hundred years ago that James Martineau, British Unitarian pillar, was searching for the seat of authority in religion. In a book of that title, he examined all of the alternatives: Is the final authority in religion to be found in hierarchy, or in a holy book, or perhaps in a saintly person? Can we safely hand over our souls to any of the above? His answer was a resounding "No"; for Martineau discovered that there was only one place for the seat of final authority in matters of religion and that was in the individual conscience, as duly comforted and challenged in the embrace of the beloved community.

Whether penultimate truths come to us through science or reason, intuition or action—and all are valid Unitarian Universalist classic routes—one fact is universal: we come by our religious virtues democratically. The convictions we hold are not revealed to us so much as experienced by us. As Unitarian Universalists we freely examine every idea that crosses our path, keeping for tenets of faith only those wisdoms that prove truthful to ourselves and loving of others.

FOR REFLECTION AND DISCUSSION

1. Sophia Fahs (1876–1978), our preeminent religious educator, stated:
    A deeply religious person is one who is sensitive and alert to the evidences of an invisible creativity. He/she is one who seeks to find the sacred everywhere.

    Where do you personally find prominent evidences of the sacred in your story?

2. It has been said that Unitarian Universalism embodies a "relentless commitment to Reality." Discuss what this might entail for our individual and institutional lives.

3. Patrick O'Neill, our minister in Brooklyn, New York has noted:
    Even if no divinity exists, for me the relationship of all living things, each to the other and to the world which sustains us, is sacred.

    Is that true for you? Can the sacred exist without the presence of divinity?

4. *Whatever for you is set apart, solemn, breathtakingly special— that is sacramental. Sacraments are very special because through them we enter the mystery and holiness of our common life, and see a vision of God.*
    —Clarke Dewey Wells

    List five moments or experiences that are sacramental for you.

5. One of our current Unitarian Universalist troubadours
   is Peter Mayer who wrote the classic "Holy Now" (1999).
   Here are some of the words of that stirring ballad:
   *When holy water was rare at best, it barely wet my fingertips, but
   now I have to hold my breath, like I'm swimming in a sea of it...
   It used to be a world half-there, heaven's second rate hand-me-
   down, but I walk it with a reverent air, 'cause everything is holy
   now.*

   Ponder and comment.

6. The Hebrew word *erets*, meaning "earth," occurs at least
   five times as often in the Hebrew scriptures as the word
   shamayim, meaning "heaven." What might that fact mean
   for your theological perspective and conduct?

SILENCE

Nature's silence is its one remark, and every flake of the
world is a chip off that old mute and immutable block.
The Chinese say that we live in the world of ten thousand things.
Each of the ten thousand things
cries out to us precisely nothing.
—Annie Dillard

Put your ear close down to your soul and listen hard.
—Anne Sexton

WORDS

Like some of you, I make my living as a wordsmith, piecing together the alphabet to lift people's spirits. That wasn't always true for me, since I was unusually reserved as a baby and young child, saying little that was intelligible until I entered kindergarten.

What a blessing merely to possess language! The remarkable power of words to silence or motivate, to harm or heal. Even as some of our beloved elders, in cognitive decline, are surrendering language, there are newbies, like our own three-year-old grandson in Santa Barbara, Zadin, who's prattling away like gangbusters, birthing words by the minute.

Words echo inside our chambers whenever we're inspired or angry, despairing or joyous. Somehow human experience isn't quite complete until we try to frame it in language. And love unspoken fails to reach its destination.

The second chapter of the Bible recounts that God breathed into the nostrils of a human, and it became a "living being." The early Aramaic translation of that phrase, from 2000 years ago, reads: "Adam was given the spirit of speech." The very breath of life pours into us this magic potion; through language we become enlivened souls.

Nary a people, from the beginnings of time, has been found without the gift of speech.

Nonetheless, as a religious pilgrim, neither my livelihood nor my life is composed merely of words. My existence readily shrivels without song and silence, touch and action. In truth, deeds are the bottom line of Unitarian Universalism. Our lives are ultimately judged not by our chatter or even our character but by our conduct.

You and I belong to a word-focused, reasonable faith, but we're scarcely a band of intellectuals. Rather, in the final analysis, we're called to be truth-doers: people who lug, with our own hands, the necessary timbers to build a more just and joyful world.

Nonetheless, our words count! We're here on earth primarily to *do* the truth but we can never forget to *speak* the truth as well. Unitarian Universalists belong to a distinct legacy of prophets who have assiduously assailed the social and theological orthodoxies of their day, both with deeds and with words. We have grown accustomed to lighting fires in cold rooms.

In fact, a cornerstone of the eight steps to enlightenment taught by the Buddha some 2500 years ago is "right speech." In a world of exaggerated advertising, horn-honking road-ragers, hate radio, internet abusers, and political spin-doctors—simply a ruder American culture than ever before—producing right speech is no mean feat in 2011. Yet that's our theological mission: to think deeply, to speak kindly, then to act honorably.

Even when we have something difficult, or perhaps harsh, to say to somebody, and we will have those times, the key is to speak our truth in love. Jesus in the gospel of Matthew was asked to sum up the 613 laws of Leviticus in the Hebrew scriptures. He did so by encouraging us to "reprove our neighbor with kindly and gentle intent." Not to bash or judge our neighbors; on the contrary, whenever we must correct or challenge them, to do so in a mood of respectfulness.

One of our Unitarian Universalist religious professionals recently took the five mindfulness precepts of the Buddha in a formal ceremony. Rachel told us she was devoting her life to the cultivation of deep listening and loving speech in order to bring greater joy to others, starting with her partner and children. She said: "I vow no longer to spread news that I don't know to be certain and to stop criticizing things of which I'm not sure. I will also refrain from uttering words that might cause discord or spread bitterness. I will aspire to speak my truths in love!"

Try as we may, our words often do harm.

We live in an "argument culture" where there's increasing glorification of onslaught in public discourse. Everything in the media seems focused on contention and debate. In a debate, reason is often misused to trounce the other person. Just look at the origin of the word. *De* is "to the utmost," *bat* is "beat"—you see it in words like battle and combat.

Debate, in today's world, is seldom civil and decent; rather it's a way of proving we're right, more than finding out what's right. What we desperately need in our families, congregations, and larger society is more dialogue and less debate. Dialogue is a constructive way of discovering new ways of seeing. In courteous theological discourse, both sides have a chance to change and grow.

Throughout the course of any day, we're likely to locate moments of gossip, unfair rage, and jealous criticism. Almost unknowingly we can spout untruths or misleading half-truths. Our words can harm. So, let's vow to stop, or at least reduce, our harmful language at home and work, in our congregations and in the greater world, as card-carrying Unitarian Universalists. Hopefully, usage of THEOLOGY ABLAZE, its essays with ensuing discussion, will enhance respectful theological dialogue in our ranks.

Remember Hippocrates' cardinal tenet: "First, do no harm." Haughtiness is a subtle sin as well. We may be different than other religious folk, but Unitarian Universalists can never presume to be better. Any "holier than thou" attitude is foreign to our theology.

As Unitarian poet Carl Sandburg put it:

Look out how you use proud words. When you let proud words go, it's not easy to call them back. They wear long boots, hard boots...Look out how you use proud words.

In this poetic fragment, Sandburg is delivering a primary lesson for individuals, classes, and nations alike. Note the clash of proud words that occurs in Congress day in and day out. Arrogance pitted against arrogance. We experience elected officials pursuing not justice but self-righteousness. They aren't the only culprits. All too often, you and I say cruel and destructive things, because it's easier to be clever than kind, to raise our own status by lowering that of others. In the long run, smug, nasty words are often the ones that undermine our homes, our communities, our parishes, and global harmony.

Stuck-up words often ride roughshod and aren't easy to call back. The best practice is not to send them. When prone to revenge, may we enter the silence, even walk away. There's a time to bite one's tongue, to leave things unsaid, to participate in what might be called a word-fast.

Words not only wound; they can also instruct and inspire. Words capture souls and quicken imaginations. Being around grandchildren regularly, I'm reminded of the amazing clout of our adult verbiage; how, whenever we speak to our little ones, we need to insure that we deliver fair and friendly words, from heart to heart. As children hear words throughout life, they're creating a dictionary of terms of censure as well as terms of comfort—words they'll regularly use on their own.

Tens of millions of Americans annually observe "The Great American Smokeout" as well as "Earth Day," one concerned with eliminating contamination of our bodies, the other with reducing the pollution of our planet. Someone has recommended a continental "Speak No Evil" day, an observance that could work to purge the pollution of our spiritual atmosphere, the realm in which we commune with others.

A rabbi once asked listeners if they could go for 24 hours without saying any unkind words about or to anybody. A minority raised their hands signifying yes, some people laughed, while quite a large number called out "no!"

He then responded: "All of you who can't answer 'yes' must recognize how serious a problem you have. Because if I asked you to go for 24 hours without drinking liquor, and you said, 'I can't do that;' I'd have to tell you that you're most likely a practicing alcoholic. And the same scenario holds with respect to smoking. So, what keeps us from realizing our addiction to the negative use of words?" The rabbi makes a telling point, doesn't he?

A special day may seem silly, but we've got to start somewhere and what's wrong with starting here and now, where we live and move and have our beings? What better way to celebrate our golden anniversary as a religious movement than pledging to speak respectfully with neighbors and strangers, friends and foes, with ourselves and our loved ones?

Once we get into the habit of right speech, it might just prove hard to break.

QUIETUDE

Words are wondrous vehicles, and we Unitarian Universalists will never abandon them by descending into utter stillness and hush. Yet their fragility—indeed, inadequacy—is being acknowledged more and more as we reach mid-life maturity as an Association. One of the paramount lessons of growing up theologically is discerning when words are necessary and when they're futile, potentially harmful.

In the mystical tradition, it is said: "Before the Word, there was silence." Before creation, before proclamation, and before chaos… there was silence.

We can't hear humans talk, let alone entertain "most excellent speech," unless there's silence. The more complete the silence, the more expressive the speech. Therefore, after any powerful outpouring of words, we welcome quiet, rather than clapping. There's no gratitude comparable to the gift of appreciative silence.

In the presence of exquisite art, the stillness of a forest, the quietude of the vast desert, the solemnity of the majestic mountains, the tranquility of gently falling snow, the ocean when waves are resting, composure in the face of unspeakable tragedy or the ineffable wonder of human love; in the presence of all these and much more… silence resounds. As the Psalmist declares: "There is no speech, nor are there words…yet their voice goes out" (19:3).

We can understand why Thoreau capitalizes Silence.

The story is told of Ralph Waldo Emerson and Thomas Carlyle choosing to sit opposite one another for hours on end, without words. After this weird and wonderful session, both literary and philosophical giants commented on the ineffable depth of their wordless encounter.

In Buddhist tradition there are some 21 different terms for silence. Resourceful individuals are familiar with an infinite variety of forms of quietude. Friends and lovers, as well as congregational gatherings, are nourished by routine word-fasts. There's a Hasidic saying: "The altar dearest to God is the altar of silence." The nearest altar as well.

Some religious folks seem to think that the number of times they mention the word God during conversation or worship predicts, even hastens, the presence of the Infinite. Hardly. One church member, coming from a fundamentalist background, was initially disconcerted, in our San Diego ministry, by the paucity of times that God's name was spoken during our worship services.

However, after months of increasing involvement in our sacred circle, Marsha paid our band of freethinking mystics a high compliment: "I've never worshipped in a religious community where the 'word' God is so rarely mentioned yet the 'reality' of God so recurrently felt. I now feel balanced as a Unitarian Universalist, bridging both heaven and earth. Hallelujah!" Indeed, as Marsha grew to recognize: spiritual equilibrium is the objective in our religious quest, where the intellect and soul, hush and utterance, rationality and intuition are equally affirmed.

Silence is a particularly potent and evocative lurking-place of God for verbal Unitarian Universalist types. Garrison Keillor pointedly jests: "The rule at the Unitarian monastery is complete silence, but if you think of something really good, you can go ahead and say it."

In truth, modern-day Unitarian Universalists underpractice quietude in worship and underappreciate freedom from turbulence and self-assertion at work. Our lives are prone to being cluttered with chatter. Yet periods of sufficient inwardness enable us to be receptive to otherness—be it the sound of nature, the sounds of our own interior castle, or the sound of divine humming.

There's the Sufi story where the governor on his travels stepped in to pay homage to the Master. "Affairs of state leave me no time for lengthy dissertations," he said. "Could you put the essence of religion into a paragraph or two for a busy person like me?" "I shall put it into a single word for the benefit of your highness." "Incredible! What is that unusual word?" "Silence." "And what is the way to Silence?" "Meditation." "And what may I ask is meditation?" "Silence."

Nineteenth-century British Unitarian James Martineau claimed that words were fragile containers in conceptualizing the theological quest, but ultimately needed to be used. He maintained:

> All belief and speech respecting God is untrue yet infinitely truer than any non- belief and silence. The confession of ignorance once made, we may proceed to use such poor thought and language as we find least unsuitable to so high a matter.

Perhaps. To be sure, words are essential in conceiving, then conveying, messages about anything theological, including the Unknown. However, we dare not underrate the power and relevance of silence as a uniformly valuable (not lesser) vehicle for luring the sacred into our sphere or us into its embrace.

We join the Buddhists, among other seekers, who claim that the Void can furnish a worthy vessel for the sacrosanct. Ralph Waldo Emerson, in pointing to the numinous, said: "I like the silent church before the service begins better than any preaching." For, as he stated elsewhere: "Let us be silent, that we may hear the whispers of the Gods." This counsel was delivered from a consummate wordsmith.

How about God's silence? In fact, the Eternal spirit has proven to be progressively quiet and uninvolved, according to Jack Miles' analysis in his book *The Biography of God,* where he notes that action yields to speech, which yields in its turn to silence. As Miles states it:

God's last words are those he speaks to Job, the human being who dares to challenge not his physical power but his moral authority...God never speaks again, and he is decreasingly spoken of.

And in the Christian scriptures God speaks but once, to say: "This is my beloved son, in whom I am well pleased." Jesus talks a lot but not the Creator. So God, in both the Hebrew and Christian chronicles, seems to grow gradually more reserved, if not distant—certainly mysterious.

Furthermore, there are contemporary Jews who lament not only the silence of God in the closing ten books of their holy writ but also his inscrutable nonappearance during the holocaust. For some, this state of affairs leads to passionate atheism; others are left in the clutches of agnosticism; and still other Jews, in the face of God's quietude, muster affirmations of his presence, even partnership.

Despite what God may or may not be up to, there remains ample moral challenge, so claim Unitarian Universalists, for humans to pursue. Our work is fairly transparent. And a portion of it is to keep our lives lubricated with adequate periods of solitude, stillness, and silence.

Entering the silence is a holy vow accessible to all God's creatures—women, men and children, animals and plants, too. The Greek root *mys*—found in the words mystery and mystic—means shutting the eyes, ears, or mouth, because in the presence of luminous things, we are driven, more often than not, to silence. Truly, the sacred enterprise beckons us to be speechless and dumb sometimes, to still our mouth, then our mind, finally our will—to shut up fully before we dare to open up freshly to the bidding of the Spirit. It calls us to enter the silence, so the mystery within us might connect with the mystery beyond us.

In the monastic tradition, they call the time from dusk to dawn the Great Silence. Between the last evening recreation and first morning meditation, one is required to be quiet. The Great Silence intimidates contemporary folks, so we rush to fill our solitude with social busy-ness, bodies, food and drink, TV, and miscellaneous inanities instead of mustering the courage to embrace holy emptiness.

Befriending the Great Silence is a hallowed, occasionally harrowing, imperative for the religious pilgrim. So, one day when we cross over into our final silence, the ultimate darkness, we will be spiritually seasoned, ready to connect with the Silence as God.

FOR REFLECTION AND DISCUSSION

1. In the life of your congregation recall encounters where
    words have been agents of healing...as well as occasions
    for hurt.

2. Has your congregation ever produced a worship service
    where the time of silence was central not merely a mo-
    mentary interlude? If so, describe how you felt. If not,
    would you consider generating a service devoted to more
    silence than talk or song?

3. What are the words you regularly employ (and the atten-
    dant situations) that tend to do more harm than good?
    And how might you alter your behavior?

4. Are there times, during the day, when you feel sum-
    moned "to enter the silence," to engage in a period of
    word-fast? If so, have such times of silence enhanced your
    spiritual life?

5. Honestly speaking, are there times when you're intimi-
    dated to speak...and also moments when you're daunted
    by silence? Unpack those times.

6. Give thought to the connection between moments of
    silence now in your existence and the ultimate Silence
    (death).

LOVE

We do not need to think alike, to love alike.
—Francis David, 16th-century founder of Unitarianism

What is essential is never to allow
the limitations of time and the
erosion of memories to deaden
the longing of the heart in
its morning demand for love.
—Paul N. Carnes, UUA President: 1977–1979

We can always make choices to add love to the world.
—Gini Courter, present UUA Moderator

After the apostle Paul's classic ode to love in the 13th chapter of I Corinthians, he begins the very next chapter with the words, "make love your aim." As if to say, knowing all you do about the intricacies and difficulties of love, dear people of Corinth, I exhort you to get on with actually living love. Former Starr King School for the Ministry president Bob Kimball succinctly put it: "The purpose of religion is simply to increase the odds on love."

Unitarian Universalists live by our aims not by our accomplishments. Consequently, our opening worship anchor is often called the *Aspiration* not the *Achievement*. We say words such as: "May love be the spirit of this congregation..." In short, may love be our aim and guiding force as persons and villages.

The story goes that Winston Churchill was dining one night at a deluxe restaurant in England. After a scrumptious meal, he ordered pudding to crown the evening. Churchill found the dessert displeasing and summoned a waiter to this table: "My good sir, the pudding is interesting but lacks a theme!"

Loving and being loved constitutes the governing theme in our

Unitarian Universalist pudding. Only love, at its core, can touch people and transform our congregations; only resourceful love can redeem civilization. The proof in our pudding is love…a robust love within, among, and beyond our selves. An Infinite Love, so claim our forebears, that has created and sustained life today, tomorrow, and forever…rest assured. A love that invites us all in, a love that never let's us go, and a love that won't let us off…off from growing a just and merciful community, within and beyond the walls of our Association. As Gordon McKeeman drolly observes:

> Universalists believe that all of us are going to end up together in heaven, so we might as well learn how to get along with each other now.

There are four primary, indivisible destinations of our loving in the full-bodied religious life: love of self, neighbor, nature, and God. Our progressive religion is not a multiple-choice test where we can pick the favored spot for our affection. To stay theologically ablaze, we must pay homage to every zone of existence. In celebrating our 50th anniversary of existence as a consolidated movement, we recognize the broad power of these linking loves in our depth theology.

Healthy loving is expansive not exclusionary; it reaches within, without, and beyond in order to be both fulfilling and fulfilled. It is internal, interpersonal, and international. We're not permitted to hoard or bask in love's gleam but urged to spread it. The entire creation hankers for and banks upon the best of our human love.

Note that all four are referenced, in one way or another, in our Purposes and Principles: we advance "the transforming power of love"; draw from "Jewish and Christian teachings which call us to respond to God's love by loving our neighbors as ourselves"; and celebrate "Earth-centered traditions which instruct us to live in harmony with the rhythms of nature."

Before I note the principal features of love, we will explicate, briefly, those four zones.

LOVE OF SELF

It all starts with self-love. Our own core must be sturdy yet supple, before we can sufficiently love neighbors or animals, strangers or deities. Unless we consistently care about ourselves in empowering ways, the rest of creation will receive from us only watered-down love-substitutes.

Unitarian Universalist songwriter Libby Roderick poignantly framed it in our new hymnal supplement: "How could anyone ever tell you...you were anything less than beautiful; how could anyone ever tell you...you were less than whole. How could anyone fail to notice...that your loving is a miracle; how deeply you're connected to my soul!"

In times of personal gloom or turmoil, are we Unitarian Universalists belting out that kind of love ballad, starting with ourselves? As we gaze at our oft-frail and pockmarked beings, do affirmations of self-love pull us back on purpose? When our own individual tapestries are torn, even shredded, can we muster strength of spirit to mend our precious webs of belovedness?

Self-regard isn't everything; it's just that there isn't much without it. Self-love is fundamental to our version of theology.

LOVE OF NEIGHBOR

"Love thy neighbor as thyself": these paired commandments from both the Hebrew and Christian scriptures are effortless to utter, yet difficult to execute. Loving God sometimes constitutes a smoother task than either loving self or other, because God can remain conveniently remote, whereas humans are unavoidably in our face.

Loving thy neighbor as thyself means just what it says: "as much as" not more or less than. There's an implied equal sign in the command. In short, we can't love others without enjoying ourselves.

We may idolize our neighbors, become infatuated or grow symbiotic with them, yet we cannot truly care about others without having a similar density of respect for our own beings. Those among us who have succumbed to either egocentricity or self-loathing remain stuck on feeble, shaky images of ourselves, whereas sufficient self-love impels us to nourish both neighbor and earth with exceeding tenderness.

We can't give away what we don't possess in ample measure ourselves. Plainly, these love zones are yoked. "As thyself" implies that the survival of self is the limit of ones love for the neighbor. To be effective in loving others we have to preserve our own strength and integrity. A good neighbor doesn't burn out or play martyr.

The law of boundaries is abrogated at great expense. In terms of evolution, those plants and animals that selectively limited their growth-boundaries survived, while the dinosaurs perished through excessive development. The same principle applies in human intercourse. Our response to the needs of neighbors must be discriminating, lest we become overwhelmed.

Nonetheless, Unitarian Universalism, at its most authentic, never fixates on self-fulfillment. It ultimately pursues communal salvation, the continuing sustenance of the Beloved Community…a large, welcoming, ever-expanding reality that dares to open wide its heart, its benefits, and its enlightenment to the least, the lost, and last among us. From our theological perspective, either everybody is saved or nobody is saved!

There are no ulterior motives in caring for our neighbor. Compassion is never to be used as a warm-up or softener for religious conversion. Service isn't a means toward some end; it is the end.

The Beloved Community—the real article—is rarely embodied by one place, one time, or one group but ever widens its fabric to include outsiders, strangers, those dwelling on the edges of existence. One more step, one more embrace, one more thread…a tapestry always woven thicker than the imaginable.

As country-western singer Ashley Judd croons: "Love can build a bridge, between your heart and mine…love can build a bridge, don't you think it's time, don't you think it's time…"

LOVE OF NATURE

Universal love exhorts us to bring not only races and nations but other species within our moral circle of concern, consciousness, and connectedness. Universal love refers to revering all living entities within the cosmos.

We share earth's home. Native Americans conduct a ritual called "the making of relatives," where they pledge to adopt all living beings as kith and kin, related yet separate wonders, of a unified creation.

Our linked-charges as Unitarian Universalists are to gaze lovingly toward ourselves, our neighbor, and the earth…to gaze inward, outward, and beyond…into the farthest nooks and crannies of the cosmos.

For as *Unitarians* we know that despite the welter of life forces buzzing throughout creation, there abides an indisputable oneness at the heart of reality. Creation is a uni-verse, where every *unit* of existence matters.

That's the core message of every Earth Day: where Unitarian Universalists are urged to live, work, and act in a loving, respectful way toward this unspeakably precious blue boat we call home…an Earth comprised of animal and fish, bird and plant, human and tree, spirit and rock.

As *Universalists*, we claim that our own lives and those of every other sister and brother, indeed the entire universe, rest in the grasp of an infinitely loving power.

Unitarian Universalists sign up and sign on as full-fledged stewards of the Great Living System. We enlist as loving tenders and menders of a beloved web that keeps on weaving, from the unit to the universe…never finished…only surrendered, when our own hands relinquish the task to other hands waiting in the wings.

Recently, our youngest San Diego grandchild, eight-year old Owen—something of a theologian-in-training—popped up with yet another imponderable, as children often do: "Grandma, does the earth talk?" And Carolyn wisely retorted: "Well, what do you think, sweetie?" "I think it does; when we hurt the earth, it sneezes, and when we're good to it, it's happy and smiles."

Thus stateth Owen's gospel: for, in clumsily yet courageously loving self, neighbor, and earth, our job is really nothing more and nothing less than igniting more smiles than sneezes.

LOVE OF GOD

Even when our hearts are broken by our own failure or the failure of others, even when we have done all we can and life is still broken, there is a universal love that has never broken faith with us and never will.
—Rebecca Parker

There exist two meanings to these three simple words: love of God. First, it denotes God's love toward *us*; and, second, it references our love toward *God*. Both meanings are worth noting in our exposition of the overall theme of Love.

Remember from our Universalist roots in America, John Murray (1741–1815) exhorted: "Give them, not Hell, but hope and courage. Do not push them deeper into their theological despair, but preach the kindness and everlasting love of God."

According to this classic Universalist proposition, human hope and courage are ultimately grounded in and surrounded by the embrace of the divine. The Universalist theological stool will wobble, eventually collapse, without all three legs in place: hope, courage, and God's love.

What does "the kindness and everlasting love of God" reference? It means that no matter how hard we humans work, we cannot create or earn our salvation, which remains a gracious gift of the Eternal One. Additionally, no matter where we hide or how far we run, we cannot elude God's inescapable presence. Even human free will, however obstinate, is no contest for the Universalist deity. No matter how fractious the divisions and how extensive the destruction wrought in human history, God's love will ultimately prevail.

Unitarian Universalist John Taylor aptly phrases it: "We need to learn the art of holding on easily. Much is going to be taken away, slip away, or be destroyed. We can let go. What holds on to us is far more important." This day, one's entire life, the full-blown cosmos rests in the grasp of a loving and Eternal Spirit. Such is the overruling Universalist affirmation of our heritage and identity.

Our human compassion, then, is in response to such divine mercy. We can never repay the Creator, only respond. When we feel unconditionally loved by the Universe, then we're filled with hope and activated by courage. We transmit God's love, insistently yet imperfectly, to other sisters and brothers, soil and sky, animals and plants, to all who hunger for healing and assurance.

However, we're not only loved by God; we're also charged to love God. Loved, we love in return.

Remember when Jesus uttered the great commandment about loving God, it was unconditional: "Thou shalt love the Lord thy God with all thy heart, and with all thy soul, and with all thy might!" When he spoke of loving thy neighbor, the word "all" was not used.

In essence, both the Hebrew and Christian testaments are declaring that we need to love God—that is, our own understanding of God—with as much of our total being as possible. We do this by surrendering, without subjugating, ourselves. For authentic love requires treading the fine line between surrender and submission. Appropriately, the Hebrew word *yadah*, for knowing God, is the same term used for knowing one's lover sexually. The key in surrendering to God is to enter the being of God and to allow God to enter ours—without either of us losing our respective identities. Our divine–human love is a meeting not a merging.

The Hindu way of religion emphasizes three pathways to communion with Brahman: the way of knowledge, the way of devotion, and the way of action. Each has its own merits. Surrendering emphasizes the way of devotion: love and affectional bonding. It reminds us that depth theology is based on relationality, requiring ample heart as Jeremiah stated it: "When you search for me, you will find me, if you seek me with all your heart, I will let you find me, says the Lord" (29:12–14).

The key for Unitarian Universalists, then, is to love God as whole-heartedly as proves reasonable to do...actually, in some profound sense, not unlike loving self, neighbor, or nature.

LIFE'S CENTRAL VOW

Our Unitarian Universalist version of religion is ultimately not about beliefs but about behaviors, not about creeds but vows—in short, keeping life's central vow...loving and being loved. What might this mean?

First, love is primarily a verb rather than a noun. Our purpose in life is not to define love, once and for all. It can't be done, plus the exercise doesn't prove all that useful. Our mission on earth is to love—to share, create, give love, to bear love—to be lovers of nature, ideas, humans, projects, animals, plants, and the deities. Greek literary giant Nikos Kazantzakis put it deftly: "If I were fire, I'd burn; if I were a woodcutter, I'd strike; but I'm a heart, hence I love!" Yes, our goal is to become a theology ablaze.

A second reminder. Love isn't a feeling or sentiment so much as an activity or deed. Yet robust love is something not just given but given *and* received—and, oh, how hard it is for earthlings to receive love, particularly for dynamic, outpouring Unitarian Universalist types. The receiving of love may be for many of us a more rigorous and riskier act than the giving of love.

As full-fledged lovers, we're summoned to live ambidextrously between the active and passive voices. Progressive 20th-century minister Howard Thurman used to say, "My heart must be a swinging door that opens in and opens out." Authentic lovers need to allow others into our hearts, encourage others to nurture and caress us, permit others to take care of, even carry, us upon occasion. As the folk ballad says: "He ain't heavy, he's my brother; she ain't heavy, she's my sister!" For life's central vow is loving and being loved.

Third, most of us are trained to love in bursts but falter over the long haul. While the juices flow and enthusiasm sparkles, we love passionately. The theological hallmark of love demands more continuity. It would have us attend during the lulls of our quest.

"Attention, attention, attention," wrote Zen Master Ikkyu centuries ago when asked to write down the highest wisdom. "But what does attention mean?" pressed his questioner. Master Ikkyu replied, "Attention means attention." The etymology of attention stems from the Latin *attendere*, meaning to "stretch." One way or another, for good or ill, in dependable loving our souls are stretched. Our hearts and minds and bodies are stretched as well. As the poet Marge Piercy observes: "Loving leaves stretch marks."

Loving hallows the underrated virtues of hardiness and durability. While taking the vow of stability, those who love are flexible and resilient, bendable as bamboo in the storm rather than stiff trees that fall victim to obsessive control. Lovers aspire to remain at our affectional posts, especially during the inevitable seasons of upheaval and bleakness.

Fourth, our loving is fake unless demonstrated toward those near and dear to us, including family and friends, and, yes, ourselves as well. One of life's tragedies is that people are often more adept at delivering love to strangers than kinfolk, those far off while dodging the imperative of loving upclose.

Another easily bypassed reminder about life's central vow is that genuine loving can be difficult, even painful, far messier than we ever anticipate or want.

It's relatively easy to love when we're feeling grand or to disappear when the going gets rough or stifling. What's strenuous is "holding to the difficult" (Rilke), acknowledging one's thorny past or dreary present. "Holding to the difficult" mandates facing another human being rather than fighting or fleeing. It entails staying awake while staying put. It requires diving into the depths, when we'd prefer to wade in shallow waters. This brings to mind a passage from Ramak-rishna:

> *There are pearls in the deep sea, but one must hazard all to find them. If diving once does not bring you pearls, you need not conclude that the sea is without them. Dive again and again.*

"Love being difficult" impels us to be strong enough to discipline a child, brave enough to abandon bad habits, and large enough to enfold society's dirty outcasts. Just when we think our task is done, love insists on yet one more appropriate demand. Just when we'd rather stay on the periphery of our congregation's life, love calls us to renew our membership vows, to mount the stage of responsible action. Just when we're lured to coast in a friendship, love reminds us that truthful, trusting communication is required. Just when we'd rather remain comfortably speciesist, love impels us to recognize the rights, even the souls, of animals.

Which will it be for you, right now in your theological evolution: love or fear? If you choose love, then you'll have no choice but to sit down and ponder: what and who have I been put on this region of earth to love? As love cracks open our shell, it'll tell us exactly what this beautiful and broken world requests from us, right now.

There are lots of things in human existence that we can't dictate, but we can control one major thing: refusing to renege on our commitments when trouble arises; refusing to walk out on social causes when they become unpopular; refusing to abandon our faith community over a disagreement; refusing to abandon our friends when they're beleaguered; and refusing to compromise our values when they're challenged or rejected.

Loving and being loved is life's central vow.

Current UUA President Peter Morales puts it eloquently:

> *We are one people united by what we love. We love compassion, we love life, we love freedom, we love justice, and we love one another. That love*

endures. Candidates, resolutions, and General Assemblies come and go. Love endures. And love will guide us.

FOR REFLECTION AND DISCUSSION

1. Zen Buddhist John Tarrant seems to grasp love's fierce, twisting nature:
   Like the stars over dark fields, love is the gift of the eternal forces. We do not know why it appears; it is just the song the universe sings to itself. And, like other beauties, it is a demanding guest. As soon as love arrives, we have to serve it—we were naked and now must put on clothes and work.

   Reflect and discuss.

2. Periodically, our congregation will sing Libby Roderick's exceptional ballad of self-love during a worship service, while we're together as an intergenerational community. First, we have our adults sing it to the children facing them, while seated in the front of the sanctuary; then the children return the favor; finally, we all sing it together. Something to consider.

3. Who is the most difficult of neighbors for you to honestly and honorably love? In your congregation, neighborhood, and in the larger world?

4. When we are summoned to love nature and all therein, what entities are included in your present embrace?

5. Noted contemporary theologian Karen Armstrong contends that the way to God, Brahman, or the Way is through living a compassionate life. As she puts it: "first you must commit yourself to the ethical life, then disciplined and habitual benevolence, not metaphysical conviction, will give you intimations of the transcendence you seek." In what ways does Armstrong's approach square with yours?

6. How do you balance your loving between the active and passive voices

PRAYER

For me, prayer, among other things, means a conscious contact with that
which has created all that exists and which is creating me at every moment.
—Arvid Straube

When all the rest of it falls away out of busyness or distraction, I can still,
each morning, lift up those I love and those in pain, through prayer.
And fortunately, there are those I know who pray for me.
—Anita Farber-Robertson

In the life of the Indian there was only one inevitable duty—the duty of
prayer—the daily recognition of the Unseen and Eternal. Daily devotions
were as necessary as daily food...Each soul must meet the morning sun, the
new sweet earth and the Great Silence alone!
—Ohiyesa

One of the questions that has been asked most frequently of our faith during the past fifty years is this: "Do Unitarian Universalists believe in prayer?" Our short answer is: "Well, some do and some don't. That's the nature of our noncreedal religion, but probably all of us agree on one thing—prayer is an intensely personal matter, not an exercise to be turned on and off at the pressure of any tradition or minister!"

The crux for religious progressives is to distinguish between prayer that seems abusive to humans as well as the divine and prayer that seems useful to both realms.

There exist at least two narcissistic modes of prayer—one I call manipulation and the other, breast-beating. Over the years, I've used them both, especially during my younger years. Perhaps you'll recognize them as well.

In its crudest form, prayer is an attempt to bribe or cajole a cosmic force into giving us what we want: be it rain from the sky or riches from the lotto, peace of mind or military victory. Our soul leans upon the universe so that it'll tilt in our favor. Such prayer is basically an effort to manipulate reality without changing ourselves one iota. It reminds one of the child who prayed every night for a new bicycle. Then he realized that the Lord doesn't work that way, so he went out and stole one, then quickly pled for forgiveness.

That wasn't the way I did it, but, certainly, in my youth, there were times when I tried to jockey the Almighty to produce desirable results: whether on a date, shooting free throws in a basketball game, or taking a crucial math test.

I've grown to find this form of prayer unacceptable on various grounds. First off, it often doesn't work. Pat Robertson, you may remember, once claimed that his prayers caused God to divert a hurricane that was approaching his Virginia headquarters. Now I ask you, where was Robertson when one of the recent Floridian or Honduran "acts of God," let alone Katrina, wrought devastation? Why didn't he fly down to New Orleans and pray like crazy? Or is it only his own property that deserves God's favor? Or doesn't God listen to Pat Robertson anymore? It's all rather puzzling, isn't it, this public praying for your own private needs?

At some juncture in our staying theologically ablaze as Unitarian Universalists, we begin to realize that it isn't God's necessity to mesh with our personal wishes so much as our job to align our life with the values of goodness, with the universe, if you will.

Furthermore, imploring God for special treatment often permits us to shirk self-responsibility. In our theology, grace and effort are joined in holy union. Both the divine and human realms need to carry our own fair share of life's moral load. Liberal theologian Reinhold Niebuhr's serenity prayer offers just the right mixture: "God grant me the courage to change the things I can change, the serenity to accept the things I can't change, and the wisdom to know the difference."

So, prayer invariably demands human sweat and exertion: in fact, sometimes prayer and action are synonymous. As we say every Sunday morning, in many of our Unitarian Universalist aspirations: "and service be our prayer." I think that's what the abolitionist Frederick Douglass meant when he said: "I prayed for twenty years but received no answer until I prayed with my legs." I know that I never felt more prayerful than when I was marching for racial equality from Selma to Montgomery, Alabama back in 1965.

We also resonate with the story about a Catholic Worker House in New York City, desperate for more funds to continue their work with the poor. The tradition was to pray to St. Joseph for assistance. They did so for several days with no response, whereupon Dorothy Day and her colleagues marched to St. Patrick's cathedral. There they picketed the statue of St. Joseph. After a short time, Cardinal Spellman felt compelled to come out and deliver the necessary money. Never confuse prayer with passivity.

A second form of prayer I utilized, then outgrew, was what I would call breast-beating. A healthy confession is good for everyone, but no god worthy of the name ever benefits from our self-belittlement, nor do we. Sadly, many people still get relief or even kicks from pelting themselves with phrases of "miserable offender" and "there's no health in me." Instead of groveling, our Unitarian Universalist version of God would prefer that we join forces in evolving a more just and merciful universe.

You may recall the story of Ethan Allen, the American patriot, who, after the capture of Ticonderoga, hurried home to his family in Vermont and while there attended a Thanksgiving service. During the long prayer in which the Rev. Dewey was giving all the credit for the victory to the Lord, Allen interrupted: "Parson Dewey, Parson Dewey, Parson Dewey!" At the third call, the minister paused and opened his eyes. "Please, please," said Allen, "mention to the Lord about MY being there!"

Whether our praying is composed of words or silence, song or action, we earthlings have a critical role to play. We aren't the center of the universe, but we aren't extraneous either. We're cohorts, full-fledged partners in the interdependent web of existence.

Let's move on to some reflections on the positive force of prayer. There has been a pronounced upsurge in "comfort with praying" in our Unitarian Universalist ranks in recent years. We feel more relaxed praying, both privately and publicly. Nonetheless, in our liberal faith, we must each still make peace with our own growing grasp of what prayer does and doesn't mean in our daily lives, so here cometh working notes on the subject from *one* practicing Unitarian Universalist.

William Tyndale was right on target, I believe, when he said: "I have a solemn regard for the feelings that prompt prayer." That's probably the best place to start talking about healthy prayer. No one who lives deeply, that is religiously, is stranger to the wealth of feelings that prompt prayer: feelings such as grief, joy, hope, love, anger, and gratitude. Authentic prayer starts not in theory but in feelings, not in the head but in the heart.

Prayer can be heard in the lullaby of parents nodding over their child, in the wailing of the bereaved, and in the exuberant expression of the singer. As St. Paul described: prayers are "inarticulate sighs, groans too deep for words." Praying emerges from our human groans, be they groans of delight or anguish, groans simply too powerful for words.

I remember driving from San Diego to Los Angeles on Christmas Eve 1987, around 8 p.m., mere hours after my father died, to be with my mother, and, while driving, spilling forth in unchecked tears, memories, and song fragments, sodden in a cascade of emotions that my father's life and death evoked in my heart. I don't recall; I may have said some words outloud, but no formal prayer was made. I was simply swimming in an ocean of the feelings that prompt prayer.

The choice of praying or not praying, then, in some profound sense, is often not ours to make. We "hunger and thirst after righteousness"; we dance before the Ark; we simply gush with tears; we walk trembling yet confidently into the Red Sea, believing in our desperation that somehow a path will open to us.

Prayer is "deep calling unto deep" as the Psalmist puts it. When we pray, we do something seemingly impossible: we talk to somebody who's actually not somebody else, yet as near to us as our heartbeat. We discover the eternal as a spirit deep within us—a nudge, a solace, a co-conspirator of sorts. Praying enables us to be accompanied, to proceed unalone.

Prayer isn't created by thought any more than the wind is made by the weather bureau. We stumble upon exquisite beauty, and we're driven to exclaim: "God, that's beautiful!" We discover a startling breakthrough in our love relationship, and we break forth into thanksgiving or tears of joy or are driven to our knees.

We feel deep sorrow or fury or frustration, and we can only stammer. Sometimes we can't even speak, we dare not speak, yet the praying still flourishes amid our silence. As someone sagely penned: "Silence is the language God speaks, and everything else is a bad translation." Whenever we experience, then exude, these indescribably strong feelings, we're impelled to prayer of one sort or another, in some form or another…whether or not you even choose to call it prayer.

I was visiting a congregant only in his twenties, a guy grappling heroically against the relentless erosion of cancer. I spent considerable time with Robert, and over a period of weeks, his humanity gushed forth prayerfully:

There are times I'm so weak that I lose all will and want to throw in the towel. Other times I'm frozen with terror about my future. And yet underlying all my fear and pain and rage abides some hope. No one seems able to either give me hope or take it from me; I just feel it in my very bones. And living or dying, I simply refuse to compromise myself by destroying all shred of hope.

I still have so much to give. Why me? Why now? God damn it! And I

don't even know if there's a God or not. All I know is that these feelings
I'm feeling are my prayers, and I have to verbalize them, because I can't
stuff them inside. I need to let them out. I want them to be heard. And I
keep spouting them whether or not anyone in heaven or on earth hears
them!

Sincere, heartfelt prayer emerged right from Robert's gut, the kind of praying we'll never find in the standard books of common prayer. When we touch such depths, as my parishioner-friend Robert was able to fathom, when our spirits truly resonate with the well-springs of joy and sorrow, wonder and gratitude, love and despair, then we're brimming with the feelings that incite prayer. Indeed, we're praying, however unorthodox our manner, however clumsy our words might be, and whether they're spoken to a power beyond or within.

Naturally, there'll always be those planned prayers that Unitarian Universalists are asked to deliver at community meetings and worship services, or blessings on the spot for family dinners and the like. Our main guideline is to offer fresh sentiments, streaming from the depths of our soul, and sometimes take a risk or two. If anything, prayer's got to be real rather than rote.

In fact, the Latin root for the word prayer is *precarious*, which reminds us that prayer, the genuine article, remains an uncertain, even scary, adventure. Does prayer work? Well, it depends. Sometimes, a person recovers from sickness, sometimes not. Yes, prayer is precarious, just like everything else during the course of our living and dying.

In times of dire tragedy, Unitarian Universalists don't pray for a result so much as for resolve, for strength, for hope even when healing is unlikely…and for sufficient love to fill the room, our hearts, and our tomorrows. We invoke the creative spirit of Infinite Love within, among, and beyond us.

Plus, our best praying is usually short and simple. Long prayers telegraph either anxiety or arrogance. Furthermore, praying, whether alone or with others, isn't the time to get fussy about words. It's not the time to impress humans or overwhelm God with extraneous information. All that's important is that we be earnest and heartfelt.

Unitarian Universalism also believes in consciously holding people in our thoughts and prayers. We light candles and offer chants on behalf of our sisters and brothers. We believe that our souls generate healing energy. We're not talking about superstition or magic, but prayer as an act by which we place another's burden in the center of our consciousness.

In a newspaper recently there was a report touting the medicinal value of prayer based on research conducted at the Heart Institute in Kansas City. The results were published in a respected medical journal. Overall, patients who were prayed for did 11% better than the patients in the control group, based on an evaluation of 35 medical measurements. It should be noted that those praying and the patients did not know one another.

A theology ablaze uses prayer primarily to center our own spiritual state rather than to reap specific rewards. However, here's the other side of the paradox: as mystical humanists or naturalistic theists or whatever theological crossbreed we might be, Unitarian Universalists generally refuse to be stunned by any scientific study that proves the medicinal value of prayer.

Why? Because our spirits sit wide open to mysteries beyond our creation and blessings beyond our prediction. In the name of human compassion, we regularly hold fellow kin tight in our prayerful thought. I know I do. Of course, prayer may or may not change reality, but it does change those who are praying and being prayed about. Of that I'm sure. Prayer keeps the gift of love surging, and love opens the human heart and fortifies our human bonds, which is the best we earthlings can ever manage anyway.

Taking a quiet moment to hold in conscious love the images and names of those we care about is an act of theology ablaze.

One last point: it's our conviction that the spontaneous process of praying should be going on all the time in our lives…if we're going to stay vital, human, and religious. As the Bible invites: "pray without ceasing." Pray from the soul, while walking and working, dreaming and dancing…yea, every moment of the daily journey.

Then our very breathing becomes an unending prayer.

FOR REFLECTION AND DISCUSSION

1. Our late UUA President Paul Carnes remarked that Unitarian Universalists are usually folks who like passing resolutions better than saying prayers, failing to note that our resolutions, addressed as they are to the Universe at large, may, in truth, be the functional equivalent of petitionary prayer.

    What do you see as the linkage between prayers and resolutions?

2. Unitarian Universalist mystic Jacob Trapp references:
    …our involuntary turning for help, a sense of awe, and wonder before the sublime and the mysterious—these are both not only eons ago but today, pre-theological experiences. They are a natural and primary kind of prayer.

Is prayer voluntary or involuntary or a combination of both? Surely there are prayers involving help, awe, and wonder during the flow of your life. If so, share examples. Are there any other forms of prayer that are real for you?

3. UU minister Kathleen McTigue reminds us:
    "There is something particularly touching about having someone say to us, 'I'll remember you in my prayers.'"

    Is that a practice that appeals to you, individually and congregationally? Do you have a prayer circle in your congregation? Does your parish weave prayer shawls as is the practice in several of our flocks? If so, describe how they are used?

4. Colleague Roger Cowan liked to remind folks that:
    I am a humanist who prays, who begins each morning with devotional readings and a time of silence and prayer. Why do I do this?

    > *I need a quiet time.*
    > *I need to express my gratitude.*
    > *I need humility*
    > *I pray because, alone, I am not enough and also I am too much.*
    > *I express my gratitude for the gift of aliveness.*
    > *I assert my oneness with you and all humankind and all creation.*
    > *When I pray, I acknowledge that God is not me.*

    What do you think?

JUSTICE

*Unitarian Theodore Parker said that the moral arc of the universe is long,
but it bends toward justice. The bending, however, is not automatic, nor is it
inexorable. It is dependent on people who feel compassion, equity and justice
as imperatives of their faith.*
—Richard Gilbert

*We need to develop a passionate discontent, an anger that picks us up and
shakes us by the neck and will not let us go. The Holy Spirit, you know, isn't
on the side of order and stability.*
—Marilyn Sewell

Justice is a place where we all arrive together.
—Jeanne Pupke

In daring and determined ways, yet with mixed results, Unitarian
Universalism has labored, over the past 50 years, to do its best to
bend the moral arc of the universe a bit farther toward justice. We
can rejoice in our efforts, without resting on any laurels.

Our sprouting Unitarian Universalist commitment to and support of the GLBTQ (gay and lesbian, bisexual, transgendered, and
queer) community started in 1970 and has produced innumerable
Welcoming Congregations across the continent. The number of
women in central associational leadership positions has mush-
roomed, plus more than half of our currently settled ministers are
women, not to mention that the majority of students preparing for
ministry are women, which bespeaks extensive growth in feminine
consciousness and gender justice throughout our progressive religious movement since 1961.

Our Journey Toward Wholeness program has built upon the set-
backs and detours of our persistent, albeit blemished, commitment
to racial justice over the past five decades. Unitarian Universalist

minister Mel Hoover, pillar in the ongoing implementation of JTW, puts our moral struggle in perspective:

We can't change the past, but we can learn from it and build on it. We can't control the future, but we can shape it and enhance the possibilities for children and grandchildren. More than 6,000 of our Unitarian Universalist children are multiracial. We can dare to face ourselves in our entirety. To feel the tears of the individuals and groups who feel marginalized...and of the individuals and groups who risk and make mistakes.

Most every level of our association has been trained to address the pernicious demons of racism and oppression. Yet as Unitarian Universalist theologian Paul Rasor rightly notes: "Our primary form of engagement has been intellectual...multicultural work represents a danger that must be embraced bodily."

As recently as 1970, one of our consummate historians, David Parke, wrote that at a Unitarian Universalist-sponsored dinner in Philadelphia, when he publicly condemned the easy tolerance of racial and ethnic jokes told at the expense of others, "I was criticized as being grim and humorless."

Forty years later, there plainly exists a heightened intolerance of such slurs. We're readier to care for a child, so an overworked mother can have a day that is her own. We're more willing not only to assist women caught in harm's way, but also to support women in times of their ascending power and glory. In 2011, we're more likely to challenge gay-baiting or lesbian-bashing humor. Racist affronts are usually countered in our congregational life, and Unitarian Universalists from around the land trekked to protest the harsh anti-immigration legislation instituted in Arizona. As UUA President Peter Morales exhorted in this noncompliance protest in the summer of 2010: "*todos somos Arizona.*"

Clearly, immigration reform as both a legal and moral mandate will be on our Unitarian Universalist agenda for years to come.

Moreover, we're prepared to refuse to hold a district-wide men's retreat until the active presence and gifts of blue-collar men and men of color are strongly urged. Throughout our movement, women and men are active participants in the greening of our parishes, worksites, and homes.

Nonetheless, our bending toward justice falls short. Heterosexism, racism, sexism, ableism, and classism remain insidious monsters in our own basements and living rooms, congregationally and associationally.

Revolutionary religious experiments that exemplify what Unitarian forebrother Roger Baldwin called "holy discontent" are seldom popular or centrist. So justice-building Unitarian Universalist brothers and sisters must persist and plod, remaining true to our avowed purpose, marked by what Gloria Steinem calls "outrageous acts and everyday rebellions."

Liberal religionists would confess that life's infirmities and inequities will not be eradicated during our lifetimes. We cannot hold to optimism but neither are we pessimists who futilely throw in the towel. Rather we know that on occasion our faulty revolutionary talk and walk may just, as the Native Americans say, grow some corn.

For example, our justice-making effort took a leap forward with the Commission on Appraisal's recommended C-2.4 Inclusion section, which would have replaced the nondiscrimination clause in the current UUA bylaws. Clearly, this is the direction in which our religion is advancing.

This recommended inclusion paragraph directs us to become a bona fide theological force that combats "systems of power, privilege, and oppression" and the damage they have wrought in our congregations and world. If Unitarian Universalists are who we claim to be, then certain ethical and spiritual conduct must blaze accordingly. There can be no broader or more urgent press for justice than our Article II's unwavering "pledge to do all we can to replace such barriers with ever-widening circles of solidarity and mutual respect."

The third phrase bends the moral arc even wider by calling us to "commit to structuring our congregational and associational life in ways that empower and enhance everyone's participation." What is telling about this Inclusion paragraph is its focus upon Unitarian Universalists cleaning up our own households of worship first, as well as our associational life, before we rush forth to overhaul the structures of society.

LESSONS FOR BENDING TOWARD JUSTICE

Note that our association-wide program is called a journey not a destination, so we remain stubbornly committed to the work of justice. Additionally, it's a journey toward not perfection but whole-ness, recognizing that our efforts will be blemished, never pure or complete. Nonetheless, in the past 50 years we've garnered learnings that assist us in actualizing this theological trait of justice. Here are several of them.

First, along with Marian Wright Edelman, prominent Director of the Children's Defense Fund, Unitarian Universalist justice-builders are determined "to make justice our life-calling." Justice is never a three-week task force or one of our avocational pursuits. We're called to be lifers in the pursuit of "justice, compassion, and the transform-ing power of love" (Article II).

Whether we are members of an oppressed group, dwell among the oppressors, or comprise a mix of the two, our moral imperative and theological duty is to emerge from closets of hostility and fear and grow closer encounters of esteem and fairness.

One of the things that hampers our movement toward disman-tling racism is the belief that one-time experiences, such as *Jubilee* weekends—no matter how necessary and valuable—can transform either individuals or organizations. It just doesn't happen that way. Unlearning personal racism and eliminating institutional racism aren't occasional affairs but demand long-term plans, sustained vigilance, and daily practice.

Second, justice must be soaked in a sense of respectfulness, one of the least practiced aspects of human relations. Genuine respect in our families, friendships, congregations, workplaces, and the larger world is hard to come by, for it requires that we become more flexible and egalitarian than most individuals are on a daily basis. As theologian Sam Keen puts it: "Respect is love at second sight." And third and fourth.

Can we look at one another and honestly say: "You and I are equally worthwhile creations. I hold you in highest regard. Your time, your tasks, your needs, your visions are as significant as mine and will be treated as such in our relationships?" Unitarian Universalist theology contends that one of the most relevant songs in our hymnal is the short but mighty #402: "From you I receive, to you I give, together we share, and from this we live."

Authentic respect is fundamental to augmenting justice across lines of color or gender, class or orientation, conviction or capacity. Respect literally means "to look at something or someone again." Respectful persons are those who look again at what is easily ignored or missed. They look again at outworn, debilitating patterns and consider developing new habits. They look again at their own motives before casting judgment on neighbors. Practitioners of respectfulness remind all of us to look again at the history of gender disharmony and racial brutality in order to create a world beyond it. They urge us to look again at how a class or an orientation has been trivialized, objectified, physically abused, emotionally thwarted, and socially devalued.

An elder of the Achuar tribe of Ecuador, one of the oldest indigenous peoples of South America, upon being offered help by a benevolent Westerner, responded in this way:

If you've come to help me, you're wasting your time. If you've come because your liberation is tied up with mine, then we can work together.

When we're respectful, we recognize that human liberation is indivisible. Authentic respect is grounded in an active gaze and a level glance. It holds the other firmly yet freely in its sight, recognizing, as poet Denise Levertov muses: "To give another your attention is a precious thing."

Respect is the cornerstone of justice-building.

Third, every one of us can be an ally, in some sense, for the cause of justice. Sometimes we're the primary advocate; sometimes we're the butt of oppression and need others to assume the leadership. Nonetheless, at one time or another, all of us will be called upon to be allies.

To be an ally in justice-building requires steadfast courage. When Nikita Krushchev delivered his famous denunciation of the Stalin era, someone in Congress is reported to have said, "Where were you, Comrade Krushchev, when all these innocent people were being slaughtered?" Krushchev stopped, looked around the Hall, and said, "Will the person who said that kindly stand up?" Tension mounted. No one stood up. Then Krushchev said, "Well, you have your answer now, whoever you are. I was in exactly the same position *then* as you are *now!*"

Being an ally means insisting that racism and class elitism, homophobia and sexism—and all other malicious structures of bigotry, named and unnamed, in which we flounder—be eradicated. Being an ally means declaring that injustices are mutually reinforceable and need to be opposed in the open.

Let me speak to the issue of being a pro-feminist man, an ally in gender justice work. I understand, even applaud, and have tirelessly supported the process of men venting festering agonies and woes. Wounded animals are the most dangerous, and mature men must aggressively face our own injuries on the path toward healing. Being wounded is only part of our gender story. Men are also wounders, and we must answer for that. We need to heed the unbearable pain and terror that women and children feel, living in a world where one in four women will be raped and one in six children is the victim of sexual abuse.

Mature masculinity and our theology ablaze require that we heal both the body personal and the body politic.

Gender justice reminds men that women's rights and concerns have not been satisfactorily addressed yet and that sexism has not be conquered—even in our "enlightened" Unitarian Universalist fold. Justice exhorts contemporary men to be pro-feminist supporters up close with the partners, mothers, daughters, and other women who share our personal and professional lives, recognizing that any virtue that is practiced publicly but not privately soon turns fraudulent.

Privilege, while granting men power, causes costly, irreparable damage to our own bodies and souls. It's an undeniable lesson of our Unitarian Universalist commitment to fostering a mature masculinity that feminism lies in men's deeper interests. Working as allies with women to make the ideals of equality substantive is integral to the fullest expression of what it means to be an "evolved" man.

Both genders have much work to do, for we've still not approximated the mid-19th-century exhortation of our Unitarian foresister Margaret Fuller: "A new manifestation is at hand, a new hour is come, when Man and Woman may regard one another as brother and sister, able both to appreciate and to prophesy to one another."

Being an ally means speaking out about the unearned entitlements we enjoy as members of any dominant group—privileges we've been taught for so long to deny or ignore. As African-American seminary professor Alma Crawford prompts:

"Just never forget that you Whites have been the nonstop beneficiaries of the most effective Affirmative Action program in history."

We must surrender any delusions of grandeur. There's no such thing as a perfect justice-ally. Allies are neither saints nor saviors; our aim is to remain consistently conscious. Progress not perfection is the intent of truth-tellers and justice-builders. We will stumble, but if we admit our lapses and apologize when we show cowardice, we can always climb back on the path. Unitarian Universalist brother

Harvey Thomas, a trainer in the Black Concerns Working group, pledged to our brothers at a Pacific Southwest District men's retreat: "If the white brothers in this lodge are willing to deal with your own racism and privileges, then, and only then, can you count on me to meet you halfway!"

Beleaguered individuals must dare to be advocates for our own dignity and destiny. And with regard to those in power—the privileged gender or race, class or orientation—our mandate is to be allies. Advocates alone can't create a just and merciful world, neither can allies, but together, as the spiritual goes, "we can move mountains," one shovelful at a time.

Fourth, justice demands being uncompromising, neither tyrannized by politeness nor swallowed by righteous indignation. Speaking our truths means not being worried about offending others (which we will) or worried about undercutting the entrenched power structures (which we must).

I—as a white, heterosexual, anglo-saxon, middle-class, aging male (what is called the WHAMM condition)—reside among most of the dominants in this society. Therefore, it's my primary mission to spend the bulk of my time intrepidly speaking truth in love to fellow "whammers," in short, to those in power.

Fifth, let's look at the current signature motto of Unitarian Universalism justice-work: "standing on the side of love." Associational leader Meg Riley reminds all of us that "standing on the side of love" isn't merely a song or a banner slogan but an action to be taken.

Our charge is to stand on the side of love, through fair and foul weather, always recognizing that love actually doesn't only take sides but also builds bridges across sides, so we might become one human family: friend, stranger, and foe.

What else might it mean to stand on the side of human and divine love?

For starters, an evolving Unitarian Universalist theology holds that every unit of existence—animal, plant, or human—is sacred and to be treated as such. All are welcome at our table: whatever color or belief, gender or political view, sexual orientation or physical condition, class or age they might be. No one is excluded based on identity alone.

We inhabit a world where people are damned in the name of religion because their views are different, are assaulted because either the hue of their skin or the manner of their love is different. Therefore, those of us who are held fast in the grasp of a loving faith must demonstrate an alternative way of being: the way of full-fledged acceptance.

Unitarian Universalists contend that we were created out of love and for love, and that whenever humans struggle to share the challenges of emotional, spiritual, and sexual love, it's surely a time for observance not condemnation.

Unitarian Universalism has declared itself to be a welcoming movement for gays and lesbians, bisexuals, transgendered, and queer persons as well as all versions of "straight" people. Unconditional regard for all God's creatures is our one and only religious orientation, and we're driven to practice it for better, for worse, forever. We have made it unmistakably clear that homophobia and heterosexism are sins to be resisted and that sexual respectfulness and loving communion are gifts to be celebrated on our sites and throughout the world.

Sixth, Bill Jones, one of our leading African American Unitarian Universalist theologians throughout the decades of our merger, put it succinctly: "The mission of racial justice is nothing less than the co-equality of individuals. The concepts of assimilation and integration aren't adequate to the task of justice; only co-equality is sufficient, because it honors the full worth and value of everyone." Co-equality is what the Buddhists mean when they summon us to practice "right relationship."

Co-equality changes the power game; it redistributes resources and equalizes privilege. It radically alters our personal and communal lives. It calls us to build social justice rather than build personal egos or empires.

Seventh, justice work won't be easy, but it can be fun. It must be. Genuine justice-building is balanced with joy-sharing. Even one of our premier workhorses for justice, Theodore Parker, who harbored fugitive slaves in his home, noted the glaring absence of any exuberance among his mid-19th-century Unitarian colleagues:

> *Most powerfully preaching to the conscience and the will, the cry was ever duty, duty, work, work. They failed to address with equal power the spirit, and did not also shout, joy, joy, delight, delight! Their vessels were full of water, but they did not gush out, leaping from the great spring!*

We can end up gloomy justice-builders, if we're not vigilant. The effort to repair the broken world is serious, but never grim, labor. Tormented fanatics can be spotted in the campsite of prophets. The Seva Foundation of Ram Dass espouses three criteria in their holy work: (1) do something to reduce suffering in the world; (2) grow in the process; and (3) have fun doing it. As theologian Ada Maria Isasi-Diaz reminds us: "the typical trouble with *gringas* is failure to *fiesta* enough!"

Playfulness of spirit is not a frivolous and irresponsible luxury, even given the deplorable state of the union and the universe. We can hardly afford another humorless crusader. Compassion unsung and undanced produces a doleful, tiresome enterprise.

So, our network of revolutionary justice-builders must include an abundance of laughing, singing, clowning, and dancing. Let us march forward, rolling back assumptions and resisting prejudices, while rolling in greater approximations of justice and joy.

Eighth, justice requires staying at the table, and when someone, ourselves included, inevitably screws up, rather than beat a hasty retreat or wallow in self-pity or guilt, we must be willing to seize the opportunity to deepen the dialogue As Harlon Dalton states it in his book *Racial Healing*: "Engagement is critical to healing. We need to learn to sacrifice neatness for the messiness of reality and comfort for the occasional pain of honest dealing." Surely, power-sharing demands sacrifice and discomfort. There's "no easy road to freedom," to use Nelson Mandela's words.

Finally, justice-building means being not optimistic but hopeful. Optimism indicates that matters will work themselves out eventually among the races, classes, genders, and orientations...so we can sit down and coast a bit. Hope says: "no, we must keep the pressure on, we must remain attentive, we must dialogue and dance, meditate and march, we must repent and resist. We must risk more passion and quit trying to be so damn logical about injustice."

In sum, we are called to resist and reconcile all the way home.

FOR REFLECTION AND DISCUSSION

1. As you review your justice-building efforts, what seems to block you from being a more effective change-agent in the world? Is it perfection, or purity, or fear, or just what? And for your Unitarian Universalist congregation, please tackle the same question.

2. Taquina Boston renders a couple warnings to enthusiastic justice workers:
    Be careful of going stupid, whenever you don't wish to be held accountable. And furthermore, even when you are an ally, you still hold seats of power. The key question to always ask the other is this: am I willing to live in solidarity with you?

Sharon Welch echoes Boston's sentiment when she states: *Universal human solidarity is not our birthright, not a gift, not an essence, but a task.*

Study and discuss the challenges of these feminist activists in our ranks.

3. JoEllen Willis, in the book *Soul Work: Theology in the Work of Anti-Racism*, states:
    Intellectual courage is not in short supply among Unitarian Universalists. We are brave in our reflections. We are not so bold in our actions.

    Comment.

4. In your justice-building work in your local congregation, how have you managed to move from consciousness-raising to conduct-raising? What have proven to be the useful lessons in navigating this path?

5. Alison Cooper puts it this way: "I am a hopeful feminist, because I see things clearly yet wake up with a smile on my face."

    Can you identify with Cooper's attitude? If so, in what ways? If not, why not?

6. Do you consider Article II (our Purposes and Principles) to be a vehicle for transformative justice work? If so, be specific. If not, why not?

SALVATION

Unitarian Universalism lacks an adequate doctrine of sin.
—Huston Smith

It is our Unitarian Universalist job to help in saving the human enterprise on every level: self, others, communities and cultures, and creation itself.
—Scott Alexander

We've been willing in the years since our birth as a consolidated movement in 1961 to wrestle more vigorously with the theological themes of sin and guilt, repentance and salvation. We've grown to admit that, whereas we're no longer perfectible beings, humans are renewable, and that a rigorous process of atonement and restoration is equivalent to the classic Christian concept of salvation. Indeed, we have been fanning our flaming chalice by advancing our own brand, or understanding, of salvation.

Psychiatrist Karl Menninger launches his book *Whatever Became of Sin?* with an intriguing incident that happened during 1972 in a downtown section of Chicago, but it could have just as easily occurred in another bustling metropolis.

A stern-faced, plainly dressed man was standing on a corner. As pedestrians hurried on their way to various destinations, he would solemnly lift his right arm, and pointing to the person nearest to him, intone loudly the single word: GUILTY!

Then, without any change of expression, the man would resume his stance for a few moments before repeating the gesture: the raising of his arm, the pointing, and the grave pronouncing of the one word—GUILTY. The effect of this strange pantomime on passing strangers was extraordinary, almost eerie. They'd stare at him, hesitate, look away, glance at each other, and then at him again, then hurriedly continue on their ways.

One man, turning to another, exclaimed: "How'd he know?"

"Guilty before whom? Is a police officer following? Did anyone see? That isn't technically illegal, is it? I can make it up. I'll give it back. I apologize. I wasn't myself when I did that. No one knows about it. I'm going to quit; I really am!"

What's significant about this opening vignette is not that there's some accuser roaming the streets of yet another large city, calling people guilty, but that those who are pronounced guilty...*they* or *we* actually feel vulnerable to the accusation. The passers-by don't scream, "It wasn't my fault!" or "Sir, I don't have the foggiest notion what you're talking about!"

Why? Because we've truly wronged somebody, somewhere, at some time, even recently, perhaps this very day, and the verdict of guilty snugly fits you and me, every last one of us. Those who know love will feel guilt. Guilt is the warning tension that comes when life principles are betrayed. Good guilt reminds us that we stand accountable for what we do with who we are.

To be sure, there's neurotic guilt that pervades our lives, guilt that may be socially initiated but becomes privately exaggerated, guilt that needs to be flushed. Nonetheless, authentic guilt operates in our lives whenever we've intentionally or unintentionally wronged ourselves, others, our universe. In our modern age many of our old guilts are thrown off and rightly so. At the same time, plenty of compunctions are too easily brushed aside, and little remains sacred.

You bet we've hurt or destroyed property, animals, persons, and nations. Every one of us who dares to love will, sooner or later, violate the personhood of another. We feel guilt precisely because we have, in fact, committed wrongdoings.

You can call it alienation, a shortcoming, or a mistake, or you can reference the Greek word for *sin,* which means "missing the mark." The bottom line still holds. We miss the mark, widely and often. We've all sinned and continue to do so, and our sins come in various shapes and sizes. Plus they're more than just personal peccadilloes. Sin also involves collective irresponsibility: war, economic injustice, racial oppression, environmental degradation—such sins don't only break rules; they damage people and devastate earth. While we may not be directly *responsible* for such wrongs, we are invariably *related* to them.

Evangelicals and liberal religionists see sin differently. Evangelicals would dwell upon on our sin-sick souls, paralyzed by original sin. We're viewed as helpless and hopeless. On the other hand, the liberal blind spot enables us to deny, ignore, or skirt full recognition of our own sinful nature, our complicity in wrongdoing.

Unitarian Universalist theology, at its most mature, would have us acknowledge our sinfulness without wallowing in it. We sin, both personally and socially, but we're ever more than our sins. Sin is neither the first nor the last nor the only word about us, but merely one important word about our histories, and such recognition and ownership free us.

There exists a deep, driving desire in human nature, Unitarian Universalism affirms, to become morally responsible beings; at least, most of us want to do so. In the end, we want to confess, be judged; then, whenever possible, be forgiven. We want to stand liable in the final analysis: as a person, as a partner, as a parent, as a patriot, and as a religious pilgrim.

In his trenchant volume, entitled *The Blessings of Imperfection* (1987), Unitarian Universalist layleader Peter Fleck recalls a television skit showing a woman behind a table, and in front of her was a long line of people. The woman behind the table addressed the person at the head of the line and said in a somewhat bored but otherwise business-like voice: "Of course, you know that you are dead. So, all you have to do now is go through the entrance behind me on your right marked heaven or through the left one marked hell."

The dead man looked incredulous. "You mean, that I, uh, am to choose whether I want to go to heaven or to hell?" "That's right," said the woman behind the table." "But, is there no judgment or final reckoning?" he inquired. "Doesn't it count how I've lived, the good things I've done as well the bad things?" The woman behind the table showed the first signs of impatience. "Look sir," she said. "I can't spend the whole day on you. People are dying, the queue is lengthening. Come on, make up your mind."

The dead man by now was in a panic. "I've done some wrong and bad things during my life. I want to come clean, I want to confess, I want to be judged fairly; and, yes, I want to be forgiven..." The woman behind the table no longer could hide her impatience. "I'm not interested in your sins, and nobody else around here is either. Just make up your mind, that's all I'm asking of you."

The dead man looked horrified. He buried his face in his hands, then he stepped forward past the table and disappeared through the entrance on his left marked "hell."

The point is that we human creatures want to have a day of reckoning. You and I want to own up and come clean. In the end we desire a just and full evaluation of how we've carried out our lives. For all of us have done things we shouldn't have done or omitted things we should have done.

Unitarian Universalists don't focus on any literal hell, and historically we've believed in a loving God that will somehow reconcile us all. Yet we still want, don't we, some time of summing up the character and conduct of our days? As moral beings, as accountable creatures, we want things to matter, we want our specific days and nights to make a difference.

We want to make amends, start over, and become whole. For us that process is called "salvation." It's best done, or at least started, right on earth rather than waiting for some presumed "judgment day."

Moving from sin toward salvation, moving from brokenness toward wholeness, demands recognition and ownership of our flaws, then engagement in the arduous practice of repentance, which involves confession followed by real changes in behavior. Too many of us just want the pain of our wrongs to go away; we don't really want to make any changes. Real growth necessitates substantial, spiritual change. Calling ourselves victims or blaming others for our lot in life is to stay trapped in the status quo, furnishing a moral copout.

Genuine confession is relevant to our way of doing religion. It can be cathartic and liberating to voice our offense, either directly to the actual person or to an impartial listener. Clearly, one can overdo it. However, despite confessing to a therapeutic other, our sense of sin still needs to be dealt with in the private courts of our inner heart before any fresh start can be navigated.

THEOLOGY ABLAZE encourages us to take a fresher look at the concept of repentance, the bridge between sin and salvation. We're acknowledging repentance to be a noble word and a worthwhile endeavor. Repentance doesn't mean breast-beating, wallowing in guilt and shame. It literally means to stop what we're doing, to turn around, to change directions, to make restitution, and to get back on course. In the parlance of twelve-step recovery groups: repentance means to take a fearless moral inventory, to admit where we're wrong, and to make amends whenever possible.

As Unitarian Universalist minister Suzanne Meyer put it:

Such is the real meaning of repentance: not trying to blame bad genes, bad parents, or bad role models, or other environmental factors, but owning up to the fact that you made a wrong turn and are in need of a moral course correction. The objective of repentance is wholeness, reconciliation and reunion. Repentance in the end is all about taking the most direct way home.

Unitarian Universalism is a realistic yet positive faith: a life-affirming and hopeful religion. We believe people can change, turn around, renew, forgive, become stronger than ever, precisely where our bones or hearts have been broken. Yet such regeneration doesn't come easily, without a cost, without change. Lasting change demands repentance and amends.

While traveling in Zimbabwe, Africa in the mid-1990s, we came across a keen proverb that remains fastened to my soul: "It's important that when death finds you, it finds you alive!" When we come to die, we need to have our houses in order, or, as Pope John used to say, "to have our bags packed." We need to stay generative today, tomorrow, and every day thereafter, not knowing precisely when we will die.

Theologians on-the-grow resonate with the Midrash saying: "repent one day before you die." "But I won't know when that is!" "That's the point!" We must reform, grow, turn around daily. We must be spiritually prepared to die this very day.

Sinning is subtle and sneaky and infects everyone. All of us, whether we're active psychological or physical abusers, have, in small, even unconscious ways, violated the personhood of others, especially our loved ones. And continue to do so. To top it off, we can become astoundingly *original* sinners, you and I.

That's why my Unitarian Universalist buddy, Tomas Firle, while involved in our *Stopping Gender Violence* working group at First Church in San Diego, developed a card that could be carried in our wallets as a constant reminder.

It says:

My Interpersonal No-Violence Pledge
I will not raise my voice or use threats to dominate others; I will not raise my hands in an intimidating manner. I will not hit or hurt anyone, physically or emotionally to get my way. Instead, I shall seek help when I feel moved to the point of violence; speak out when I witness abuse by others; encourage others to take an active stand against violence.

You sign the card and keep it on your person as a moral prompt. That card will remain in my wallet all the days and nights of my journey, alongside family photos and credit cards.

Here's another example, from American history, of our spiritual aspiration to keep migrating from sin to salvation.

Perhaps you know the story behind the hymn "Amazing Grace"

and its author. In any case, it's worth repeating, because it shows how personal changes in our behavior can affect widespread social results. My version isn't new.

John Newton grew up in a rough and tumble family of seafaring folk. They had little, and without education or privilege they clawed out from the sea what they could. Following his harrowing childhood, Newton experienced a terrible career as a sailor.

He jumped from more than one ship in a foreign port, was forced into the British navy, and engaged in mutinies and rebellions galore. Newton eventually begged, borrowed, and stole enough to become the master of his own ship, and became, not surprisingly, a slave trader. He went to the west coast of Africa and bartered there for slaves. Most often it was the village elders who traded off youth and children for petty and pretentious possessions. Alcohol was one of the big items, but fancy textiles, metal utensils, and clothes were the common coin of trade.

Captain John Newton would cram 250 slaves into the hold of his small ship and take them in chains to America, where they were sold for cash or bartered for objects of high value in England. His ambition was to make enough money to be so well off he could ask for the hand of a high-class lady. He managed in ten years to put enough money away to become wealthy for the rest of his life. Newton sought out and then married the woman of his hopes.

The tale takes a turn. While at sea, between Africa and the British colonies, Newton's ship encountered a raging wild storm. They were loaded to the gills with human cargo. The slaves screamed in delirium and terror as the ship heeled over on its side, out of control and unmanageable by any crew, no matter how heroic. Seawater poured over them, and the sailors staffed the pumps in desperation and exhaustion. Newton's officers told him all was lost.

They were speaking to a man who loved his wine, women, and song. Newton, in fact, comfortably described himself as a full-fledged libertine and one who ran neck and neck with Satan. Newton's announced goal was to take the rest of humanity with him to hell. He mocked all things religious or moral and had no use for feelings of remorse. His motto was get mine and to hell with you. But as they all faced a savage death and at the end of their strength, in the face of the worst storm he had ever known, Newton smiled strangely and said, "Well, I guess we'll just all have to put our trust in God!"

Miraculously, the ship survived the storm, and this foxhole incident caused John Newton to reflect on his life and the possibility that there was something of significance beyond his own arrogance and greed. Newton began to think about others. He even changed the way he treated his slave cargo; he became more humane. He treated his crew differently too. Newton became fair and reasonable, launching a process of change that continued for the rest of his life. In short, Newton repented, moving from alienation toward repair, from sin to salvation.

Newton eventually left the sea and became a minister in the Church of England. He was sent to Olney and there, with his friend, the poet William Cowper, wrote and published a book of hymns. John Newton is known in the history of the Western Church as a leader of the revivals of the mid-18th century. He wasn't a theologian or scholar. Newton's primary method of preaching was with his hymns. The one for which he became best know was the confession of his own journey.

"Amazing grace, how sweet the sound, that saved a wretch like me. I once was lost but now am found, was blind but now I see." Newton called himself a poor wretch, and although we have predictably produced two options in our Unitarian Universalist hymnal, "soul" or "wretch", I no longer instinctively choose soul without remembering John Newton's wretchedness and, yes, my own culpability in racism and other personal and social wrongs.

Real, enduring salvation requires our grit and effort. It also requires the support and guidance of other sisters and brothers. However, transformation of the kind that Newton experienced needs grace, the gift of a power and presence beyond our creation and control.

Am I guilty, you bet I am? And so are you. Do we sin; yes, we all do? Yet sufficient sources of salvation—within, among, and beyond—exist to redeem me and you and you and you...

FOR REFLECTION AND DISCUSSION

1. Unitarian Universalist minister Marlin Lavanhar gets to the nubbins of several theological issues with these words: *What is missing in our movement is a sense of sacrifice and human sinfulness and vulnerability, an articulation of the human need to surrender to something larger than oneself and a commitment to spiritual practice.*

   Ponder, then address in discussion the various matters raised in this statement.

2. Fred Muir, in his book entitled *Heretics' Faith: Vocabulary for Religious Liberals,* does something similar to this book in exegeting different theological concepts. Reflect upon his understanding of sin:
   Sin then is anything that I do that isolates, ostracizes, or separates me or others from the human community (and by extension, from the web of life) which results in robbing or denying human uniqueness and potential.

3. Richard Gilbert, who was born a Universalist and has been a practicing minister/theologian throughout the course of our golden epoch, writes:
   Universalism is an idea whose time has come. Walter Henry McPherson said that "you Universalists are sitting on the biggest word in the language. It is time to improve the premises or get off." I would rather try to improve the premises and act on the promises than get off.

Comment.

JOY

That which is Whole is joy.
There is no joy in fractioned existence.
Only the Whole is joy.
But one must desire to understand the Whole.
　　　　　—Upanishads (VII.23)

Neither duty nor suffering nor progress nor conflict—not even survival—is
the aim of life, but joy. Deep, abiding, uncompromised joy.
　　　　　—Carl Scovel

Here's the latest issue of grandson Owen's theological pronouncements, straight from his minister's mouth:

I was visiting Owen's class as they were talking about UU heroes and heroines—Olympia Brown, in particular. The teacher asked the children: "What does a minister, like Rev. Kathleen, do?" Owen said: "They help people clear their minds." We were a little puzzled, so I asked Owen what that meant. He said: "Yes (and he paused for just a second), so they can discover peace and love and joy."

The teacher and I just stared at each other with wide eyes. Owen must have seen us look at each other, because when I turned to look at him, he kind of shrugged his shoulders and said, "Well, that's what you always say!"

Yes, peace, love, and joy are all central theological themes in our Unitarian Universalist lexicon.

Throughout religious history, matters of joy—everything from being silly to pure delight—have been undervalued, since orthodox religion's been a serious, if not grim, enterprise. For some believers, the more you suffer, the more religious you are.

A priest once said to Groucho Marx, "Groucho, I want to shake your hand for all the joy you've brought into the world." Groucho responded, "Why, thank you father. And I want to shake your hand for all the joy you've taken out of the world." Too frequently religion has devoutly dimmed, rather than lit, life's spark. That's why an affirming, buoyant, and blazing faith such as Unitarian Universalism is particularly valuable in a world where organized religion all too often majors in fear, guilt, and misery.

In a survey at Columbia University, 100,000 Americans were ranked on a happiness/unhappiness scale. It turns out that fundamentalist Baptists scored highest on the unhappiness scale, followed by Orthodox Jews and Roman Catholics. Who scored lowest on the unhappiness scale? Unitarian Universalists and Quakers! Basically, we'd like to think, because our faith has little to do with shame, terror, or punishment.

Unitarian Universalism is flawed to be sure, but we're an upbeat, joyous faith, since our mission rests squarely on the here-and-now rather than the there-and-after. We concur with the poet W. H. Auden, who urged humans to "practice the scales of rejoicing" daily.

One of the ways I practice those scales is by humming and whistling, every chance I get, every walk I take. Follow me around, and it'll be hard to smirk or frown. How do you, as a card-carrying Unitarian Universalist, practice the scales of rejoicing in the here-and-now?

Note the burgeoning presence of rousing music, banner parades, and intergenerational celebratory protests in the contemporary life of Unitarian Universalism. Additionally, neo-pagan festivals have made a considerable difference in the good-natured, fiery, almost mischievous, spirit of our 21st-century movement. If one were to salute but one monumental change in the ambience of our Unitarian Universalist gatherings in recent decades, it would likely be the sheer joyfulness of our singing. It used to be said that Unitarian Universalists were afraid to *sing* something unless we could *sign* it. That's no longer the case.

Words matter, to be sure, but tunes are joining forces with texts from various sources. Our new hymnals exude melodies, from multiple cultures, that are uplifting and soar off the pages. Although our choirs are burgeoning, and the Musicians Network has proven a major lift to our movement, there is a groundswell of musical passion from within our own souls. Consequently, we're belting out songs in our local tribes.

Perhaps Unitarian Universalists are realizing that singing is physically accessible and financially reasonable. One's larynx comes with birth. Every one of us possesses our own encased instrument, to be employed at our beck and call. The human voice box isn't cumbersome to lug about like a saxophone and doesn't have to be borrowed like a friend's piano.

Eminently portable, we can sing where we live, love, and have our beings: whether running or gathered around a campfire, in the shower or during a speech, at social justice rallies or in church—yes, church. And one can sing during all seasons of the soul, whether we're sad or mad or glad and odd combinations thereof.

King David, despite his prodigious wisdom, never tried to prove God; he simply sang the Creator's praises. The Hindu poet Tagore says: "God respects us when we talk, but loves us when we sing." Song and dance are embodied theology; what one clergyperson considers, "a body of practical divinity."

Authentic joy should furnish sufficient nutrients for all the regions of the Self: body, spirit, mind, soul, heart, and conscience. Singing does just that. As Paul says in I Corinthians 14:15: "I will sing with the spirit, and I will sing with the mind also." That's certainly the spiritual balance we seek in choosing tunes that awaken the spirit and stretch the mind as well. Singing definitely spurs the growth of the conscience, for there has never been a social protest movement that hasn't been saturated in song. Justice-building is irrevocably linked with joy-sharing.

On a personal note, as a practical theologian, when I come to die, if I'm lucky enough, after I utter some goodbyes and shed the attendant tears among my beloveds, I would like to be alone, and as my voice is willing, sing some sort of thank-you to the Great Spirit and fellow-pilgrims for an incredible jaunt beyond my imagining. As the Psalmist resounds: "My heart is ready. O God, my heart is ready! I will sing, I will sing praises!"

I hardly know what melody or medley I'll choose to sing, since there's so much music crowding my soul. I just want to go out singing, or at least humming.

Furthermore, Unitarian Universalists are more playful of late, have you noticed? Not just our children and youth at intergenerational festivals. Play, at its finest and fullest and freest, is becoming an end in itself not just as a means to regenerate the body or replenish the soul, to win friends, to appease the gods, or to beat depression.

Unitarian Universalist theology is recognizing that we're playful animals by nature. We exist on earth, among other things, just to play for play's sake—not to play with a why in mind, or with an opponent, or with a finish line, but to play because we are frolicking, fun-loving creatures. There's rarely a workshop or retreat, nowadays, where we don't intentionally intersperse creative, play-fair games throughout the course of oft-weighty social debate or theological discourse.

If singing doesn't work for you, I invite you to try "whistling," which I consider to be breathing with a bounce. When I whistle, I warble. My body bobs, yet settles down. My sounds can be sweet or shrill, soft or clamorous. I grow lighter of heart. My eyes twinkle. A smile emerges. Whistling derails my aging brain from life's insistent seriousness and clears my soul of pointless clutter. Paradoxically, when I whistle, I'm not mindless but actually mindful in an uninhibited, joyous fashion. It invariably fans the flame of my faith.

My selections vary. I've been known to whistle the classics, folk tunes, country-western favorites, as well as offbeat, silly ditties—but largely popular stuff, being an inveterate romantic. Like Anna in the Rodgers and Hammerstein musical *The King and I,* most of the time "I whistle a happy tune," but not always. Whistling might suggest a bout with some sorrow or gratitude for the unspeakable marvels of this singular day. Striding along by myself, nocturnally, I've been known to whistle through my fright. Whistling, you see, covers the waterfront of our emotions from mad to sad to glad.

Since I've become a grandfather, I warble lots around our local grandchildren—Trevor, Corinne, and Owen—trying to transmit this ancient and sacred art and hoping that my whistling proves infectious.

Then there's laughter. Only when religion has honored both its serious and funny bones will it settle safe in human hands. It's appalling to learn that children laugh about 400 times a day, while we adults average 25 chuckles. That's hardly enough mirth to sustain a joyful journey. May we Unitarian Universalists keep on laughing all the way to our graves and beyond, where we just might join a chorus of chucklers surrounding the Almighty.

Our theology of joy is compelling, because Unitarian Universalists consider it folly to squander this single, precious life and miss its soul-deep satisfactions and sorrows. The cemeteries are filled with corpses of those who've bartered their souls in anticipation of promises to come.

One of my favorite stories on this score is of the woman who'd worked hard all her life, pretty much denying her deep desires along the way, waiting around for the time when she'd formally retire. The way she put it: "When I stop working, I'll reach my happiness haven. And I'll fire up and be free to do all the things I really want to do."

Lo and behold, when parishioner Marilyn retired, a dreadful thing occurred. She plumb forgot what the things were that she loved most, and Marilyn was left empty-hearted, without much of anything exciting to seek or accomplish. Accordingly, she frittered her final laps away. Marilyn had failed to develop and practice the scales of rejoicing, day-in and day-out, along the way.

THEOLOGY ABLAZE posits that the Egyptians were right when they speculated that, shortly after death, we'll be confronted by the god

Osiris with a quiz that has to be answered honestly. After forty-two rather routine questions concerning how the deceased has lived, Osiris asks one crucial question that has two parts: first, "Did you find joy?" and, second, "Did you bring joy?"

Note the emphasis of Osiris isn't on our products or our possessions, not even on our creative talents or our noble works, but on the basic purpose of our earthly journey, namely: Did you locate joy and did you spread joy during your lifetime?

We can't lie to Osiris, and a lot's at stake. If we answer these questions affirmatively, we're given back a measure of continued existence. If not, we're lugged off and forthwith eaten by a hippopotamus. In truth, hippos are vegetarians, so we're more likely to be gobbled up by a crocodile or lion instead! Pleasant thought, right?

So, despite steady attempts throughout religious history to squelch our hilarity, to shut down our dancing, to condemn singing as irreverent, despite all these stifling efforts (especially in the Western world)...religion, at its finest, has been marked by irrepressible joy.

Linguistically, the linkage between religion and joy is unmistakable. For, example, *enthusiasm* literally means "being god-filled." And the old Sanskrit word *lila* signifies in Hindu culture both the enjoyment of this earthly moment and the playfulness of God.

I like the way the poet Kafiz puts it:

Every child has known God—not the God of names, not the God of don'ts, not the God who never does anything weird. Rather the God who only knows four words and keeps repeating them: "Come, dance with me!"

Woody Allen's warning that "most of the time we don't have much fun, and the rest of the time we don't have any fun at all" is a rude wake-up call for us, especially during the dank and difficult times of modern life.

It's so tempting to get spiritually stuck in the extremes of despondency or shallowness. Therefore, depth theology offers a few reminders for staying joyful during the "daze" of our lives.

First, without losing ourselves in esoteric distinctions, it's important to recognize that whereas the reality of joy may include physical and mental contentment, even bliss, it goes deeper than that. The cycle of pleasure is usually short; it arrives, contributes its sensation, then leaves. Joy's a thick not a thin virtue, enduring rather than mercurial, and doesn't appear merely when we summon it, or by wearing a smiley-face T-shirt or by cracking jokes.

Joy, the real article, is the product of effort, time, and sacrifice. It arrives at offbeat times and in strange guises. As the Hindu scriptures sagely note, joy comes only as a Whole: replete with bouts of sorrow combined with moments of ecstasy. The genuine article blends both gift and grind.

Second, joy dwells inside. The fullness of joy comes from tending our own garden rather than coveting the plot of our neighbor. Joy is lodged in the corners of our beings and must be fostered there, first and foremost.

Unitarian Universalists allege that if we want to have a happy partnership, then we need to be the kind of person who exudes positive energy. If we hope to have a more cooperative child, then we need to become a more understanding, caring adult. If we want to be trusted at work, then let us be trustworthy. We need to live inside-out, by first nurturing the hub of happiness within our own interior castles.

Third, we're charged to entertain joy at sneaky times and in serendipitous places. Be surprised by joy! You and I are seldom able to buy much joy during our lives, no matter how hard we try; so loosen up, let go, and be surprised by the real thing.

Let joy crack open amidst the most ordinary of our daily events and we may—no promises, remember joy is an unmerited surprise—be showered with a spray of life-giving radiance.

Jesus reminds us in the Christian scriptures that the realm of God dwells in the midst of us, right where we live, not on the other side of the fence, not behind or beyond or above us.

Instead the realm of God, holy joy itself, is discoverable smack dab in our very midst, where we're least likely to look: in well-worn relationships, in difficult work, in startling objects, in quiet moments, in the eyes of strangers, yes, even in the tedium and trivia of life.

Which reminds me of our now 15-year-old grandson Trevor's various Little League teams, which I've assisted over the years. One season, the head coach right away told the kids to keep their eyes on him whenever they were seated in the dugout. Fair enough. "What else do you have to do as Little Leaguers?" he firmly inquired. Child after child, wouldn't you know it, delivered "don't" after "don't": don't throw your glove or bat; don't argue with the umpire; don't climb the fence; don't hit anybody; don't spit; but then one kid (I think growing weary of all the negatives) shyly piped up: "Coach, I want to have fun, is that alright?"

I knew, right then and there, that this little boy had unlocked the gate to life's prime purpose. This youngster knew that the point of being on earth was finding and delivering some joy, whether or not he ever played another inning of Little League baseball.

The Koran and the Talmud, sacred books of Muslims and Jews, respectively, teach that we will be held accountable for every permissible pleasure life has offered us and that we've refused to enjoy during our earthly sojourn. In a similar vein, we adults stand responsible for developing a world that makes it grueling for our little ones to bask in and unravel their own inner joy. We must labor to create the context wherein children's lives are filled with genuine revelry, so, as comic Shelby Friedman quips: "They can see the delight at the end of the tumult!"

A fourth reminder. Joy, in addition to being found midst the mundane surprises of our days, is also likely to turn up amidst the torments of existence. A balanced religion, such as Unitarian Universalism attempts to be, avers that joy and sorrow are woven fine (Blake), mutually enriching forces that can't be torn asunder.

Note the baptism of King Aengus by Saint Patrick in the middle of the 5th century. Sometime during the rite, Saint Patrick leaned on his sharp-pointed staff and inadvertently stabbed the king's foot. After the baptism was over, Patrick looked down at all the blood, realized what he'd done and begged the king's forgiveness. "Why'd you suffer this in silence?" the Saint wanted to know. The king replied, "Well, I just thought it was part of the ritual."

As we welcome its sharp poignancy, sadness makes life holy, not just a sentimental outburst of superficial merriment. Sadness is part of life's ritual.

Note sadness isn't the same thing as depression; don't confuse the two. Depression signals that one is mired in self-denigration and despond and likely in need of some medical assistance. Whereas sadness can't be removed from life, depression needs to be combated, certainly controlled.

Feeling blue need not indicate or result in despair. Indeed, healthy people are *schemerzenreich,* as the German word evokes, "rich in our ability to contain not erase sorrow."

Healthy religion helps us live more realistically and gracefully with sadness: both ours and that of others. An evolving theology doesn't attempt to cure sadness. Why? Because sorrow and joy are equally potent realities.

Ministerial colleague Judith Walker-Riggs tells a story that summarizes the certified linking of joy and sorrow, especially during the Christmas season.

Judith once viewed a most unusual crèche, where the little carved figures were not painted, but made of different colors of wood. One of the wise men, for example, wore a gown in pale ivory that fell in curved folds around his brown feet. There was power and vitality and grace in the carving of each figure. The crèche was from Africa.

More than that, the woods were not mahogany or rosewood, as you might think at a glance. For these figures were carved from thorns from the *egun* tree in Nigeria. They were big thorns, very wide at the base, but sharply narrowing, and they grew in the three colors used in the crèche.

Judith relates how strange and beautiful to have carved something out of thorns for a holiday that's the epitome of "coziness." Perhaps the thorn is the death of a loved one, and this may be our first holiday without her. Or the thorn is someone having moved away, or we've moved away from him. A severed relationship or a new illness diagnosed: all these and countless other conditions can represent dreadful thorns. In their presence Christmas will no longer be simply a matter of continuing family customs per usual. A new Christmas must be carved from life's thorns.

A fifth way to stay joyful is through being of service to those in need. Our culture is suffering from a great illness. We're suffering from a grave disrespect...for other human beings as well as the earth. Yet the way to cure our ills, the way to get healthier is through service. There's nothing that will make us well like compassion will. There's a Hebrew word, for which there is no precise English translation: *simhah*, usually translated as joy. However, what this term fully means is "the happiness we make by sharing."

People sometimes ask Unitarian Universalists why our faith places such emphasis upon justice and mercy, and we reply, well, because "service is our prayer," or as Alice Walker reminds us, "service is the rent we pay for our stay on earth."

Furthermore, we believe service to be one of the rare places where deep, abounding joy is truly given and received. I exhort us to find ways always to be of assistance to others, especially those in dire financial or emotional need. Dare to spread some joy. As Unitarian forebear Emerson said: "Happiness is a perfume you cannot pour on others without getting a few drops on yourself."

There have been effective ascetics as well as martyrish prophets in human history, but the bulk of exemplary spiritual pioneers have embodied the power of joyful justice. They have merged activism with ecstasy—good deeds with good times. Martin Luther King, Jr.

was known to be clownish in his innermost circles.

Without a passionate, sustained commitment to serve society, our lives will dissipate into soulless pleasure in no time at all. For joy-sharing is a puny experience if unaccompanied by its life partners, justice-building and peace-making.

You and I belong to a religion that claims that each of us can make a significant difference in the ongoing creation of our cosmos. We can meet the challenge of the Egyptian God Osiris by finding and bringing joy, because the source of joy is planted deep within every one of our souls, if we but unleash its power. When we do, the entire Creation reverberates with a loud hallelujah!

An evolved theology maintains equilibrium between receiving and distributing joy. Happy people are both givers and receivers, unstuck in one or the other condition. Again, we say, the key to a fulfilled theological journey is sharing "Wholly Joy."

Let me close this hallmark with a charming story that may assist us in staying joyful during all the seasonal changes of the year. It's a story concerning the translation of the Christian scriptures from English into Inuit language.

Problems arose for the translators when they encountered certain words in English for which there was no corresponding term in the Inuit language. For example, there's a passage that tells that the disciples are filled with joy upon meeting Jesus. Since there's no word for joy in the Inuit language, the translators had to find another way to express the meaning of the scripture.

In their research, they discovered that one of the most joyful times for an Inuit family is when the sled dogs are fed in the evening. The dogs come barking and yelping, running about and wagging their tails furiously; the children are squealing with delight, and the neighbors join the delightful commotion as well. It's truly a blessed time for the Inuit people.

Consequently, the translators used that particular event to help convey the meaning of the aforementioned biblical passage. As a result, when the scripture was translated back into English, it read, "When the disciples saw Jesus, they wagged their tails."

As we face lives replete with both challenges and delights, heartaches and memories, may we do so with a soulful of joy—barking and yelping, bounding about and wagging our tails as excitedly as possible, so that our joy might become contagious and all creatures of the universe might join in the scales of rejoicing.

FOR REFLECTION AND DISCUSSION

1. A crucial part of Universalist theology has been the conviction that "holiness and true happiness are inseparably connected." That seems to mean that we can't truly be joyful without leading exemplary lives, worthy and holy lives. Conversely, if our journeys are drab and void of joy, then that doesn't qualify as a sacred quest either.

    Happiness and holiness are as Siamese twins; when torn asunder, they both wither and die. Do you find that true in your personal and congregational existence?

2. Popular inspirationalist Robert Fulghum, who is also a card-carrying Unitarian Universalist minister, states that he needs his fix of laughter (or internal jogging) at the close of every day:

    To end the day, I do a funny thing before I go to sleep. I read something humorous in bed. Joke books, cartoon books, I'll read anything to help me to bed with a laugh in my mind. This annoys my wife, because I get to laughing and shaking the bed, and then I have to read her the story or the joke.

    Assuredly, humor is at the heart of the joyous spirit. Do you enjoy any custom such as this?

3. Unitarian Universalist poet Doris Vernon contends that we need an eighth UU principle: "It is our solemn duty to dance, laugh, sing and enjoy our life."

    What do you think?

MYSTERY AND WONDER

The essential nature of Unitarian Universalist religion contains at its core a rational mysticism. Some lean toward the rational, others toward the mystical. At our best, we are able to embrace both worldviews.
—Lex Crane

Let us go remembering to praise,
to live in the moment,
to love mightily,
to bow to the mystery.
—Barbara Pescan

In writing my book entitled *Freethinking Mystics With Hands: Exploring the Heart of Unitarian Universalism* (1998), it became apparent that whereas the rationalist strain in our Unitarian Universalist heritage has been well-established, our mystical inclinations lie rather concealed. We've been lampooned as a demystified religion suffering from an "ecstasy" deficit. Even while praising Unitarian transcendentalists such as Ralph Waldo Emerson and Margaret Fuller, we have often failed to acknowledge their enveloping mysticism.

Nonetheless, as President Louis Cornish of the American Unitarian Association, expressed in 1937: "We belong among the mystics." He was insisting that our faith includes the company of those pilgrims who experience the cosmos numinously.

Considerable strides have been made since consolidation, especially with in-resident theologians such as Crane touting self-refined versions of mysticism. Whether we are devoted naturalists, humanists, theists, agnostics, pagans, or existentialists, the mystical temper is enjoying front-row status in our ranks. We are ever-awakening to the countless mysteries and wonders that radiate throughout our daily lives. Unitarian Universalist theologians are becoming students of the miraculous.

During the past 50 years there have been pamphlets produced by the UUA such as the splendid one written by Arthur Foote in 1976 entitled "Can I Be a Mystic and a Unitarian Universalist?," where this prominent minister makes an ardent case for all "who hunger for genuine religious experience." A crucial characteristic of our particular brand of mysticism is that it discourages irrationality, since "gullibility and credulity are not human traits we admire."

One could surely designate "Spirit of Life" by Carolyn McDade (composed 30 years ago in 1981)—our signature theme song—as an ode to mystical activism. It was written, as Carolyn relates, during the middle of the same night following the assassination of Harvey Milk, the gay mayor of San Francisco. It was penned directly from her spirit to ours, mainly as a prayerful anthem.

> *Spirit of Life, come unto me. Sing in my heart, all the stirrings of compassion. Blow in the wind, rise in the sea; move in the hand, giving life the shape of justice. Roots hold me close; wings set me free;*
> *Spirit of Life, come to me, come to me.*

One can posit the Spirit of Life, an Eternal Spirit, or the Great Spirit and still feel stirred by the mystical sentiments of McDade's words and melody.

In 1989, "Spirituality: Unitarian Universalist Experiences" was another pamphlet well-received in our ranks. It was introduced by Rosemarie C. Smurzynski:

> *A new note is being heard in Unitarian Universalism. Not a sixteenth note, not an eighth note or a quarter note—it is a whole note. It is spirituality. Not entirely new, we have heard this note sounded before in the liberal Christianity of William Ellery Channing, in the Transcendentalism of Ralph Waldo Emerson and Margaret Fuller, and in the Humanism of Clinton Lee Scott. Now it is gathering momentum. We hear this note as a crescendo in the roar of the ocean, in the quiet of our hearts, in the voice of fellowship, in the call to justice.*

In 2002 there was the formation of "Unitarian Universalist Mystics in Community," yet another theological perspective being legitimated as an affiliate organization in our movement. The purpose was: "to encourage personal witness and service reflecting the wellsprings of connection and compassion which open in us through the mystical life."

In the *Embracing Our Theological Diversity* volume (2005), over 90% of questionnaire respondents claimed "wonder and awe" as a very important part of their identity, be they humanists, naturalists, or theists. Unquestionably, since merger, our overall theology has been realizing that a sense of mystery and wonder precedes any desire to explain the origins of the world or locate a code of conduct.

Let's delve into these two theological virtues that are clearly yoked in our Principles and Purposes: "Direct experience of that transcending mystery and wonder…"

MYSTERY

One Unitarian Universalist minister suggested that we are prophets of the strangeness of God. I like that notion. For it is precisely the strangeness and mystery of things which calls from an awareness of a category beyond categories. Mystery may be the one absolute!
—Linda Weaver Horton

I call myself a mystical agnostic because even though we cannot know about a creator or sustainer, we do know, I believe, that the proper response to the miracle of existence is wonder, awe, worship, allegiance.
—Stephan Papa

Belief and disbelief can meet on the common ground of mystery.
—Chris Schriner

The substance of our faith points to an ineffable yet undeniable connection with sacrality. Unitarian Universalist mystics would affirm two braided convictions: our lives are embraced by a mystery that is baffling yet trustworthy, and our earth-bound purpose lies in surrendering not solving it.

It remains disheartening how few organized religions really choose to wrestle with mystery. Conventional religion has customarily been concerned with mastery over mystery—reducing Life and Spirit, Death and God to creedal phrases and clever doctrines.

In fact, there are orthodox theologians who claim closure on any and all mystery. Conversely, there are other religions that major in the exotic and esoteric. They often dwell in muddled thinking and obfuscation. Clarity is apparent only to the initiated. Such occultists bask in secrecy or mystification.

On the other hand, there exists the danger of parched and barren rationalism, where the universe is scrubbed clean of its imponderables and life is shrunk to the logical and literal. Unitarian Universalism, at our truest, aims to be a faith that neither explains away nor drowns in mysteries. The profoundest realities are often invisible—intangible yet insistent, downright mysterious.

Furthermore, we recognize that Life's deeper mysteries are profoundly ambiguous, double-edged; they both attract and repel. Awake and exposed, humans tremble in the presence of the numinous. The mysteries of birth, love, death, sexuality, and the cosmos are uncanny and elicit a special feeling, best rendered by the English word "awe" and its derivatives "awesome" and "awful." The astonishment we experience in the presence of the Holy is reinforced by the fact that the "ah" sound is present in the name of most deities: Adonai, Yahweh, Allah, God, Rama, Shiva, and Krishna.

Those who remain content to encounter rather than decipher divine mystery affirm that God is but a symbol or sign pointing to unfathomable realities beyond naming. Universalist Clarence Skinner talked of "God as a majestic symbol for the sublimest reality which the human mind can conceive."

Indubitably, mystery remains central to our Unitarian Universalist appropriation of depth theology. We refuse to imprison the vast and exploding marvel of infinity in shapely statues or petrified symbols. The atheists among us declare that the endless mystery that surrounds us is puzzling, perhaps even meaningless; the agnostics perceive it to be fathomless and unknowable but not to be ignored; and the affirmatists celebrate ultimate mystery as a treasure-trove of insight and direction, sometimes deigning to call it God.

Could it be that classically "reasonable" Unitarian Universalism might turn out to reside among the spiritual leaders in exploring the profundities of mystery? Between an arrogant and dry rationalism and an occultism that thrives on camouflage and mystique, dwells mature Unitarian Universalist thought and action. It is where our elusive spark blazes.

We neither revel in nor eradicate mysteries. We belong to a religion that pushes our minds as far as they can go and then bows before the mysteries. We resonate with the song, "Ah, sweet mystery of life!" The primary mystery of existence is life itself, a reality we all share. It's not always fair or sweet or beautiful, but it's a gift, a marvel, since each of us is a statistical miracle. We didn't earn this gift, and we can't repay it; we can only take immense pleasure in it.

Behind mysteries lie other mysteries. It's incumbent upon spiritual adventurers to leap into, or at least lean toward, the mysteries of existence, exposing our souls to their perplexity and power. Unitarian Universalism beckons us to engage life, meet death, surrender to love, wrestle with God. Blessed are those who rather than avoiding or explaining mystery have the courage to encounter mystery, from beginning to end.

I close this segment on mystery with a poignant piece from the Reverend David Eaton in *Been in the Storm So Long* (our 1991 meditation manual):

Birth–Life–Death
Unknown–Known–Unknown
Our Destiny: from Unknown to Unknown.

I pray that we will know the Awe
and not fall into the pit of intellectual arrogance
in attempting to explain it away.

The Mystery can be our substance.
May we have the faith to accept this wonderful Mystery
and build upon its everlasting Truth.

WONDER

Religion and poetry do the same thing.
They connect little things to big things.
—Lynn Ungar
Science and religion together reveal to us a world of wonder. They make us
grateful to be part of it, even in the face of the fear, pain,
loss, and evil that are also part of it.
—Helen Lutton Cohen

Mystery and wonder seem yoked in our fiery theological quest. The former denotes moments when we're deepened; the latter occasions times when we're dazzled. Often one is foreground; then they change places. They're both elemental virtues in the robust religious adventure.

Unitarian Universalists are encouraged to be wonderers all our days and nights. Jacob Trapp in his splendid hymn (1981) "Wonders Still the World Shall Witness" telegraphs that the Creation isn't finished with revealing its marvels: "wonders still the world shall witness never known in days of old, never dreamed by ancient sages, howsoever free and bold."

It remains one of our primary theological aims to marvel at things too beautiful for words and to wonder at sorrows too piercing to be answered...to stand astonished in the presence of meadows, animals and flowers, birth and death and all the experiences in-between. The capacity to feel awe, to experience miracles in the daily, to be ablaze when the world is dreary…is a rare and wonder-ful calling. Wondering may prove to be the most magnificent endeavor bold theologians ever pursue.

As colleague Clarke Wells poses in his poetic essay entitled "Sunshine and Rain at Once":

> *Once upon time there was a magician who didn't know he was one because nobody ever told him he was. He lived simply and worked at his job hard as you would expect an ordinary man to work at an ordinary job. When one day he died it was an ordinary sort of death…Some time after the funeral the magician's children discovered a diary which they did not know their father had kept, and they opened it and a jaguar jumped out, and yards and yards of rainbow silk, desperate, beautiful, unwinding…*

In every human story reside untold miracles. The challenge is to reveal our magic while alive, to open our pockets, our hearts, and let the wonders tumble forth. There are "jaguars and yards and yards of rainbow silk, desperate, beautiful, unwinding…" in each of our spiritual travels.

Unitarian Universalist educator Sophia Fahs claimed that our earliest religious beliefs grew out of direct encounters with the bedrock wonders and phenomena of the natural world—the earth and sky, growing things and animals—and from intensely personal experiences of birth, love, sickness, joy, death and the mystery of inner thoughts, dreams, and feelings. That's where children live and fashion their religious sensibilities. And that's where we adults could profitably spend more time. The very presence of children can liberate grown-ups from our rigid, jaded sensibilities due to what Fahs calls the "untiring, wondering curiosity" of little ones.

I took up "magic" eight years ago for two principle reasons: first, to impress our grandchildren and, second, to lessen the pain in my arthritic hands. It's worked wonders on both counts. I've even performed a half-dozen times for elementary school classes and during intergenerational worship times, sharing moments of incomparable glee, despite the ungainliness of my new hobby. I specifically invite children to call me Mr. Tom or Mr. Fun, nothing fancier than that. While I'll be a reverend all my days, something like Mr. Joy will be featured on my calling cards, from this day forward.

Manipulating balls, coins, ropes, cards, or silks is about as sensual an endeavor as one can fathom. Being a shameless merrymaker via magic affords a splendid opportunity to flub and falter as I juggle patter and handling simultaneously. I've also amused random adults with sleights of hand, once in a nearby Laundromat while washing clothes. The other day I bred the audacious notion that when I formally retire from settled ministry, I may just engage willing peers in sessions of "elder" magic.

I venture to say that children and adults "fooling around" together may just rank among the most wonder-filled sights the gods and goddesses ever witness. Among the happiest events I've enjoyed in my ministerial service have been all-congregation parties where everybody dances with everybody: where the children, youth, and adults of our tribe are having a festive, uninhibited time, without chemical lubrication, playing with neither opponent, clock, score-card, nor end zone in view, luxuriating in what Sarah McCarthy calls "our own liberating ludicrousness and practicing being harmlessly deviant."

When the youth graduate from our RE program and go off to school or work, we've held exit interviews, asking them one basic question: "What do you most recall from your religious education experiences at First UU Church of San Diego?" Occasionally they remember specific Unitarian Universalist personages or dates. Then, if pressed, they might recall some of the basic principles of our heritages. Specific peers and adults usually come into focus, but above all else, they recollect the intergenerational revelry they've enjoyed in our midst. Our program has failed those who wander off wonderless.

They talk vividly about holiday candlelight services, community protest marches, and Martin Luther King, Jr. celebrations. They mention the Saturday work projects, where their contributions were esteemed by the adult members of the tribe. They retain with stunning clarity and delight those moments when they and we were embodying *wonder*: our holy vocation as an intergenerational community.

Every day counts, doesn't it? The Navajo people teach their children that each morning the sun comes up is brand new in all respects. A luminous solar body is born every dawn, lives for the duration of one day, and in the evening it expires, never to return again. As soon as Navajo children are old enough to understand, adults take them out at sunrise and say, "The sun has only one day. You must live this day in a good way, so that the sun won't have wasted time." Acknowledging the specialness of each 24-hour span is a marvelous way to reconnect with our basic birthright of wonder.

The Bible often talks about the concept of being *fulfilled*. I take that to mean filled full—packed to the brim, neither with waste nor haste, but with episodes of meaning and grandness, such as mystery and wonder.

Mature theological pilgrims internalize the ancient Celtic imagination that welcomed nature, divinity, and human existence as equal partners in one unified cosmos, every bit of it rampant with soul and radiance. Animals are our brothers and sisters, flora and fauna ooze sacrality, rivers and streams are the outpouring of earth's vast reservoir of tears.

Standing tall before the advancing dawn, while facing the morning sun, may we bow in prayer and humbly utter:

Spirit of Mysterious and Wondrous Life,

    Thank you for another day—a blessing I did not earn.
May I become an unfettered beholder during my waking hours.
Open my eyes that I might see,
Open my ears that I might hear,

Open my nostrils that I might smell,
Open my mouth that I might speak,
Open my throat that I might croon,
Open my hands that I might touch,
Open my soul that I might entertain
    mysteries eluding capture and wonders exceeding comprehension...

So may it come to pass.

FOR REFLECTION AND DISCUSSION

1. The Unitarian poet and minister Robert Terry Weston wrote at the close of his poem on the evolution of the universe:

   This is the wonder of time; this is the marvel of space; out of the stars swung the earth; life upon earth rose to love. This is the marvel of life, rising to see and to know. Out of your heart, cry wonder: sing that we live.

   Soak in these inspiring sentiments. Then compose your own prayer or poem.

2. Another verse from one of our finest, Jacob Trapp:

   Let me listen to the music of daybreak within me.
   Let me march to a strain unheard by mortal ear,
   Let that in me which surpasses me have glimpse of the unsurpassable.

3. One of our prominent mystics since merger has been naturalistic humanist Ken Patton:

   I am my soul. The mystery is not _in_ the flower; the flower _is_ the mystery. All things are the mystery. They are. That is all. They cannot be explained, so take them as they stand. Do not look for anything behind or beyond them. Do not look for a mystery extraordinary. Every awareness is the experience of mystery if we have become sensitive to it. The secret is in the day.

4. Name some of the particular ways in which your congregation occasions moments of mystery and experiences of wonder during the course of a calendar year

SELF-CARE

*To be nobody but yourself in a world which is doing its best, night and day,
to make you everybody else—means to fight the hardest battle which any human can fight, and never stop fighting.*
—E. E. Cummings

I'm working on a lifestyle I can honestly recommend to others.
—Richard Boeke

*You need only claim the events of your life to make yourself yours. When you
truly possess all you have been and done...you are fierce with reality.*
—Florida Scott-Maxwell

If we ignore our spirit or ravage our body, enslave our heart or vacate our mind, avoid our conscience or forfeit our soul, we're literally abusing the singular gift of creation that is you, that is I. Our peculiar being is God's distinct gift to us; self-care is our best way of saying thank you. It's an imperative of staying ablaze and growing up theologically.

Over the course of the past fifty years, Unitarian Universalist culture is acknowledging that authentic self-care is among the most important gifts a congregation can grant to itself as well as to each of its members. A parish where self-care is hallowed as a virtue is a healthy one; the same lesson holds true for individual voyagers.

However, the virtue of self-care isn't the same as being stuck on your self. The extremes of narcissism and neglect are dead-ends, whereas self-fulfillment is a central mark of being religious. Unless we take good and continuing care of the beings we are, then sooner or later, our effectiveness as professionals, as partners, as parents, as patriots, and as spiritual pilgrims will suffer as well.

Suppose you were to come upon someone in the woods working feverishly to saw down a tree. "What are you doing?" you might ask.

"Can't you see?" arrives the impatient reply. "I'm sawing down this tree." "Well, you look exhausted, how long have you been at it?" you reply. "Over five hours, and you're right, I'm beat! This is hard work." "My goodness, why don't you take a break for a few minutes and sharpen that saw? I'm sure it'd go a lot faster." "What do you mean? I don't have time to sharpen the saw," the person says emphatically, "I'm too busy sawing!"

That's the point. If we fail to take time out to sharpen our tools, those same tools are bound to break down. If we bypass healthy and holy breaks amid our frenetic days, then our bodies and spirits will surely decline. According to a rabbinical saying: "Any human being who has not a single hour for their own every day is no human being!"

A major dis-ease of contemporary American society is being worn-out, whether it comes from physical exhaustion, emotional stress, compassion-fatigue, or a worldview of cynicism. The gauge, for too many high-achieving and deeply caring people, Unitarian Universalists included, reads "nearly empty"—empty of passion, zest, and spirit.

To make matters worse, those who work themselves to the bone nowadays are often accorded more rewards and esteem than those seeking a balanced life. Some analysts even view the new heightened desire for work as something ultimately insatiable, a drive having less to do with money and status than with some mysterious urge to self-destruct, even if in glorious fashion.

To be sure, some burnout comes with the territory of being a morally sensitive person. There exists in the robust religious life both what Hans Selye called *eustress* (good stress) and *distress* (unhealthy stress). The art of balanced self-care is purely to embrace the former and diminish the latter.

As we all know, unless there's some tension in the strings, the violin simply can't play. Stress or tension is a precondition for growth. Therefore, depth theology seeks a rhythm of peace and unrest,

serenity and struggle. Remember that Jeremiah in the Hebrew scriptures warned that there exist any number of false prophets running
around "healing the wounds lightly" and preaching "peace, peace,
when there is no peace."

2011 is no different. There are false prophets peddling literature
and pushing groups on how to lead semi-tranquilized lives. Personally, I don't want nor do I recommend a worry-free existence. Being
a spiritually attuned mortal means living with abundant concerns—
both local and global—weighing upon our hearts. Those who systematically skirt all anguish or unease quickly turn into zombies.

Living well starts with a commitment to regularly scheduled Sabbaths. Running, walking, doing yoga, chanting, tai chi, just sitting
quietly in a corner of your house…you and I must find the ways to
launch our day so that we might stay centered while moving, grounded while soaring, for the remaining hours. Sabbath literally means
to draw a deep breath, without which our lives quickly succumb to
frantic swirling. We need to catch our breath…regularly.

Taking care of one's self is correlated with conducting an accountable life. Unitarian Universalists are heretics, literally, "choice-
makers." Within our limits of background and resources, we possess
the power to make personal decisions. We currently live in a culture
of victimization. Of course, there exist those among us who have
been victimized in one way or another, even severely, and we need
both internal and external resources to disentangle from our past or
present anguish.

But constantly tagging ourselves as victims and blaming others
for our lot in life is to remain spiritually struck. Being fueled by a
sense of victimization is futile. Rabbi Harold Kushner's child died
of a tragic and irreversible degenerative illness. In *When Bad Things
Happen to Good People*, a proven classic during half of our fifty years,
Kushner puts it sanguinely: "Expecting the world to treat you fairly
because you are a good person is like expecting the bull not to charge
you because you are a vegetarian!"

There are no guarantees in life, only opportunities. Life is not fair, but within life there exist sufficient options to make it livable, even meaningful.

Whenever I feel utterly stuck, I recall the advice of a counselor who pressed me once saying: "Hey, Tom, remember that you're only immobilized from making some sort of decision if you're either dead or unconscious—otherwise, you always have another move!"

We aren't masters of our fate in some absolute way but neither are we powerless victims. We're responsibly free to render adequate decisions to make our lives and the lives of all those whom we touch more lovely and beautiful. Unitarian Universalist theology urges us to seize our god-given capacity to be a choice-maker, indeed, as healthy a choice-maker as possible during our earthly stay. What does it matter to believe in the inherent worth and dignity of everyone, as our theology fervently does, if we don't equally affirm and nudge everyone to use his or her integrity and dignity responsibly?

Another governing principle of good self-care is starting right where we are. Heed Ashley Brilliant's comic line: "I may not be totally perfect, but parts of me are excellent." You and I possess everything we need, internally and externally, all the necessary resources, to lead better, not perfect, lives. Of course, we have to tweak here and there, yet, ultimately, we must make peace with the body and mind and soul with which we've been graced since birth and make the most of who we are as unique beings progressing toward whom we might decide to become.

According to the Genesis story of Creation, when finished, Yahweh said that "it was good, very good." That pronouncement included us frail, imperfect humans. Yes, we're good, very good. Good enough and absolutely sufficient for what will be required during our earthly sojourn. We possess defects, all of us, but we're not defective persons. We're products of the evolutionary process, gifted with enlarged brains that make it possible for us to understand an orderly universe and to honor its laws.

One more caution. Being a highly disciplined guy, I have to be careful, maybe you do too, that my pursuit of self-care doesn't add to my stress level. You and I can become frustrated by the very spiritual disciplines we pursue for refreshment. As one sage remarked: "Stress, in addition to being itself, and the result of itself, is also the cause of itself."

No uniform self-care program will work for every Unitarian Universalist. We're all different, and disciplines that succeed for you won't necessarily bring me growth. The paths toward self-nourishment are countless: songs, play, walking, silence, fencing, guided imagery, prayer or meditation, knitting, deep conversation, tai chi, reading, mastering magic tricks, dancing, writing, and on and on. We can learn from mentors and buddies, but eventually we're answerable for finding, then tailoring, the disciplines that will sculpt our idiosyncratic being into healthier shape.

Unitarian Universalism exemplifies a holistic theology, and, as such, summons us to shepherd our *whole* beings. We have bodies, spirits, minds, hearts, souls, and consciences and each of these discrete realms of the Self must be nourished daily in one way or another. There's no hierarchy of regions: the soul's no more important than the mind, nor the heart than the body. They're equally crucial. In fact, the zone that's foremost is the one we're neglecting.

Then there's self-pity, one of the most popular, nonpharmaceutical drugs in our society. It's narcotic because it gives momentary pleasure and separates us from actuality. Self-pitying types are forever wishing they were someone else who had more energy or money, possessors of fewer wrinkles or odd bumps growing on our bodies. As some wag noted: "On life's totem pole of bargain basement emotions, jealousy and self-pity are the tackiest."

They're oft-entwined, since when we're the whiniest, we tend to be envious of others, especially the younger and stronger. Occasionally, we won't be able to follow such counsel, for we're truly immobilized. Other times, we need an outside goad to jolt us off our pity-pots. Mature pilgrims pursue self-renewal rather than get derailed by self-pity, dealing directly with the natural disappointments and diminishments we'll face in life.

However, we need to maneuver a fine line between mature self-love and narcissism or what Martin Luther termed *incurvatum in se,* meaning "turned in upon oneself." It's all right to stare at our navels, if when we do so, we also acknowledge our vital connection to other people.

Earthlings aren't complete unto themselves. It's only in the context of community we ever become fully human. When the apostle Paul observed that "we are members one of another," he used the word members in its original sense—limbs. We're frequently one another's arms and legs. Lacking one another, we're incomplete, maimed, less than human.

We're beckoned to nourish, on a daily basis, the entirety of our beings—body, spirit, heart, mind, soul, and conscience. Some brief notes on each area of self-care.

BODY

Our body is flawed to be sure, but it's ours, the only one we'll ever inhabit. So let's pledge to feed it, exercise it, and caress it with utmost care. We need to treat our bodies as sacred temples rather than temporary dwellings or disposable commodities. Plus, we don't just have bodies. We *are* our bodies. We are what we eat, and we are how we exercise.

When I spent a month alone in the woods some years ago, I tentatively learned the practice of self-massage, lightly caressing my own skin, for five or so minutes a day. That's about all this shy guy could handle. It was somewhat disquieting to affirm my body, upclose, with my own hands, but, after all, as I grew to understand, my body's mine, and it likes to be touched, especially by its owner. In addition, I'm the most convenient person around.

Is some direct physical self-care too much for you and me to experience daily? Humankind would be healthier and holier if we practiced more self-massage rather than pining away for others to always meet our sensual needs.

SPIRIT

The theological theme of self-care would have us ponder, ingest, and heed the first Beatitude: "Blessed are they who are at home in the spirit." Might we not begin to engage one another daily with the traditional Quaker greeting: "How goes it with thy Spirit?"

At core, the spiritual journey begins with our paying attention to our basic breathing. As Thich Nhat Hanh says: "Breathing in, I calm my body and spirit. Breathing out, I smile." Or I breathe in hope and love; I breathe out hurt and bitterness. As near as breath itself is the Eternal. Moving in and out of us as we breathe is the One, the Holy, the Spirit.

We travel toward our common center along different spokes of the sacred wheel of life. Some reach the core of their Spirit through meditation, others through prayer, still others like myself through chanting. A chant takes a basic truth and anchors it through repetition. Chants are so versatile. You can chant while walking or sitting in your office. Chants can be learned in a minute. Remember, there's no single way, let alone one correct way, to stretch or anchor your spirit. There's your way. Find it, then practice it.

HEART

Heart-work has to do with nurturing the entire range of our relationships. Noting that our word courage comes from the French word for heart (*coeur*), we aspire, struggle to be open-hearted, strong-hearted, clear-hearted, and full-hearted persons in all our ties with humans and animals and deities. We resonate daily with Carlos Castenada's query: "Does this path have a heart?" The heart has everything to do with empathy, compassion, and joy, and the primal heart-bonds of my existence request, nay require, gentle, firm tending, day in and day out. How is your heart sourced and resourced?

Are your bonds of intimacy as current and caring as possible?

MIND

Our intellect is a gift of the creation, and we must cultivate it carefully. As religious forerunner Ralph Waldo Emerson noted: "Too many religions impel us to leave our mind outside the sanctuary when we enter!" On the contrary, an ever-evolving theology makes sure we employ our minds fully whether we're inside or outside the sanctuary. Our mind isn't just for gathering information or even garnering knowledge so much as receiving and sharing wisdom on the pathway toward becoming sages and crones during our earthly jaunt.

Unitarian Universalism fosters a reasonable faith. I personally expand my mind through journaling, through mastering magic tricks, through the recitation of poetry (primarily out loud to myself), and through writing books. How do you stretch your mind as a means of intentional self-care?

SOUL

If the spirit has to do with making intuitive and transcendent connections, soul-work for me, along with the Jungians, has to do with raking the ashes, confronting the shadowed underbelly of existence where anger, anguish, and angst abound. It's tempting to avoid dealing with our rage, our fear, and our sorrow, but any self-care regimen worth its weight must face squarely the uncomfortable regions of our netherworld.

We start with facing our fears. The Christian scriptures claim that "perfect love casts out fear." I beg to disagree. Love doesn't rid us of our terrors and anxieties. It only enables us to live more sanguinely amidst them.

My experience is that the bolder one loves, the more complicated, even scarier it gets, whether young or old. Angst customarily settles at the bottom of love, keeping us on our relational toes.

The poet Rumi reminds us that "our greatest fears are like dragons guarding our greatest treasures." If we slay our dragons, the priceless assets and abundance of our life will lie unprotected.

Fear is the finger pointing out where the problem is—if we go in the direction of fear, it will often push us toward growth. As one writer puts it, "hug your monsters," for as long as we run away from our conflicts, they will harass us wherever we go.

There's a fine line, of course, between bravely facing our angst, and being downright foolhardy or taking stupid risks with valuable things. The dragons of our spiritual journey cannot be ignored, denied, or wished out of existence. They can't be suppressed or seduced. They must be engaged.

In healthy self-care our pesky fears are welcomed into the field of enhanced awareness. We begin to call our personal beasts by their true names: be they sickness or doubt, vanished dreams or failing strength, broken bonds or joyless spells. We invite such creatures into our living quarters, our hearts, and our hours—if desirable, perhaps for a cup of tea in the late afternoon.

CONSCIENCE

The sixth self-care zone, not in hierarchical order, is our conscience, which often goes unmentioned in standard self-care programs. Why? Because it's tempting to forget that taking good care of ourselves is inextricably linked with showing compassion toward our neighbors and displaying respect for the earth. Unitarian Universalist minister Stephen Fritchman, in a 1976 essay for our Unitarian Universalist Service Committee, registered a compelling insight:

> *Surgeons can today transplant hearts, kidneys and other human organs, but no one in the health sciences can yet transplant a conscience. So feed and care for your conscience as you do your brain; neither can be replaced.*

In summary, this core theological theme reminds fellow Unitarian Universalists to take good, full care of ourselves, starting here and now, because doing so may prove to be our steadiest resource and our greatest accomplishment. Through a theology of self-fulfillment we not only say thank you to the Creation, our lives also blaze with energy and crackle with resolve. We may not gain any more time for living through rigorous and comprehensive self-care, but we will live a lot more fully, because our senses will be more alive and open to the entire universe.

Self-care begins and ends linked with another theological trait: *courage*. Indeed, the poet Ben Jonson considered courage to be the primary virtue, because all the others could only materialize if we are brave enough to pursue, then embody, them.

Eda LeShan tells the story about a dinner party, when she sat next to a woman who was an oceanographer. At one point LeShan was asked if she had ever wondered why lobsters could weigh one pound, three pounds, even ten pounds when they had such a hard shell. How could they grow? Eda had to tell her dinner companion that resolving this fascinating quandary wasn't high on her list of priorities.

The woman smiled and proceeded to explain that when a lobster is crowded in its shell and can't grow anymore, it instinctively travels to some place in the sea, hoping for relative safety and begins to shed its shell. It's a terribly dangerous process—the lobster has to risk its life, because once it becomes naked and vulnerable, it could be dashed against a reef or eaten by another lobster or fish. But that's the only way it can grow.

In a mature self-care regimen, when we seriously commit to theological growth in our personal and institutional lives, it can become a difficult, even dangerous enterprise.

Such is the challenge of our midlife maturation as a movement: to shed our shells, to go to the reef, to break through self-imposed, constricting barriers, to become more resourceful theologians, more of our best selves as Unitarian Universalists.

Therefore, every day let us stretch our minds with a fresh notion.

Every day let us warm our hearts by touching the being of another. Every day let us stir our consciences by doing something, however minor, to make our globe more safe or sane. Every day let us lift our spirits by sitting still or exploring natural beauty. Every day let us ground our souls by facing a fear, unearthing some hurt, and showing a bit of righteous rage. And every day let us feed our bodies with healthy nutrients, keeping our temples fit and energized.

Most of all, THEOLOGY ABLAZE reminds us to be kind to ourselves, fortified by St. Paul's phrase: "Let your steps be guided by such light as you have." Unimaginable sources of light are present in every being, during every epoch, just waiting to be turned on. We don't have to carry the lamp of another or bask in the refracted glory of a fellow pilgrim. Our lives need only be steered by such light as we possess.

"This little light of mine, I'm going to let it shine," runs the spiritual. We will be duly amazed when we switch on our inner lights, here and how.

There's no way we'll ever accomplish full self-care, but Unitarian Universalism, our chosen faith, encourages us to be pulled by our aspirations rather than resting on our accomplishments. We plod, we persist, we keep our eyes on the prize. We demonstrate our appreciation for existence itself by taking good, not perfect, care of our whole beings.

And that will prove enough, yes, that will be enough…for this one, precious lifetime.

FOR REFLECTION AND DISCUSSION

1. Enumerate the reasons that self-care qualifies in the Unitarian Universalist pantheon of theological themes, both for individuals and congregations.

2. How do you intentionally and regularly nourish the different arenas of your Self? Address each of them, one at a time: body, mind, heart, spirit, conscience, and soul.

3. In what specific manners does your parish support the self-care programs of both its religious professionals and its laity?

FORGIVENESS AND RECONCILIATION

We must get better at Universalist values of love and forgiveness, hope and
courage...these are the virtues of the work of the Spirit.
—Rosemary Bray McNatt

If we Unitarian Universalists have made any progress on issues of gender,
sexual identity, race—or problems of simply living together as families and
friends—it has begun with the acknowledgment that we will screw up and
we will need forgiveness...Forgiveness is not one act. It is a relationship.
—Laurel Hallman

FORGIVENESS

The process of forgiveness enables us to face the worst and the best in humanity, our most grievous impasses and highest resolves. In what has become one of the most widely used readings in our new hymnal (#461), Reinhold Niebuhr hallows forgiveness as the "final form of love."

Recognition of the power of forgiveness has become an especially rich and rewarding process for Unitarian Universalists, since it's forced us to admit our inadequacies and culpabilities. During our five decades since consolidation, forgiveness has enabled us to avoid wallowing in the diminishing emotions of resignation, vengefulness, inertia, and self-justification, while still facing our shortcomings. It has challenged us to anchor hurts and wrongs in the past, while advancing with our lives. Practicing forgiveness has stretched progressives to experience the full course of hurt, bitterness, healing, and reconnection.

Forgiveness has also summoned Unitarian Universalists to humanize rather than demonize wrongdoers. It has compelled us to shape distinctions between justice and retaliation. It has obliged us to grasp that forgiveness is a choice not a compulsion. Forgiveness is integral to growing up theologically.

It has proven to be a quantum leap for our movement, which had uniformly bypassed mention of forgiveness in its formal documents over the past 50 years, to produce what was a groundbreaking recommendation in the proposed revision of Article II (2009):

Capable of both good and evil, at times we are in need of forgiveness and reconciliation. When we fall short of living up to this covenant, we will begin again in love, repair the relationship, and recommit to the promises we have made.

This chapter will unravel the complexities of forgiveness, followed by related thoughts on reconciliation and repair.

"To forgive or not to forgive" is perhaps the trickiest theological query of them all. Over time, I've modified my own views on forgiveness due to public events, personal soul-searching, and ministerial counseling. Situations vary and as Unitarian Universalists we can't be rigid about profound emotional, spiritual, and moral matters such as forgiveness.

It's quite tempting to turn forgiveness into a "should." If there's any *ought* involved, it's not an ought of obligation but more like an ought of opportunity. As Unitarian Universalist author Dwight Lee Wolter puts it: "To err is human, to forgive is an option." Indeed it is. Forgiveness comprises a theological option akin to grace, unfolding, if at all, on its own timetable.

Under this hallmark, we'll review benefits of the forgiving act, while also paying homage to occasions when forgiveness may not be warranted or, at best, partial forgiveness is in order.

Let's start with a live illustration of the fierce ambiguity inherent in the forgiving process.

You may recall, years back, of the Pontiff's pardon of the man who had tried to take his life. In a bare, white-walled cell in one of Rome's prisons, John Paul tenderly held the very hand that had held the gun that was meant to kill him. For 21 minutes, the Pope sat with his Turkish, would-be assassin, Mehmet Ali Agca. The two talked softly. Once or twice, Agca even laughed.

The Pope forgave him for the shooting. At the end of the meeting, Agca either kissed the Pope's ring or pressed the Pope's hand to his forehead in a Muslim gesture of respect.

One must ask: is forgiveness a purely personal transaction or can it be applied in a political way to reconcile enemies? The Pope seemed to be suggesting that such acts would at least dampen some of the more vengeful desires that are constantly set loose in hotspots throughout the globe.

Understandably, there are complexities of forgiveness that involve the question of justice. Personal or divine forgiveness isn't public justice, and it shouldn't be permitted to override justice. The Pope forgave Agca, but Agca remained in jail and should.

Despite its enormous difficulties, even drawbacks, there remains a formidable power to the gift of forgiveness, both personally and globally. Forgiveness doesn't look much like a tool for survival in a bad world, but that's what it is. Forgiveness frees people from spiritual slaveries of all sorts—forgivers and forgiven alike.

Nonetheless, we all exhibit periodic resistance to the forgiveness process.

First, humans are prone to bypass forgiveness, racing with lightning speed from our hurts to conciliation without recognizing what must be forgiven before any durable healing can take hold. Truces are often made and signed, then broken even before the ink is dry. That's happened all too frequently in the Middle East and Ireland. America's been party to its share of busted treaties as well.

There has to be sufficient pause between the hurt and any reconciliation, so that genuine forgiveness can evolve. How tempting it is to rush toward redemption, especially when our own heart isn't on the block, engaging in what has been called "forgiveness lite." I recall, early in my ministry, inviting a grief-stricken person to begin the process of forgiveness toward someone who had murdered his wife. And he plaintively cried: "Oh, Pastor Tom, not yet, not yet!"

I was moving toward a premature pardon, out of some noble theology combined with my own raw uneasiness, rather than caring about this person's fresh loss and indescribable suffering. To do the opposite: to confront our hurts, to pursue responsible restitution, to allow people to grieve properly...are crucial steps in the process toward genuine reconciliation.

Is forgiving the same as excusing? Not at all. My life-partner, Carolyn, and I excuse one another all the time, indeed regularly throughout the course of our 38 years together. Forgiveness needs to be reserved for serious offenses that are without precedent or explanation, and we've shared those moments as well. Being wronged is what separates forgivable from merely excusable acts. When wronged, one must boldly say, "I'll never understand why you hurt me like that. You didn't have to do what you did. It wasn't written in the stars or in your genes. You did it of your own free will, and I despise you for it. At least, I hate that part of you, and I blame you for it. I can't get around or over it, absolve or understand it. You not only hurt me, you wronged me."

Forgiveness has nothing to do with excusing, explaining, or forgetting but everything to do with remembering. And forgiveness isn't tolerance. Many offenses can be forgiven but not tolerated. Real forgiveness is concerned about full accountability—"with justice not vengeance," to use Simon Wiesenthal's phrase. Gandhi's forgiveness was accompanied by his actions to end British imperialism in India. Martin Luther King, Jr. forgave lynch mobs, even as he worked for laws to protect all citizens from such mobs.

However, the process toward full-fledged reconciliation remains excruciatingly difficult. Some psychologists, ethicists, and theologians would contend, and I can't disagree, that sometimes it's just not possible.

There are times to be a moral unforgiver: telling the truth, asserting fundamental rights, and opposing injustice, while refusing to forgive.

Here's a story of partial forgiveness, all too familiar in our modern world. A gay man is ostracized by his born-again Christian parents who are active members of *Return Incorporated*, an international evangelical organization dedicated to converting gay people to heterosexuality. The parents claim to hate the sin and love the sinner but have stated publicly: "our son's homosexuality is worse than a death in the family."

This young man's parents' entrenched, sanctimonious refusal to admit their hostility toward their son is a nonnegotiable obstacle to full reconciliation. To disapprove of his sexual orientation is one thing; but to wage a conversion campaign, while insisting that they're acting out of compassion, is another.

Therefore, although Peter refuses to underwrite his parents' behavior by forgiving it, neither will he abandon them in retaliation; mature separation is not amputation. Peter has decided, and I think wisely, to maintain occasional contact with his folks, provided *Return Incorporated* isn't mentioned. Any illusion of family harmony, of course, is lost forever, being replaced with something limited—painful, yet real.

So it goes for Peter and countless others who've faced comparable dilemmas in their own lives, where either unforgiveness or partial forgiveness offers the only healthy choice.

Learning not to forgive, after a life in which forgiveness has been knee-jerk, compulsive, or imposed, is an impressive achievement in our adult lives. When it's genuine, forgiveness must remain an option not an obsession. That's why the same person can grant or withhold it, depending on the circumstances. The ability to make discriminating moral choices signifies maturity and freedom.

Naturally, there are still times when complete forgiveness is mandated, possible, and healthy, because staying in a state of hate has its costs as well. Bitterness digs two graves. The word resentment is derived from the Latin meaning "to feel again." The nonforgiver, then, can become a resenter, someone who often feels and reacts to the pain again and again, caught in the cycle of spite.

In the long run, most Unitarian Universalists desperately want to break these vicious cycles of hatred and revenge. We want to bury the hatchet, move beyond animosity toward some semblance of forgiveness.

We desire to accomplish what Rev. Rob Eller-Isaacs references in his "Litany of Atonement" (#637): "We forgive ourselves and each other; we begin again in love."

When we're able to do so, here are some suggestions.

First, it isn't necessary to tell the person we're forgiving that they're the subject of our efforts. If sharing such information helps, fine, do it. If sharing worsens an already thorny situation, then avoid doing it.

Forgiveness need not always be a two-way street. Sometimes we gather the courage to extend forgiveness only to find the other side unwilling, reluctant, or unable to cement a truce. It appears to be a no-win situation, until we remember that forgiveness doesn't have to be reciprocal...to be genuine to you.

At the very least, when we venture some degree of forgiveness, we're left with the freedom of no longer holding a grudge or bearing a resentment. Venturing some level of forgiveness enables us to secure a wrong in its own time, so neither the wrongdoer nor the wronged have to lug it around as a burden. You don't forget the wrong, but it belongs to past history.

Second, even though the person who hurt you and is in need of your forgiveness is distanced geographically or has even died, it's never too late or impossible to forgive. You and I can forgive as long as we have breath.

Third, who needs to be forgiven? The list is endless, and we're all on it. Institutions, parents and children, congregations, countries, enemies and friends, lovers, even God. Forgiving ourselves is the nubbins of it all, since we're invariably the toughest nut to crack. We stand in constant need of separating ourselves from our failures and affirming our own worth, even while disapproving of things we do or have done.

We need to forgive ourselves, because, if we don't, we'll never be able to receive another's forgiveness, let alone that of the Eternal Spirit. When we forgive ourselves, we don't take away the wound, because we're forever wounders and wounded people, and, yes, we will likely feel the pain again and again, but there's still some release and relief. Our souls can rest more easily, when uncluttered with remorse, resentment, and recrimination.

At the core of the Unitarian Universalist thought articulated in THEOLOGY ABLAZE lies the conviction that, whatever else we may be, we're renewable beings. We can always open another door to fresh hope. Forgiveness has the power to save us from despair and bitterness. That power is huge and signals the ultimate form of love.

RECONCILIATION

Our liberal and liberating religion charges us to create an inclusive, fair-minded, and nonviolent community where we live, work, and worship. In short, we must resist demonizing, resist hate crimes, resist dogmatism, and resist intolerance, wherever they rear their ugly heads.

As Coretta Scott King emphasized: "It's vitally important that we endorse zero tolerance for bigotry!"

While being full-bore resisters, Unitarian Universalists remain devoted reconcilers as well, and occasionally with the very same individuals or groups. Our way of religion summons us to be spiritually ambidextrous, to confront and conciliate, to crash barriers and build bridges. To complicate matters, some of us who resist are, in fact, temperamentally combative, while others who reconcile are unduly compliant. So, we need reconcilers who have spine and resisters with suppleness.

In any case, genuine bridge-building is never to be confused with passivity or acquiescence; for King, Gandhi, and all bona fide activists continually teach that reconciliation is an act requiring enormous nonviolent strength and prodigious moral force.

I belong to a small San Diego band of peace-makers called the Fellowship of Reconciliation—an international, interfaith organization founded in 1914. It wasn't christened the Fellowship of Peace, Justice or Mercy because the founders wanted to challenge us, and they did; for reconciliation is perhaps the most difficult of life's encounters, since it entails the coming together with some measure of harmony among individuals who've been sundered. There's no more demanding religious art or skill than finding common ground and making beneficial compromises—be it between partners, work associations, congregants, nations, races, or faiths.

To illustrate this point, I've never lost sight of a disturbing phrase tucked away in the familiar, comforting 23rd Psalm in the Hebrew scriptures that reminds us of the ever-present call to be reconcilers and reconciled: "Thou preparest a table before me in the presence of my enemies." Setting a table before family or friends usually poses no special challenge, unless, of course, you're at odds with your own kin, or have to turn silent when talking about religion or politics. However, being called by God to be companions with our foes, literally, to break bread with our enemies, constitutes a grueling spiritual test.

What is necessary to diminish hostility...internally, interpersonally, and internationally? What will it take to find, then cultivate, common ground with our opponents—some of whom, some of the time, may even lie under the same roof with us or be one of our relatives or friends?

The first building block to becoming a reconciling presence is a willingness to give up our sense of rightness. We have to start at home and work. Unquestionably, one of my trickiest life-challenges is to relinquish my sense of being in control, being correct, being rated the "good guy" in fair or foul weather. I have to regularly remind myself that the purpose of my holy union with Carolyn is mutual growth *not* individual triumph, shared satisfaction, never personal virtuousness. Being right is the booby prize; staying healthfully together—ah, that's the goal.

On the global level, a perfect example is Jerusalem. Recently, more than 100 U.S. rabbis claimed that there's no theological rationale for Jewish control of the disputed Temple Mount in Jerusalem and that both Jews and Moslems should *share* control of this holy site. As they put it:

> *The temple Mount, which contains the ruins of the ancient Hebrew temple, as well as two major Islamic shrines, should be a "house of prayer" for all peoples.*

The first step, then, in finding common ground is giving up our own inflexible sense of rightness.

A second, related reminder is negotiating compromises on a customary basis. Too many people see compromise as a sign of weakness rather than strength. Backbone and tenacity are certainly virtues, yet they wreak havoc whenever arrogance and obstinacy creep in. "Right relationship" banks upon individuals willing to resolve conflicts through compromise, not through trying to bully or lure others to the "superiority" of our position.

Creative compromises don't always mean giving in to the other side, but they do entail giving up being right all the time. Every relationship requires yielding and shifting, time and time again: giving up something so that the welfare of the overall union, institution, or coalition might be served. Compromise means each person *promises* to contribute something *for* the benefit of the larger relationship, the greater good, instead of abetting our separate egos.

Compromise is the trademark of the human species and a source of adaptability in our evolution. Only 15% of our brain is grown before birth, and 85% is developed afterwards; so we're far more adaptable than imagined. As one analyst noted about the grand achievements of Eleanor Roosevelt: "She mastered the art of compromising *up!*" Mature theological discourse is about compromising *up!*

Blessedly, there are mediation workers, nowadays, who are trained to serve those of us who honestly struggle to forge bonds across seemingly unbridgeable gulfs. Did you know that dialogue between pro-choice and pro-life supporters has been growing from the grassroots? There exists the *Common Ground Network for Life and Choice* in Washington, D.C. that offers linkage and recourse to people engaged on local reconciliation efforts.

Common Ground is an approach to dialogue in conflict situations that emphasizes areas of agreement while respecting profound differences. Common Ground isn't some mushy, middle ground, but an attitude that offers opponents a space in which "to sit down together, to hear each others stories and to re-humanize people on the other side of any given chasm." The aim isn't to agree but to understand—without sacrificing ones prophetic morality to do so. As Unitarian Universalist Jay Atkinson affirms: "Being agreed with isn't a human necessity but being understood is."

In small groups, participants are invited in Common Ground to share the story of how they came to call themselves pro-choice or pro-life. No one can argue with a person's experience. Feelings are facts. It's amazing how often the common denominator is a painful experience; that's usually why there's so much heated passion on this particular issue.

Common Ground works for people who don't have to keep on creating an enemy in order to do their moral work. Participants realize they may meet the same people next week at a clinic on opposite sides of the sidewalk. Many have grown to say, "When I go there now, I'm looking at people differently, because I've re-humanized them in another safe and trustworthy space."

At the heart of relinquishing our claim to rightness and practicing the art of creative compromise resides the sincere desire to listen deeply. The Chinese verb "to listen" is composed of five characters:

"ears, you, eyes, focused attention, and heart." When we listen with our whole selves, we're validating others with all our attentive equipment. Listening brings us closer; for differences don't build walls, judgments do.

When we listen intently, we're saying: "I respect your views, your feelings, and your thoughts. You have a right to them and a right to express them, and I welcome them in order to build our relationship, on the road toward creating a more beautiful and loving world!"

Finding common ground means embracing the bedrock humanity we all share, and the profoundest dimension of our common civilization is the fact that we've all mourned. At one time or another, every sister and every brother among us will grieve the loss of a dream, a job, a relationship, a loved one to death. There's nothing that binds us more closely across races, genders, countries, classes, and orientations than acknowledging our share in life's unyielding anguish and calamity.

In short, we'll make no progress in reconciliation with the fiercest of our foes, until we've empathized with their soul-deep aches and torments.

There isn't a more dramatic story of such bridging than what happened in my hometown of San Diego. It's the story of the *Tariq Khamisa Foundation*, committed to breaking the escalating cycle of youth violence and planting seeds of hope for our children's future.

While delivering pizza on a cool San Diego night in January of 1995, a shot rang out and young Tariq Khamisa fell, mortally wounded. At the other end of the gun was a 14-year-old gang member.

From the beginning, Azim Khamisa, the dead boy's father, saw "victims at both ends of the gun." So he reached out to the shooter's family. Azim embraced the boy's grandfather, Ples Felix, and asked him to join forces against youth violence. Out of that remarkable union was born the *Tariq Khamisa Foundation* whose sole purpose is to stop children from killing children, to break the escalating cycle of youth violence and plant seeds of hope for our children's future.

TKF brings its message of peace and nonviolent choices to school children through the innovative Violence Impact Forum program, a lively, multimedia presentation. It has been presented to over 10,000 children, in the fourth through ninth grades, with the resultant reduction in attitudes that lead to gangs, revenge, and violence.

Remarkably, the senseless shooting of Tariq Khamisa has sparked the creation of a powerful violence prevention program that works. As Azim puts it: "I will mourn Tariq's death for the rest of my life. Now, however, grief has been transformed into a powerful commitment to change. Change is urgently needed in a society where children kill children."

That's a mighty dramatic illustration, unlike most we may ever encounter firsthand in our own journeys, but you and I can *feel* into this tragedy at some poignant, visceral level. Why? Because there's been or will come a time in our lives when we too must be united with our opposition, and the unifying cement requires our respect, our compromise, our listening, and our shared inconsolable pain. Perhaps it's a divorce that ripples on, or a seemingly irretrievable break with a child or a sibling, or an unsuspected firing from our job, or a devastating church-hurt.

During our lifetimes we humans experience, in common, the reality of massive sorrow and inexplicable joy, and, more than that, we also share the gift of earth and the challenge of dying. Those primal experiences alone should make us committed to doing our damnedest to stop the cycle of human violence.

FOR REFLECTION AND DISCUSSION

1. Amplify upon what it means to claim that forgiveness constitutes an ought of opportunity rather than an ought of obligation.

2. Describe two examples, one from your personal life and another from your congregational experience, where the process of forgiveness has been successful.

3. Where have you found unforgiveness or partial forgiveness to be the most viable options in your spiritual life? Describe as fully as you wish.

4. Colleague Anita Farber-Robertson has said:
   Unitarian Universalists have made a covenant to be held accountable. It is a difficult covenant, faithfulness is hard. We break it individually and congregationally. And continually we work to repair the ruptures we have wrought.

   In the current life of your congregation, what are the processes, guidelines, or covenants that keep you accountable to one another?

5. Unitarian Universalist thinker Harry Meserve offered this prayer in our current hymnal:
   God of our mixed up, tragic, aspiring, doubting and insurgent lives, help us to be as good as in our hearts we have always wanted to be.

   Ponder and dialogue.

HOSPITALITY

Anybody can create community with people who believe just like they do. The true test of community rests in the ability to create it with people who disagree with us.
—Lee Barker

Our Unitarian Universalist "good news" affirms that God prefers the pluralism of a world of strangers to the uniformity of a sacred society…we are called to create holy communities where strangers are not only welcome but where all are enjoined to do the work of healing and transformation by wrestling with the strangers within themselves.
—Abhi Janamanchi

Over the past fifty years, there has been no more seismic shift in our Unitarian Universalist theological landscape than the widespread allegiance to hospitality in our movement, in terms of both inreach and outreach. Imperfect to be sure, our visitor and new member integration processes have been fortified. It's been rumored that we attract more visitors than the Mormons do, yet our retention rate pales in comparison. Hence, we're laboring on warmly welcoming and actively keeping newcomers in our ranks. Several of our congregations, when considering new paid positions, turn to hiring membership coordinators.

In our *Embracing Our Theological Diversity* book, commissioners were responsive to the need for greater respectfulness toward the first-timer:

> *In our congregations cultural competency includes the practices of humility, listening, patience, graciousness, and the holiest of curiosity. Rather than asking a newcomer, "What brings you here? How did you find us?" what if we were to ask as the Tibetans used to do, "And to what sublime tradition do you belong?"*
>
> *However we do it, when we communicate graciousness, generosity,*

and openness, we represent Unitarian Universalism at its best.

Some comic wrote that religion mainly focuses on all saints, while Unitarian Universalism welcomes all *sorts*. That line draws a chuckle, for, indeed, we comprise a fairly unconventional crew in terms of theologies and lifestyles. We like it that way, and a healthy faith can poke fun rather than taking itself too seriously. Yet, labeling us all sorts misses our unswerving commitment to being a faith of all *souls* as well.

We're interested in saluting not only the known greats of history, but also the last, the lost, the least among us—indeed, every sister and brother who's walked this earth. That's why more of our congregations across the land are named *All Souls* than any other moniker. Unitarian Universalism aspires to become a religion of universal embrace.

On a practical level, regardless of how open-minded Unitarian Universalism may profess itself to be, we're habitually leaving someone out of our sacred circle. In a sincere effort to widen our horizons and embrace, local congregations must regularly take stock: Who's missing on our campus? Who's not here but might be? What perspective has trouble being heard in our parish? Then our job is to find ways to invite the absent ones into our company, if they choose to enter. We do this not out of a need to convert but out of a mandate to converse: for a robust theology can always benefit from another voice and fresh viewpoint.

Our conviction about the inherent worth of every person is the cornerstone upon which everything else in our theology is built. Our ancestors were considered heretics to be hunted down and burned at the stake. Monarchs and priests considered people evil and sinful by nature, to be suppressed and controlled. Slowly and painfully, the sacredness of human life has been wrested from spiritual tyrants and political dictators.

Still, only a small fraction of the human family is truly protected and encouraged to grow as free people. Religious freedom remains nonexistent in large portions of the world and is threatened in our own country by the intolerant positions of certain theologies. For Unitarian Universalism, full dignity isn't just a political concern, it's a religious mandate. We believe that none of us can be valued for long unless all of us are considered of worth. We bet and conduct our lives on that proposition.

The theological theme at stake is hospitality.

Most every prominent world religion has announced that there's one thing greater than the name of God itself: hospitality. As card-carrying freethinkers, some historical evidence for the relevance of hospitality is in order.

First, from a Hebrew proverb: "Hospitality toward strangers is greater than reverence for the name of God." Then, from Christian scriptures: "I was a stranger, and you took me in." Muslim theology also reports that on the proverbial Day of Judgment humans must give account of all expenditures except those of hospitality, which Allah would be ashamed to demand.

We're not saying that God isn't important. Unitarian Universalism would never dismiss the power and pertinence of a mature grasp of the Eternal Spirit.

Talking about a mature grasp of God, I confess to being unimpressed with our Unitarian Universalist advertisement in a recent (2008) *Time Magazine*. Considerable marketing ingenuity went into this clever text and certainly lots of cash as well, but the core of the ad—IS GOD KEEPING YOU FROM GOING TO CHURCH?—bothered me.

The ad is simply degrading to those in our ranks who happen to believe in their own understanding of the Infinite One. As for the skeptics and nonbelievers in our movement, in what ways could that ad prove favorable to their religious voyage? A portion of the ad truly appeals to me–namely, the part that says: "Nurture your spirit. Help heal the world." It celebrates our yoked commitments as Unitarian

Universalists to growing our own souls while making the world a better place. When that slogan is embodied, our theology catches fire; our flame is fanned.

God will remain God whether or not discussed, advertised, or worshiped by human beings. In my estimation, God wants human beings to spend our energy where it matters most: taking good care of the universe, not quarreling over any name. The Great Spirit's urging us to be concerned about earthly service not heavenly speculation. Hospitality toward strangers is greater than reverence for the name of God itself.

There's even more scriptural evidence for the importance of hospitality. According to Jewish tradition, the sin of Sodom wasn't homosexuality, as we're led to believe by religious orthodoxy (and by the rash of recent discriminatory proposals passed across America against marriage equality), but rather the sin of Sodom is insensitivity to the needs of the stranger. Abraham was famous for his hospitality, keeping his tent open during the day in all four directions, and whenever he saw strangers approach, Abraham would rush to greet, then feed, them.

Abraham tried to prepare food for messengers who came to tell him of the fulfillment of his dream to have a child with Sarah before he even knew who they were. Those same messengers proceeded to the house of Abraham's nephew Lot in the town of Sodom, where they were accosted by an angry mob who demanded Lot hand over the strangers.

Rabbis have long argued that this was consistent with the Sodomites' general refusal to treat the powerless in a welcoming and generous way. It is for this sin—inhospitableness not homosexuality—that the city of Sodom merits the fire and brimstone and people turning into salt.

One more biblical illustration to confirm the virtue of hospitality, then we'll move on to its relevance in our personal and institutional lives as Unitarian Universalist theologians.

The Judgment Day, in Christian scriptures, is depicted as a final banquet where everyone will be invited to partake. People from the East and West, North and South will join you and me for a scrumptious feast. Make no mistake: there will be folks present whose tongues we won't recognize (sorry, English won't be the assumed language), persons from places we've never seen and places our homeland has even bombed, and they'll surely be plenty of people who wouldn't be found on any of our personal guest lists.

Furthermore, we won't be merely gathering for hors d'oeuvres; we're going to sit down and consume a lavish, full-course meal together. Strangers and enemies will be summoned to unite as one people; for in sharing food together we become companions, literally "those who eat together."

That's how huge and holy the charge to hospitality is.

Hospitality is rooted in a sense of radical openness. We're called to live with open hands that both hold those near and serve those afar and to live with open eyes, or as the Buddhists phrase it, to see life with "unfurnished" eyes, that is, eyes empty of mental clutter and inherited furniture.

Openness means living with minds receptive to surprise inklings of the holy. It also summons us to open our throats: loosening our jaws in order to unleash our voices in singing the wonders of creation or in bellowing against its wrongs.

Ironically, one of the first sermons delivered during my seminary days back in 1965 was entitled *Ephphatha*, based on the biblical passage from Mark where Jesus engaged a deaf man who also had an impediment in his speech. He said to the man: "Ephphatha, that is 'be opened,' and the man's ears were opened, his tongue was released, and he spoke plainly."

Even though I preached from a different theological angle back then, its basic truths obtain. Being opened up to the new idea and the strange person, then remaining open, still signals a governing motif of my depth theology: to stand wide open to self, to others, to nature, to the Eternal. To be open to all that scares, blocks, or burdens us. As Unitarian Universalists we contend that theology ablaze is marked by exhibiting an open hand, an open heart, and an open home.

In my 44 years of ordained ministry I've witnessed stunning transformations where lives crack open and pour forth in gratitude and compassion, where ears have been deaf to fresh counsel, and then, with a gentle caress, open up. Oh, the marvels of opening up and staying open that you and I have experienced as progressive religious pilgrims.

The truth is that we come into existence with our fists clenched as babies, but when we arrive at death's door, our hands are open. During the intervening span of days, our mission is to gradually unclench our fists, peeling back our fingers one by one, relinquishing level after level of clinging and cloying...opening our hands in love and concern toward all that crosses our path. That complete process is called hospitality.

What does it mean for our local congregations?

It surely entails greeters, potlucks, name-tags, regular orientation sessions, pictorial directories. All of that and far more. Reasonable hospitality goes beneath warmth and extends beyond welcome. It signals a revolutionary way of being religious, of doing congregational life. It means being a people of open minds, loving hearts, and helping hands...for starters, within our parish walls; then in our given society, for sure; and finally throughout distant corners of the universe—being open to all that greets us along life's path: ideas, things, people, animals...the whole of Creation.

Hospitality isn't mere social grace; it's a spiritual vocation with an inescapable moral cost. It evokes our most basic religious need to know and be known, to embrace and be embraced. In truth, our spiritual sanity and international safety bank on hospitality. If we don't practice it, locally and globally, we'll grow increasingly aloof, alienated, then hostile.

We start by putting a name and face on the people we encounter daily—at the gas station, grocery store, and flower shop. These folks aren't incidental to our lives; they're our traveling buddies. I often tell our young people that if they really want to know what my religion looks like as their minister, I encourage them to follow me around during a typical day and see how I, a frail and faulty creature, aspire to treat things and touch people. In turn, I'll be honored to spend a day at their haunts. These youngsters will also need to review my check stubs, along with seeing how I negotiate my spare time, and I want to see how they're spending their loose change and idle hours as well.

The scope of authentic hospitality is far-ranging, as expansive as the entire Cosmos, starting at home, beginning with our very own selves. Far too many of us need to grow better acquainted with our inner beings...before we die. We suffer from severe self-estrangement. The paradox of human existence remains: we'll never achieve any better relationship with others than what we've mustered with ourselves.

Hospitality doesn't stop with self-exploration. As religious travelers, we must enter ever-widening circles of respectful, loving engagement. Unitarian Universalism affirms the supreme dignity of every person, contending that even the most troubled and troubling among us are redeemable. We believe in an Infinite Spirit that holds every creature in its loving caress and challenges us to follow suit.

Hospitality forces a congregation to take a spiritual audit about how it's actually addressing issues of inclusion and affection, how it's balancing the core values of independence and intimacy. No congregation is perfect. Our San Diego parish labored hard, for a quarter of a century, to create an intentionally diverse and welcoming congregation, and we were always what an intern sagely labeled as "imperfectly healthy."

We repeatedly fall short of our noblest ideals. The goal of hospitality remains progress not perfection, to stay at the table and planted on the path, to grow gradually more inclusive, paying attention to who might be left out in our hymns or readings, leadership circles or social action efforts, and in the manifold encounters of daily congregational life.

We seldom lack moments for just and merciful service, but too often we lack heart. Hospitality, above all else, dares to stretch our puny, brittle, wary hearts. Hospitality signals harkening to the deeper sounds of every precious human being, especially the cries of the abandoned and the misunderstood.

Unitarian Universalist theology contends that all of us, in one way or another, at one time or another, are the caves in which others might find shelter and kinship and we in them. Friends and strangers, hosts and guests constitute one humanity groping toward our original unity.

Which brings us back to God. It's our Unitarian Universalist persuasion that the Infinite Spirit of Love is cheering humanity on as we struggle to practice hospitality. If God could speak, I imagine God would be saying something like this: "Come on sisters, come on brothers, I know you can do it. Remember that's why I created you. So get to work. Above all else, my name included, be hospitable, open your mind, open your heart, and open your hands, because none of my creatures are going to be saved until everyone's saved."

As Unitarian Universalist theologian John Nichols proclaims:

Our Universalism is a heresy. We believe that if there is a loving God, this God will save all souls. If, in some other realm, there is a great clubhouse of souls, everybody's getting in. Catholics, Protestants, Jews, Muslims, agnostics, atheists: everybody's getting in.

FOR REFLECTION AND DISCUSSION

1. Charles Howe, in his volume on Universalism entitled
    The Larger Faith, tells a relevant story:
    The Humiliati *held yearly retreats from 1946 until 1954 in
    which this group of ministers addressed issues in theology, wor-
    ship, and liturgy. Committed to the renewal of their denomina-
    tion via a universalized Universalism, they adopted the symbol
    of the off-center cross enclosed by a circle, which represented the
    all-embracing nature of Universalism...the off-center cross rec-
    ognized Universalism's Christian roots while at the same time
    implying that Christianity was no longer necessarily central to
    the faith.*

    This symbol also reflects, with its expansive open space,
    our contemporary commitment to creating a theolo-
    gy that always has room for the new person or notion.
    What's your interpretation of this evocative symbol?

2. Rosemary Bray McNatt challenges our commitment to
    authentic inclusivity and diversity with these sentiments:
    *What I know about being inclusive, crossing from culture to cul-
    ture, learning the language of diversity, is that it's the work of
    a lifetime. It is had to accept people who are not like you, who
    do not talk the way you do, or believe the things you believe, or
    dress or vote as you do. It is even harder to appreciate them for
    the things about them that are not like you...the truth is this: if
    there is no justice, there will be no peace...and if we cannot bring
    justice into the small circle of our individual lives, we cannot
    hope to bring justice to the world.*

How does her statement relate to the call to be hospitable?

3. Denny Davidoff, former Moderator of the UUA, in a sermon preached in 1998, closed her talk on "Loving the Questions" with words from Alice Walker:
    Our last five minutes on Earth are running out. We can spend those minutes in meanness, exclusivity, and self-righteous disparagement of those who are different from us, or we can spend them consciously embracing every glowing soul who wanders within our reach...Perhaps the greatest treasure left to us, maybe the only one, is that we can still choose.

    Share your thoughts.

4. Robette Dias had these challenging words to offer on the theology of hospitality:
    It is the Journey Toward Wholeness program that sustains me as a Unitarian Universalist. It's what gives me hope that someday somewhere there will be a Beloved Community. With this diverse group, we make mistakes and get angry with one another, apologize and forgive along the way. Yet we had to learn to stay in relationship with one another, stay at this UU table, stay with respect and dignity and see this anti-racism job through. It brings out the best of me. I can finally bring my UU self that operates in the dominant society together with my Native self that keeps me connected to where I come from and who I really am.

    Reflect and discuss.

HOPE

We embrace a sense of possibility—an openness toward that which is un-known—the not-yet, the new, the different—an openness that fosters quali-ties of authenticity, curiosity, creativity, courage and compassion, all of which nurture hope and healing in our world.
—*Embracing Our Theological Diversity* (2005)

What gives hope its power is not the accumulation of demonstrable fact but the release of human energies generated by the longing for something better. The capacity for hope is the most significant fact in life.
—Norman Cousins

From within this world, my despair is transformed to hope, and I begin anew the legacy of caring.
—Thandeka

Shortly after I entered our Unitarian Universalist movement in the late 1960s, there was a continental contest for framing our faith in 100 words or less. The winning statement by Edward Schempp still rings true, as a realistically hopeful assessment of our progressive theology:

> *Unitarian Universalism is faith in people, hope for tomorrow's child, confidence in a continuity that spans all times. It looks not to a perfect heaven but toward a good earth. It is respectful of the past, but not limited to it. It is trust in growing and conspiracy with change. It is spiritual responsibility for a moral tomorrow.*

Jim Wallis, another progressive theologian, has noted that hope is believing in spite of the evidence and watching the evidence change—no, helping the evidence change. Hope is the dynamic of history and the energy that stokes the fire of transformation.

Hope is necessary to cultivate from the moment we emerge from

the womb. The real division in our world is between those who believe human beings are incapable of managing the incredibly hard
and complex problems confronting us and those who look at the
same problems and feel we have a real chance and are willing to give
it their best shot. The chasm lies between the void of vision and the
enervated on the one hand, and on the other hand, the buoyant and
hopeful people.

The philosophy expressed in *Theology Ablaze* is committed to
navigating a way of living between the romantic extremes of utopia
and doomsday, between delirium and depression. We belong to a
hopeful faith. Hopers stay on purpose even when not immediately
successful. St. Paul said: "Now faith, hope, and love abide, these three,
and the greatest of these is love." We counter: they're all crucial, but
hope—the unsung virtue of the lot—dare not get lost in the shuffle.
For we can neither keep faith nor share love, if we're not brimming
with genuine, durable hope.

Our religion doesn't suggest that the world's problems are
solved, far from it; however, good and hopeful news frequently slips
beneath our contemporary radar screens. It's the job of those who
belong to a life-affirming, this-worldly faith-on-fire, such as Unitarian
Universalism, to stand tall and shout forth evidence of good news.

Awhile back, an issue of the *UTNE Reader* highlighted a slew of
hopeful data and stories. Here are sample findings.

Labor, community activists, and women's groups have mounted
a spirited campaign against the behemoth of behemoths, Wal-Mart,
and a California jury awarded $172 million to thousands of employ-
ees at Wal-Mart Stores who were denied such basic rights as lunch
breaks, with 40 similar lawsuits pending in other states.

Although the world's population has doubled between 1960 and
2000, the rate of growth is now declining. Families on every continent are having fewer children, and in the past 30 years the global
average fertility rate has fallen from 6 children per woman to 2.8
children per woman.

Literacy in the developing world has jumped from 47%, at the time of our merger, to 70% today, meaning that more people have tools to improve their standard of living.

With respect to the environment, global production of ozone-depleting chemicals has dropped more than 80% since an international agreement was reached in 1987.

As for health, a child today will live, in developing countries, an average of 8 years longer than a child born 30 years ago. Life expectancy is more than 60 years old in all regions of the world except for sub-Saharan Africa, where, because of HIV/AIDS, it's just under fifty years.

Negative stats exist as well, but hopers don't let us forget the positive facts. Progress isn't a pipe dream, but an indisputable possibility when people put their hearts and minds into making the world a better place—for folks of all classes, colors, convictions, and conditions. In a *progressive* religion, our goal is to keep on advancing, progressing, evolving toward our espoused hope of "nurturing your spirit, help heal our world."

What dreams, both private and public, are you realizing in your daily and congregational life? Are you saying Yes to loving more deeply those near and dear to you? Are you saying Yes to greater mercy and justice where you work, play, and worship? Are you saying Yes to a one-world family, to a planet at peace, to the well-being of all living entities? Are you saying Yes to an ever-thickening theology?

Unitarian Universalists have deliberately thrown our lot with an unrelentingly hopeful faith, and by hope we're not referring to optimism. The optimist tends to be fanciful and dreamy-eyed, leaving the world's problems up to George or God, Gertrude or Goddess to solve while remaining a bouncy, mindless cheerleader on the sidelines. The optimist resembles the proverbial person who gazes at the stars but is perennially at the mercy of puddles in the road.

Instead, the hoper isn't convinced that something will happen yet remains willing to work his or her rear off to make sure that it might just come to be. The optimist lies back; the hoper moves forward. The hoper is an activated human being, one who arouses in self and others a passion for the promising. Hopers stay on purpose even when not presently rewarded.

We shouldn't be surprised that the words *hope* and *hop* come from the same root, one that means "to leap up in expectation." Hopeful folks are filled with a palpable eagerness for what is to come. When we're hopping, we're real hopers, and conversely, when we hope, we're likely to be hopping about.

The hoper differs from the pessimist as well as the optimist. Realism would often demand pessimism. Nonetheless, the hopeful person talks not in terms of crisis, a concept that usually overwhelms and immobilizes us, but in terms of issues, challenges, and jobs…with our names scrawled on some of them. Everything grows manageable when reduced to doable tasks.

The pessimist (who's but a cynic in the early stages of the disease) says: "Blessed are they who believe in nothing, for they shan't be disappointed!" Hopers, on the contrary, agree with that portion of the *Desiderata* that says: "Whatever your labors and aspirations in the noisy confusion of life, keep peace with your soul. With all its sham, drudgery, and broken dreams, it's still a beautiful world."

Hopers know that the best anti-depressant available on the market involves movement of mouth, movement of body, movement of conscience, movement of heart…moving outside our own com- miseration to connect with the universe in loving deeds.

Cynicism lies all around us; in fact, in the past few years, a new sort of progressive cynicism, if you will, has arisen. Progressive cynics harbor the conviction that Western culture and American society are *hopelessly* oppressive. Unitarian Universalists agree that our culture is drenched in racism, sexism, homophobia, and a whole array of interlinking oppressions.

I know, for as a white heterosexual male I'm the Pharaoh in most freedom-fighters' Exoduses, merely because of my given identity.

But while reality is profoundly oppressive, it isn't terminally so!

Years back, a disheartened and desperate, albeit repentant, former evangelical minister came to our Unitarian Universalist parish. Ron was saddled with a child molestation conviction. He was paying the necessary penalty for his grievous misbehavior, even as he was consciously trying to restore his life. Sanctions kept Ron from being within 100 yards of any of our children and youth; consequently he was unable to attend worship services on Sundays but was interested in participating in several of our men's spirituality experiences on weekday evenings.

Ours was a parish that had been active both in the mature masculinity movement within Unitarian Universalism as well as combating gender violence programs for years: sponsoring support circles for victims of sexual abuse as well as rehabilitation efforts for perpetrators of relational violence. We harbored a supportive community within which Ron could intentionally rehabilitate his life.

Ron was involved for over two years at First Church, sometimes awkwardly, yet persistently aspiring to redeem his existence. Our faith-community proved to be a useful haven for his arduous recovery. Several years later, after Ron had left our area, he called me, out of the blue, and thanked our "beloved community" (his words) for companioning him during his travail as well as delivering continual rays of hope:

> *During my worst times, you were there...always representing the burning hope of the flaming chalice. I want you to know that I'm still firmly planted on the road of rebuilding my moral and spiritual identity. I remain hopeful in my recovering. You were instrumental in saving my life...thank God, thank you First Churchers.*
>
> *Filled with hope...your spiritual buddy, Ron*

Our hopeful theology leads Unitarian Universalism to assert that no problem in human relations is ever truly insoluble. We may never solve it during our lifetimes. Nevertheless, you and I belong to a religion that stays ablaze by refusing to quit on justice, quit on mercy, quit on redemption, quit on humankind. We keep on keeping on, because we're incurable hopers!

Our Unitarian Universalist aim is faithfulness not success. Especially in the greater world, it's downright crucial for each of us, in her or his own way, to go on record as opposing evil. It's important to be effective in halting some of the rampant injustices in society; but if we can't stop them, then at least we must oppose them.

As author Barbara Kingsolver rightly urges: "The very least we can do in our life is figure out what we hope for. And the most we can do is live inside that hope."

In counseling, whenever someone feels despondent, the best therapeutic advice I can muster is to help break down their seemingly monstrous malaise into controllable pieces and then to locate one or two relatively easy, beginning homework assignments—actions they can effectively achieve in order to nibble away at their "mountainous" misery.

The tasks may be modest, they usually are, apparently inconsequential, but slowly and surely a breakthrough may emerge. When we're weary and beaten down, it's wise for us to do small rather than think big, to take a step rather than fantasize a leap.

The essence of hoping is its capacity to generate new directions, to turn problems into bite-size options. Optimism leaves us imagining; pessimism leaves us paralyzed; hope gets us going.

Sadly, morally progressive folks like Unitarian Universalists often fail to act until all the facts are in, which never happens. Or we fail to act until the experts agree, which seldom occurs. Or we fail to act until a more favorable time, which doesn't arrive. Lots of well-intentioned people never witness to our ethical commitments and spiritual charges. In short, we weasel out.

We can't say or bear everything, but we can say some things and we can bear a lot. And we must. If not now, when? If not us, who?

St. Augustine was right: "Hope has two beautiful daughters.

Their names are anger and courage: anger at the way things are, and courage to see that they don't remain the way they are." If we really want to understand, let alone live, hope, then it's smart to honor these two children.

First, we need to insure that our anger is used for impact not injury. Second, we need to be careful never to mistake courage for foolishness, where we commit crazy Evel Knievel sorts of stuff. In short, don't confuse anger with vengeance or courage with folly. Anger is rage for a worthy result, and courage is boldness for a useful outcome.

We've been privy in the last few years to so many sterling examples of anger and courage, since the terrorist bombings in New York and Washington, D.C., the wars in Iraq and Afghanistan, the genocide in Darfur, the horrendous fires in California and the devastating hurricanes in the South and in Haiti. Think of all the angry and courageous—therewith hopeful—people, who've dared to convert their fury into brave deeds of justice and mercy.

We humans are capable of answering hate and handling tragedy with sufficient anger and courage…born of hope.

In this day of unpredictable change, of great interhuman crises, of pervasive boredom and meaninglessness, despair often seems to be the last word. Folks decide, by preference or default, to conduct, in Thoreau's classic words, "lives of quiet desperation." Conversely, Unitarian Universalists choose to risk lives of hope, one day at a time, one struggle at a time, one possibility at a time.

A case in point is the homeless. The reality is that homelessness is getting worse. Therefore, the pessimist mopes, watches the tube, and vegetates. The optimist contends that homelessness is the government's problem and believes politicians will solve it someday for the rest of us.

The hoper says: "There but for the grace of God go my relatives, friends, associates, or myself. Homelessness is my problem as a member of the human race. I will protest it with my words and deeds. Whenever my sister or brother suffers, I suffer too, and stand accountable to do what I can to alleviate the suffering. Homelessness is not merely an aesthetic problem to be cleaned up. It is a social, moral, theological challenge to be faced, because it includes the sisters and brothers of my human family."

In the Hebrew scriptures it says, "For to those who are joined to all the living there is hope." The hoper believes that. When we affirm our irrevocable connectedness with one another, hope will flourish; we naturally become more compassionate toward fellow members of the global family.

May we never belittle the efforts we can manage everyday on behalf of hope: efforts at work to right a wrong, efforts to support affordable housing or foster a more inclusive Boy Scouts organization or elect a more fair-minded school board, as well as efforts to create more justice and joy in our own jobs, households, and congregations. There will never be a shortage of ways for each of us to do what we do best...in order to fill our world with genuine hope.

Hope stands as a central theological imperative of our chosen faith. We're charged to join the caravan of the hopeful. Where? Wherever we live. When? Right now? How? Through being angry and courageous enough to make our corner of the universe more kindhearted and more peaceful.

I grew up thinking that the term *amen* meant "so be it," as if we were merely adding an exclamation point to what had just been spoken or sung in community. I have since learned that amen more correctly translates not as "so be it" but as "so *might* it be." Amen refers not to an actuality so much as an aspiration.

Therefore, whenever I voice an "amen" in private or public, I am, in effect, pledging to do everything possible to help my sentiments and convictions come true. Amen isn't another sweet superfluous four-letter word thrown in for magical measure. Amen is a promise to translate our hopes into deeds that heal and empower the cosmos we cradle in common.

FOR REFLECTION AND DISCUSSION

1. Describe how you would distinguish between hope and optimism, as well as skepticism and cynicism.

2. How can our worship services and religious education programs be filled with authentic possibilities and genuine hope rather than leaving us downcast and immobilized with either guilt or fear? Give specific responses for both realms.

3. Unitarian Universalist theologian Sharon Welch offers sage counsel when she avers:
    Rather than a hope for eventual victory, for a world without injustice or serious conflict, I describe the power of having a more modest hope, a hope for resilience, a hope for company along the way.

    What does "a more modest hope" look like in your congregational life and in the larger world scene?

4. Michael Hogue, professor of theology at Meadville Lombard Theological School, contends that creative and compassionate theology needs to become "doxological." In other words: "What do we praise, what do we desire, what do we sing about, and for what do we hope?"

    Reflect and discuss.

DEATH

*Religion is our human response to the dual reality of
being alive and having to die.*
—Forrest Church

*I would like to believe when I die that I have given myself away like a tree
that sows seeds every spring and never counts the loss, because it is not
loss, it is adding to future life. It is the tree's way of being. Strongly rooted,
perhaps, but spilling out its treasure on the wind.*
—May Sarton

*In truth, everything arises in order to disappear; everything we have, every-
thing we think we are, must at some point be surrendered, for it is only on
loan from the bounty of the Divine.*
—Alistair Shearer

Our appreciation of "earth-centered traditions" would beckon
Unitarian Universalism to acknowledge life *and* death as yoked
realities in "the sacred circle of life." Nowhere else in our current
Article II is there any explicit recognition of our human finitude and
mortality. A commentary upon the core theological theme of death
is timely, as our association celebrates its midlife passage and forges
its future, cognizant of the fact that not only human beings die but
religious movements age, even wither as well.

Our movement matured considerably when dealing openly and
caringly, during the recent decades, with the AIDS deaths of so many
of our own members as well as community fellow travelers. Unitarian
Universalism, in countless villages, was one religious site that would
honestly and properly memorialize those who fell to this dread dis-
ease. One of our gifted and beloved ministers, Mark deWolfe, in a
sermon preceding his own premature death to AIDS, penned these
words:

It takes courage to face death, and it takes courage to live in the face of death. The sources of such courage are not in the outside world, they are not in special revelations or in the inspirational messages of gurus. The sources of courage are found in the inner soul, nurtured with love, inspired by faith, united in the worshipping heart.

DeWolfe found and embodied such courage, both living and dying as a servant of our sacred heritage.

THEOLOGY ABLAZE contends that death is real and to be treated as such, especially in our death-denying culture. We pronounce in our Unitarian Universalist memorial celebrations, at the very outset, that "Joanna Doakes has died; you and I are alive"; so we know who's still breathing in the room and who isn't. The spirit may endure, but the body of the dead person exists no more, and that difference is saluted in our memorials rather than camouflaged in euphemisms like "she's gone away" or "he's passed on."

Death cannot be tamed. Death is unknown. Death is mysterious. Death is death, and a central key to living fully is acceptance of that fact.

Death's not only inevitable, it's also natural in the overall sweep of things.

About 500 million years ago, all of life was composed of algae and amoebas, of a unified, continuous existence, growing at one end and shedding at the other. Into that world of endless glop came the transfiguring event of death. Without death, life could never have risen out of the immortal slime. Now, death and life are inextricably linked; both constitute necessary gifts of a unified reality.

Unitarian Universalist theology proceeds further. Death is desirable as well as inevitable and natural. Death's presence intensifies both our capacity to love and our impulse to create meaning. Life possesses daily urgency and importance, because we won't always be around. We embrace life all the more, since it's limited.

As we round life's unfolding bends, we personally begin to realize, given the cosmic sweep of things, that our individual lifetimes have been altogether brief. We have 10, 20, maybe 30 autumns remaining, so the final elder assignment means coming to grips with our transience.

Shedding objects and dreams is one thing, but shedding our body, the same shell we've carted around all our waking moments—for better and for worse—poses a heftier challenge. Death comprises the passage where we lose consciousness, lose our connectedness, altogether lose our known universe. Life's ultimate surrender requires consenting to die, letting go, and letting be...as we migrate toward the utter and vast unknown.

As expected, this transition is fraught with complications. There exist religionists who engage in what might be called a hasty release. Once they reach their fifties (the current vintage of our merged movement), they seem to live with one foot already planted in the grave. Every trouble or torment spells, for these folks, a death warrant. They mistake resignation for surrender. They're numbered among the walking dead; they've lost perceptible lust for life.

My Uncle Rene was the exact opposite. He showed great reluctance in letting go of anything or letting life just be, during his homestretch. Rene kept fighting every mounting loss, since, in some weird way, he believed he was deathless. As he put it: "Tommy, I plan to be immortal...now, not later!"

Possibly there have been times when you or I have also felt immortal. However, life, to be finished well, demands a willingness to accept our impermanence. To do so actually heightens our sensitivity to the preciousness of every moment.

Psalm 90 announces that humans are akin to grass, that the years of our lives may be three score and ten, or, with luck, four score. Everyone dies, sooner or later; thus the Psalmist goes on to admonish: "Teach us to number our days that we might apply our hearts unto wisdom." This passage bids us to engage every hour of existence—its sorrows and joys and blends thereof—with steady faithfulness and courage..."applying our hearts unto wisdom."

Whatever our personal Unitarian Universalist view following death might be—resurrection of the body or immortality of the soul, reincarnation or an eternal abyss—there manifestly comes a time of physical cessation, when we no longer walk this earth in our present bodily form. Mortality cannot be dodged. At some juncture, we must admit that death is natural, sometimes even safe, and that we cannot fail at it. That's a harsh recognition, nonetheless a critical one for humans to make.

When's the optimal time to die? Of course, it depends upon circumstance and condition. Your peculiar timetable may not match mine. Nonetheless, we all can likely resonate with the sentiments of Henry Cadbury, distinguished scholar and teacher who lived well into his nineties. When asked how he felt about the prospect of his death, Cadbury replied with a knowing smile: "Well, I don't want to live too long, and I don't want to die too soon." That's reasonable counsel: to die sometime between too long *and* too soon should prove just right. If we're lucky, that's how we'll meet our demise.

In any case, when we make peace with death's inevitability, we're frequently filled with a feeling of serenity; we're able to surrender to the cosmic mystery, to let go and let be. Along with Jesus of Nazareth, we can say: "It is finished." The Jewish prophet was urging home-stretchers to tie up loose ends, to resolve unsettled matters...in sum, to apply the finishing touches to our earthly trek. For, at the moment of death, not only is our physical, this-worldly sojourn over, we're also stretching homeward, bringing our journey toward a measure of graceful completion.

Surrendering is such an awkward art to master...excruciatingly so for high-control, tight-fisted, hyper-questing Westerners. It furnishes a delicate mixture of being passive yet staying active. Surrendering demands emptying. The required skill is giving our selves over to another person or principle, place or process without giving our selves away.

Surrendering means letting ourselves be who we truly are, rather than clinging to what we used to be or might have become. It means permitting ourselves to slow down, just be our own age, as robustly as possible.

Surrendering entails relinquishing "stuff" as well. As I've been drawing my full-time ministries toward completion, I've undertaken, at several different venues, a radical trimming program: ridding myself of 80% of my books, 60% of my files, and 40% of my professional collectibles.

I've done this for several reasons. Foremost, I desire to journey less laden through my homestretch years. I also enjoy placing my professional treasures directly into the hands of up-and-coming colleagues who personally relish them. This process has freed me to be awake in the present rather than rummaging around in my past. Of course, I'm making mistakes; there are possessions I should have kept and paraphernalia I've already missed. So it goes; that's the gamble of shedding.

Futile dreams, theological biases, and festering emotions need to be shorn as well. Surrendering has everything to with interior mop-up, releasing obsolete and hurtful memories…a crucial route to en-*lighten*-ment. The afternoon of existence is arguably the supreme season to reflect, sort out, and choose only what seems to remain worthy of our humanity.

Surrendering entails bowing to the needs and purposes of the universe, of the community, and finally of ourselves. Bowing daily to all that arises in our lifetime, dropping our heads in gratitude and acceptance, enables us to get off those high horses we're prone to canter as proud adults.

Surrendering dwells at the core of the Hindu greeting *namaste*, roughly translated: "I bow to the eternal spirit within all of existence that dwells within myself as well." I've found that as long as we possess awareness, no human being is too weak or wretched to utter some version of *namaste* as a fervent blessing to the unity of the cosmos.

In surrendering to other persons, to animals, to the Infinite Spirit of Life and Love, submission isn't required, but trust is. Surrendering is about forging a vow, pledging our troth, offering and keeping our dearest trust.

As we trust the flow of life's homestretch, we're able to surrender to whatever sacrifices and secrets unfold, even to death itself. Yielding unto death entails entering what Buddhists call "the Great Doubt," yet in a spirit of what our Universalists called "rest assured."

It's told of the spiritual master Krishnamurti that when he was quite old and frail, he happened to be addressing a large assembly with customary gentleness. He recognized a questioner slowly, indeed haltingly; then he tried to respond to the woman in the audience. When Krishnamurti was unsuccessful in launching a dialogue, he abruptly stopped, and with poignant vulnerability conceded that he wasn't mentally sharp anymore, so might the woman please come down to the front and just hold his hand for awhile, in deep and reverential silence. What an exquisite example of conscious surrender: emptying oneself of former capacities and giving oneself over to the mystifying present, without giving oneself away.

Additional words of Jesus flash to mind: "Father, into thy hands I commend my spirit." Dying appears to be a supreme act of confidence that the same Creation that breathed us into existence will assuredly catch, as well as clasp, us forever. The bottom line: we'll be alright when we die.

From midlife forward, we get the message that every love relationship ends in a loss: through divorce, departure, or death. We will die, and so will our comrades and loved ones. As we open ourselves to the precarious depths of love, we bare ourselves to the raw torment of loss.

Yet Unitarian Universalists experience those we've cherished living on in our souls after their earthly sojourns. We stay allied with the land of the dead, the territory of the ancestors, through the medium of love.

There's more comforting news in THEOLOGY ABLAZE. Just as we were graciously ushered into being, as a gift beyond our earning, so also there will be Love surrounding us after we die. There is no need to discuss or debate the particular form such Love might take. No one knows. It's only important that we declare with unshakable fervor and hope that the very Love that created us will surely caress and comfort us beyond our death…into illimitable seasons.

With quivering gratitude, our liberal religion seconds the sentiment of the Song of Solomon that "love is stronger than death"—yes, love outlasts death.

A capacity for mindful surrender requires remarkable, almost lifelong, discipline, doesn't it? To paraphrase Plato, the pursuit of wisdom entails the practice of dying. For whenever we die to attachments along the path, we're better prepared to release everything when it comes our turn to cease breathing. We learn that death isn't waiting for us at the end of the road. Instead, death's been shadowing us all along the way.

It's well nigh impossible to come face-to-face with death and expect to relinquish our bodies and minds rather effortlessly unless we've been practicing letting go and letting be, day in and day out, with minor as well as major possessions and preoccupations. To get ready for what no one can ever truly prepare for—the possibility of eternal nonbeing—we must bravely venture moments of dying daily.

Buddhists further claim that whereas death marks the end of our bodies, indeed the end of our individual personalities, it most assuredly doesn't signify the end of our existence. When our bodies cease to function, our core merely returns to the source of consciousness or as Ralph Waldo Emerson claimed: our souls are reabsorbed into the eternal Oversoul. The distinctive life-energy each of us embodied during our earthly existence flows back toward the center of the universe itself. The whole of cosmic reality is altered, because our unique being was present upon the earth for a stretch.

Death is an uncharted universe, a place our intellects can't adequately grasp. Ready or not, over half of us are touched every year by the death of a close family member or friend; 10% of us will die suddenly; 90% of us will face crucial decisions about health care and end-of-life care; and 50% of our medical costs are incurred in the last year of life.

In the face of such stark realities, Joan Halifax Roshi, a pioneer in providing care and companionship for the dying, charges us to wrestle painstakingly, in trustworthy circles of compassion, with open and honest questions before we die, in order to experience a potentially more peaceful departure: What are our worst fears for how our lives will end? What is our best-case scenario for our dying? What color does death look like for us and what animal might we resemble as we enter the realm of dying? Even though there exist no guarantees in life or death, what can we do now to maximize the odds of having a good death? You will add your own insistent, soulful queries.

In the end, death's justice comes to everyone, in order to make room for other creatures to birth on the scene. I resonate with the way the naturalist essayist Wallace Stegner phrases life's conclusion, in a mellow conversation with his friend James Hepworth:

> *I've been lucky. I came from nowhere, and had no reason to expect as much from this one life as I've got. I owe God a death, and the earth a pound or so of chemicals. Now let's see if I can remember that when my time comes.*

Indeed, we owe—God, this indescribably marvelous universe, ourselves, and all creaturely companions—one death, especially following a blessed and generous ride.

May this debt be willingly and gladly paid, when our turn comes to re-enter the ground of all being. I say gladly, because we're placed on earth to find and deliver joy. And when our light finally goes out, if we're fortunate, our souls will echo the glorious and soothing passage of scripture from Isaiah 55:12:

For you shall go out in joy and be led forth in peace, the mountains and the hills before you shall break forth into singing, and all the trees of the field shall clap their hands.

FOR REFLECTION AND DISCUSSION

1. In what venues has your congregation held conversations on our human mortality?

2. Describe the liturgical features that stand out in your experience with Unitarian Universalist memorial services.

3. Do you find that death's presence has intensified your capacity to love and live?

4. How do you practice dying some every day?

5. Have you given thought to the possibility that your particular UU congregation, as well as our Unitarian Universalist Association, may not last forever? That both could falter, wither, even die?

EVOLUTION

We are the trustees of evolution.
—Julian Huxley

Since the universe always changes, the truth about it must change, too. So I need not be ashamed or terrified when my own religious vision changes. It'll just be me, being part of the universe. Could the universe itself, in all its changing, teach us that security lies not in stasis, but in process?
—Judith Walker-Riggs

We have survived in one way or another for some 200,000 years. In spite of the infinite number of overwhelming and life-threatening crises we've faced, our durability has been proven. But something new is beginning to emerge at the leading edge of the development of human consciousness...and that is the instinct to evolve, to consciously evolve. It is based upon not merely the instinct to survive but an instinct that compels us toward higher, as yet unmanifest, human possibilities.
—Andrew Cohen

Ours is a theology whose cornerstone is evolution. It features our understanding of God, the universe, and human reality. Evolution constitutes the way we do religion, be it our organization or our philosophy.

It's reported that during the great debates of 16th-century Transylvania, folks scoffed at Francis David for being so changeable. "Look at this David," they taunted. "He starts out Roman Catholic, then becomes a Lutheran, then a Calvinist, and now he calls himself a Unitarian. What will he conceivably be tomorrow?" To which David is reported to have said: "*Semper reformanda*" or "always reforming." However, the period of religious openness and independence was short-lived, for John Sigismund, a frail but noble King, died three years later in 1571. A repressive monarch followed who immediately dismissed David as the court preacher and imposed censorship against any form of religious free thought. Since David was considered an unrepentant "innovator," he was banished to the dungeon, where he died in 1579, and was buried in an unmarked grave.

Synonyms for *semper reformanda* have multiplied during the past fifty years of our consolidated association. Whenever surveys have been taken in our Unitarian Universalist fold, various words and phrases pop up such as quest, transformation, search, metamorphosis, growth, "changing ourselves in a changing world" (the motto of Meadville Lombard Theological School), and "nothing is settled, everything matters." Or according to the central idiom of this book: staying ablaze.

Unitarian Universalist minister Daniel O'Connell fittingly identifies us in the following fashion:

> *Evolutionary theology promotes the idea that revelation is continuous. How our faith is revealed to us, how we reveal it to others, which parts of it get emphasized at what times in our lives, the ways we articulate this faith—changes through the generations. But the essential ideas of our liberal religious faith remain. It is what we inherit.*

In truth, Unitarian Universalists are both inheritors *and* heretics: we draw wisdom from our heritage; then as choice-makers, we shape our wisdom to match the yearnings of our souls with the cries of society. We maintain a spirit of openness of heart, mind, and hand. One General Assembly participant in a recent Commission on Appraisal hearing put it this way: "The core of my faith is the humility to viscerally understand that my positions may be wrong." Or as our 20th-century Unitarian forebear poet E. E. Cummings affirmed: "we can never be born enough."

THE UNIVERSE

Evolution is arguably one of the most profound and controversial notions ever to strike a human mind. *On the Origin of Species* flew off the bookshelves when it was published in 1859, by one of our own, Charles Darwin, and it remains a foundational book in the history of science.

Although the idea of evolution, that is, of biological change over time, didn't exactly originate with Darwin, it became a scientific theory only after Darwin articulated in the *Origin* what he referred to as "one long argument," since it took him years to write, then produce (16 years). Darwin wrote this tome only because he felt forced to do so by the evidence. He was a reluctant progressive.

Even if scientists are discovering new things about evolution in fields utterly foreign to Charles Darwin, his basic ideas still obtain from thousands of observations of species across the world: that all life is related and that species change over time in response to natural selection with new forms of life replacing previous ones.

Nonetheless, when Charles Darwin implied that humans were related to apes and monkeys, this bold naturalist incurred the derision and wrath of millions around the world. "Descended from apes!" exclaimed the wife of the Bishop of Worcester when she heard the news in 1860. "Let us hope it is not true; but if it is, let us pray that it will not become generally known."

Well, it did become widely known.

God

One of Adlai Stevenson's favorite yarns depicts a seven-year-old girl busy with her crayons. Her mother asked whose picture she was drawing. "God," the little girl replied. "Remember, my dear, nobody knows how God looks," the mother admonished. "They will when I'm finished," the child unflinchingly answered.

In truth, neither juvenile nor elder Unitarian Universalists can claim to produce a finished portrait of the indescribable Eternal Spirit, but such a realization shouldn't curb our ardor for drawing. Liberal religionists are, as colleague Dianne Arakawa notes, "basically reconstructive. Our faith involves moving toward a position of openness, of free inquiry, and a continuing commitment to seek the truth wherever it may lead."

If we stay awake and resolute, humans will keep evolving all the way to the grave. Being formed in the image of God implies that a vast and unbounded capacity for growth dwells in every human soul. THEOLOGY ABLAZE maintains that life is ever-changing, so are human beings, so is God. Unitarian Universalists contend that every hour of our journey holds some deepening claim, some corrective slant, some incredible surprise. We are born over and over again, not just once or twice. Then we die somewhere in the middle of our voyage, ready to be born yet again.

Upon encountering the burning bush in Hebrew scriptures, Moses asks God for God's moniker, but the latter only responds with *ehyeh-asher-ehyeh*, which is often misrendered by the inert English as "I am who I am," In truth, the phrase translates: "I will be who I will be." Hence, God baldly claims to be an unfinished being. Listen to how rabbinical activist Michael Lerner envisions the meaning of the Hebrew deity and our concomitant human mission:

> *What the word Yahweh really means is "the transformation of the present into that which can and should be in the future." In this sense, God is the Power of Healing and Transformation in the universe and the Voice of the Future calling us to become who we need to become.*

Process philosophers in our midst have been echoing, prior to the formation of the Unitarian Universalist Association in 1961, but with mounting crescendo ever since, the following argument: because God interacts with the changing universe, God is changeable (that is to say, God is affected by the actions that take place in the universe) over the course of time. However, the abstract elements of God (goodness, wisdom, etc.) remain eternally solid.

Unitarian process theologian Henry Nelson Wieman caught the essence thusly: "God is the growth of meaning and value in the world."

OUR HUMAN MISSION

Very early I knew that the only object in life was to grow.
—Margaret Fuller

*However many more breaths are left me to breathe, to aspire and conspire,
I know that with my final breath, I will be in the middle of learning yet
another life lesson. That makes life all the more precious.*
—Jane Bramadat

*Out of the stars, and out of the muck, out of the bestial past,
our story is not done. We stand, partners with God,
poised to believe in a destiny we will create.*
—Stephen Kendrick

Human evolution is our explicit purpose on earth, so it's spiritu-ally satisfying to believe that God's joining Creation's continuing ad-venture as well. Are humans and deities growing in our own distinct ways and places or are we maturing toward a common destiny of enhancing the well-being of the entire cosmos? Or are both asser-tions true?

Bernice Johnson Reagon of *Sweet Honey in the Rock* singing group fame, as well as long-time Unitarian Universalist fellow-traveler, states: "I'm stubbornly insistent on forward motion." We're impelled to keep on keeping on, trekking relentlessly toward the mission of growing a beloved human *and* earthly community, wherever we're planted.

Unitarian Universalists aren't interested in perfection, but we remain insistent on progress. Even when we falter and fall backward or slump sideways, ours is a life-affirming, upbeat faith, an evolution-ary theology that sets us doggedly on a forward-moving path.

As progressives, we're challenged to make decisions and take actions that advance civilization as a whole rather than negotiate moves that feather our private nests. We eschew the underbelly of any concept of progress that consciously or unconsciously promotes our religion or race, class or orientation, gender or ability as being superior to any other.

As progressives we take a fearless moral inventory of our every step: Am I making the same choice I would advise a child to make? Can I be both tough-minded and soft-hearted? Is this action sustaining the welfare of the entire universe? Am I being supportive of the weakest entities among us? Am I a gambler for love or a fearful guardian of the status quo? Do my spiritual practices result in deeds of mercy and justice, especially for the marginalized? Do my beliefs and behaviors take into account future generations of humans and animals and plants?

There's more to convey about being evolutionary theologians on a sacred journey.

For starters, we aspire to be visionaries. The European Green party says of themselves: "We are neither left nor right but out in front." Evolutionary pilgrims move about à la Leonard de Vinci who traveled with a sketch pad strapped to his belt, observing reality incessantly. We need the vision of both eagles who view the overall landscape from afar and mice who experience details at ground level. Pilgrims harbor hunches about where beauty and justice live, and, more importantly, have the courage to travel there, then coach, even goad, others to join the caravan.

Visionaries enable others to perceive what might yet become. We yank our sisters and brothers out of ruts, spurring one another beyond mediocrity, exhorting cohorts toward noble destinations. Pilgrims gladden their neighbors when vision is flagging and imagination is dormant. Emerson once wrote: "Faith and love are apt to be spasmodic in the best minds. We live on the brink of mysteries and harmonies into which we never enter, and with our hands on the door-latch, we die outside."

Evolutionists urge people to take the risk and open life's doors. We refuse to belong to a religion known as the "almost" people, where we almost touched beauty or almost incarnated justice. Depth theologians are devoted to living not on the brink but in the very midst of life's mysteries and harmonies.

Unitarian Universalists see our lives as one ceaseless adventure or discovery, as an opportunity to feed our spirits while serving the cosmos. However, we dare not get carried away with self-importance, either as individuals or as an association, as we shape the next fifty years of our religious enterprise.

We are all short-timers on this earthly plane. Each of us is entrusted with the stewardship of Unitarian Universalism for a period of time, not forever. We don't own this faith; we share it, on loan. Our mission is to become responsible stakeholders...for awhile. It behooves us to assume our Unitarian Universalist partnership, purposefully yet playfully.

Many of us would profitably identify with the Zen story that satirizes the very concept of the holy pilgrimage. The guru rests on his death bed and gasps his last words to his assembled followers: "Life is a journey."

As this closing profundity is passed around in hushed whispers, the newest of his disciples loudly and irreverently challenges this assertion. The guru himself hears this, reconsiders, and the absolutely last words his disciples hear are: "So, life is not a journey!" What a playful reminder for us to take our life-travels seriously but never grimly. Depth theology implores us to journey with a feathery touch and a light heart.

Ultimately, we're not certain of our destination, but we possess working hunches, we remain trustingly agnostic, we keep plodding, we keep our eyes glued on the prize, and we harbor enough theological resilience to stay our chosen course. We are pilgrims on an evolutionary expedition.

Human beings have collected a host of labels throughout history, such as self-conscious animals, problem-solving animals, playful animals, and spiritual animals. We're all those, of course, but we're also nomadic animals on a journey into unfamiliar lands and foreign seas, toward shrines and destinations of delight. The way continues. Our expeditions will never be completed, only surrendered.

The way leads on. We never reach our destination. We keep on growing up. We persist in fanning the flame of our chosen faith, so that ensuing generations might, in their own fashion, keep stoking the blaze of our flaming chalice...far into epochs beyond measure.

FOR REFLECTION AND DISCUSSION

1. William Ellery Channing prided himself on keeping his ministry useful and his soul awake. Indeed, the self-description upon which our spiritual forebear based his life was "always young for liberty, I trust." And he was.

    What does it mean for you to be ever young for liberty, for justice, for compassion? For your congregation? For our progressive religious movement?

2. Unitarian Universalist professor Susan Pangerl writes that for Unitarian Universalism to be a productive and worthy movement:
    ...requires our willingness to publicly reclaim our constructive task of the continuous revisioning of theology...

    What does this mean?

3. Process thinker and minister Joy Atkinson writes:
    Reality, in the process view, is made up not of things but of events. Creation is in ongoing process in every moment. The universe is created anew in every moment, as are we, and as is God!

    What might this philosophical posture mean for your congregation's image of itself?

4. Former President of our UUA John Buehrens reminds us that "part of maturity is living with this truth: there is no such thing as a grown-up person. Not me. Not you."

    Given this wisdom, how are you personally growing up, right now, as a practicing Unitarian Universalist theologian? How would you describe the theological development of our entire Association upon its 50th birthday?

5. I have kept on my desk, for decades now, a poem composed by a teenage Unitarian Universalist by the name of Shanti Foster from Maryland:
    Growing up Unitarian Universalist is searching for your head, finding it, picking it up, screwing it on...and having it fall off again and again, with hopes of a tighter fit next time.

    Reflect and discuss.

EPILOGUE

"Everyone is a theologian, either conscious or unconscious, in the sense that everyone has some conception of the nature of reality, of the demands of reality, and of those elements in reality that support or threaten meaningful existence."
—James Luther Adams, preeminent
Unitarian Universalist theologian

To be sure, we aren't all as prolific or profound in our theologizing as Adams was throughout the expanse of the 20th century, but his point still holds. You and I are eminently capable of wrestling with the manifold meanings of life. "Everyone is a theologian," from our earliest ruminations forward. Our grandson, Owen, is a case in point.

Owen was attending the kindergarten class at the Summit Unitarian Universalist Fellowship in Santee, California, the religious home of his family. Rev. Kathleen Green would periodically spend time in the Religious Education classes.

Rev. Kathleen was exploring our central symbol, the flaming chalice—its history and meanings—and asked the youngsters to sculpt their very own chalice. Eagerly, Owen created his clay piece. His minister took notice, remarking: "Owen, that's a large chalice!" Without blinking, Owen replied: "Well, yes. It has to hold a lot of light!"

It certainly does. Our flaming chalice has to generate more blaze than a mere candle. We aspire to be the religion of what our Universalist forebears called "the larger hope." Our faith deliberately embraces and honors every unit of existence. Our mercy seeks to cast a wide arc. The bowl of our chalice must be sizable enough to hold an ever-expanding fire, for our stated mission is to become a beacon of shining hope for the greater world—yea, the entire universe. As a nine-year parishioner of mine (yet another one of our younger theologians) innocently yet aptly mused: "Our god is fat"!

Fortunately, in the decades since merger, we've been maturing spiritually. We've been fanning the flame of our faith. We've been growing in theological literacy, dialogue, and depth. We've come to realize that truly "everyone is a theologian"—laity and clergy alike—including the little Owens in our ranks.

In today's burgeoning religious marketplace, Unitarian Universalists are exhorted to take our place at the table of theology. There is a hue and cry for progressive perspectives on sin and salvation, grace and God, prayer and justice, joy and mystery, forgiveness and death.

Our theology becomes radiant and fiery whenever it's purposeful. As Unitarian forebrother Ralph Waldo Emerson put It: "The purpose of life is not to be happy. It's to be useful, to be honorable, to be compassionate, to have it make some difference that you have lived and lived well." In sum, the soles of our feet must advance the souls of our beings. As pilgrims we would stay on purpose: namely, serving goodness and beauty, while healing the earth. Who we are may be God's gift to us, but who we choose to become is our gift back to the universe.

Pilgrims in the 4th and 5th centuries would travel to remote hermitages of the Desert Fathers and open a ritual exchange with the sentence: "Give me a word that I may live!" On the various main roads and by-ways of the human pilgrimage we're called upon to deliver saving words to civilization: hopeful, liberating, life-affirming words to all sisters and brothers who cross our pathway. "Good tidings" as Isaiah phrases it.

Unitarian Universalism, at our truest, comprises a shining theology that can deliver saving words to our world. It is life-affirming, liberating, and loving . . . here and now. As the current stakeholders of the noble heritage of Unitarian Universalism, it remains our charge to keep our flaming chalice ablaze…burning with clarity and compassion into seasons beyond view.

Owen's watercolor rendition of his clay chalice.

ABOUT FLAMING CHALICE PRESS

Flaming Chalice Press publishes books on Unitarian Universalism, personal relationships, and spiritual growth. If you want to learn about other books of inspiration for both mind and soul, written by Rev. Tom Owen-Towle, please contact us by phone: (619) 933-1121, e-mail: mail@tomo-t.com, or through the website: www.tomo-t.com.

To order additional copies of *THEOLOGY ABLAZE*, please send your check to:

Tom Owen-Towle
3303 Second Avenue
San Diego, CA 92103
Price: $20 (includes tax)
Shipping: $4.50